Forms of Relation

Writing the Early Americas

Anna Brickhouse and Kirsten Silva Gruesz, Editors

Forms of Relation

Composing Kinship in Colonial Spanish America

MATTHEW GOLDMARK

University of Virginia Press

Charlottesville and London

University of Virginia Press
© 2023 by the Rector and Visitors of the University of Virginia
All rights reserved

First published 2023

9 8 7 6 5 4 3 2 1

Library of Congress Cataloging-in-Publication Data
Names: Goldmark, Matthew, author.
Title: Forms of relation : composing kinship in colonial Spanish America /
Matthew Goldmark.
Description: Charlottesville : University of Virginia Press, 2023. | Series: Writing
the early Americas | Includes bibliographical references and index.
Identifiers: LCCN 2022040076 (print) | LCCN 2022040077 (ebook) | ISBN
9780813949376 (hardcover) | ISBN 9780813949383 (paperback)
| ISBN 9780813949390 (ebook)
Subjects: LCSH: Families—Latin America. | Kinship in literature. |
Kinship—Latin America. | Spain—Colonies—America—Administration. | Latin
America—Social life and customs—16th century. | Latin America—Social life and
customs—17th century. | Latin America—History—To 1830
Classification: LCC HQ560.5 .G56 2023 (print) | LCC HQ560.5 (ebook) |
DDC 306.85098—dc23/eng/20221024
LC record available at https://lccn.loc.gov/2022040076
LC ebook record available at https://lccn.loc.gov/2022040077

nlh

Publication of this volume has been supported by New Literary History.

Cover art: Details from *Cari cuna: huarmi cuna* (genealogical chart of Pedro Yaya, alcalde), from Juan Pérez Bocanegra, *Ritual Formulario,* 1631. Woodcut, 27.4 cm × 16.6 cm. (John Carter Brown Library)}

Contents

Acknowledgments

Several fellowships, grants, and institutions have supported the production of this book. A dissertation fellowship from the McNeil Center for Early American Studies; a postdoctoral fellowship from the Center for 17th- and 18th-Century Studies at the University of California, Los Angeles (UCLA); a postdoctoral fellowship from Bowdoin College; and a short-term research fellowship from the John Carter Brown Library provided the financial support, time, and community that helped this project grow. I thank Florida State University for additional assistance via the First Year Assistant Professor Award and a Humanities Book Publication Subvention. Workshops at the Tepoztlán Institute for the Transnational History of the Americas, a seminar at the Folger Shakespeare Library, a series of conferences sponsored by the Center for 17th- and 18th-Century Studies at UCLA, and the Tepaske Seminar in Colonial Latin American History gave me opportunities to refine and rethink ideas central to this book. I offer thanks for the hard work and generosity of the International Tepoztlán Collective, Ralph Bauer, Adriana Craciun, Mary Terrall, and Mónica Díaz for organizing these events.

This book is a testament to the support of mentors and colleagues who helped me grow as a scholar. I am forever indebted to the goodwill and feedback of my advisors Yolanda Martínez-San Miguel, Barbara Fuchs, and Heather Love. To the early mentors who sparked my curiosity in learning—Eyda Merediz, Juan Carlos Quintero-Herencia, and Ana Patricia Rodríguez—I give many thanks. Colleagues at UCLA's Clark Library and at Bowdoin College—in particular, Margaret Boyle, Elena Cueto-Asín, and Theo Greene—kept this project going as I crisscrossed the country. At Florida State University, I have had the great fortune of finding generous and thoughtful colleagues in Modern Languages and Linguistics who have provided invaluable feedback, and I thank Elizabeth Coggeshall and Michaela Hulstyn for their advice and insight. Finally, I cannot thank Julia Bloch, Larissa Brewer-García, Sarah Dowling, Jessica Rosenberg, Emma Stapely, Greg Steirer, and Emily Weissbourd enough. Without their brilliance, generosity, and humor, this book would not exist.

Countless others have offered their time through answers to queries, helpful questions, and invitations to dialogue. For this and more, I thank

Rolena Adorno, Kathryn Burns, Lynne Feeley, Ruth Hill, Aaron Hyman, David Kazanjian, Helena de Llanos, Dana Leibsohn, María Elena Martínez, Lina Martínez Hernández, Eyda Merediz, Anna More, Jeremy Ravi Mumford, Marcy Norton, Mairin Odle, Jolie Olcott, Rachel O'Toole, Joseph Pierce, Bianca Premo, Ben Reed, Daniel Richter, Anna Rosensweig, María Josefina Saldaña-Portillo, David Sartorius, Michael Solomon, Zeb Tortorici, Sonia Velázquez, Tamara Walker, and Adam Warren. For their friendship and kindness in offering me places to live, work, and stay (too long), I thank Fernando Alonso López, Tony Archer, Rita Borderías Tejada, Justine Chabot, Dolors Fabra Antón, Patrick Grzanka, Elizabeth Halliday Walker, Caitlin Hopping, Ana Jacinto Domínguez, Tanya Jung, Ana Martínez Lorenzo, Débora María Martín Tajada, Juan Carlos Peinado Manrique, Eva Olarte Solozábal, Marta Olarte Solozábal, Dan Taylor, Jeffrey Walker, and Adam Whitehurst.

This book would not have been possible without the patient assistance of staff at the Clark Library, the Hispanic Studies Program at Bowdoin College, and the Department of Modern Languages and Linguistics at Florida State University. The directors, staff, and readers in the Archivo Arzobispal de Lima, the Archivo General de la Nación, and the John Carter Brown Library provided invaluable help. Working with my editor, Eric Brandt, along with Lauren Bock and Wren Morgan Myers at the University of Virginia Press has been a pleasure. Their skills brought this book to press. The feedback of anonymous reviewers and contributions by series editors Anna Brickhouse and Kirsten Silva Gruesz have helped improve the book's final version. I also want to thank Dabian Witherspoon for his attention to detail, Jonathan DaSo's research skills, and Josh Rutner for his careful indexing. An early version of chapter 2 appeared as "Formal Encounters: Education, Evangelization, and the Reproduction of Custom in Seventeenth-Century Peru," in *Curious Encounters: Voyaging, Collecting, and Making Knowledge in the Long Eighteenth Century,* edited by Adriana Craciun and Mary Terrall (Toronto: University of Toronto Press, 2019), 189–205. I thank the University of Toronto Press for permission to use this material here.

Finally, to Ellen Goldmark, Vik Uberoi, Solly Uberoi, Ikey Uberoi, and Lenny Uberoi, thank you for giving me space to work, live, and laugh when I needed one. To Marcia and Glen Goldmark, thank you for the morning phone calls and Wednesday dinners. This book is for you.

Forms of Relation

Introduction

The priest of the Andean parish of Andahuaylillas, Juan Pérez Bocanegra, includes only a single image to facilitate the conversion of Indigenous peoples in his guidebook for confessors, the *Ritual formulario e institucion de curas* (*Ritual Formulary and Principles for Priests*, 1631).[1] Each chapter in the work is dedicated to a particular sacrament and includes a lexicon and model questions in Quechua[2] to help friars police catechumens' errant practices.[3] However, in the chapter dedicated to the sacrament of marriage, Pérez Bocanegra's document incorporates a woodcut. According to the text, the image displays a schema of the "grades of blood relation," including both "ancestors and descendants, men and women."[4] In this woodcut, a male figure with outstretched arms oversees a genealogical edifice structured by columns.[5] This man, identified as "Pedro *Yaya*," father in Quechua, presides over four busts of women on the right-hand side and four busts of men mirroring them on the left.[6] All eleven figures wear traditional Inca garments, with the women wearing mantles and pins (*lliklla* and *ttipqui*) along with textile head coverings (*nañaca*) while the five men wear the fringed band (the *mascaypacha* or royal fringe) on their heads, a vestment that only the elite could wear.[7] While all of the figures are given individualizing Christian names,[8] they are also labeled with Quechua terms that indicate their relationships to each other and to the primogenitor Pedro via descent.[9] This terminology is compounded by visual arrangement. Figures are bolted together by bars that cross the page in parallel and transversal lines. Each bar is hollowed out and contains both Spanish and Quechua terms operating in reciprocal translation that signify the grades of relation (first, second, third, and fourth) in reference to both Pedro at the top of the page, and in turn, to the individuals each bar connects. In all, this image seems to make the family a known and knowable entity in visual and linguistic forms.[10] The woodcut, according to Pérez Bocanegra, ensures that Inca kinship and marriages[11] can be "distinctly known and seen."[12]

Pérez Bocanegra's woodcut presents one type of kinship that Spanish colonizers and Indigenous[13] peoples navigated in sixteenth- and

Cari cuna: huarmi cuna (genealogical chart of Pedro Yaya, alcalde), from Juan Pérez Bocanegra, *Ritual formulario,* 1631. Woodcut, 27.4 cm × 16.6 cm. (John Carter Brown Library)

seventeenth-century colonial Peru: relationships labeled "consanguinity" and stamped with the bars of lineage, marriage, and blood that seem "familiar" to a modern-day viewer.[14] However, while this woodcut may appear to present the Incas as if they were a family bound unto themselves, it is better seen as part of a colonial work that *produces* what I call relations: kinship ties made through the production and use of textual forms that create dependency, organize peoples, and renew life in the colonial world. The *Ritual formulario* is a lexical and administrative product that bridges and makes kinship through a practice of writing, translating, using, and organizing bodies on the page, in the town, and in the Atlantic world. It forms relations.

Forms of Relation: Composing Kinship in Colonial Spanish America shows how texts in the sixteenth- and seventeenth-century Spanish Americas do not document kinship ties but instead produce them. It argues that kinship is made in the administration of colonial life and governance. In the process, this book expands the meaning of "form" as kinship theorists use it. In kinship study, form often refers to the human life cycle of "dependency, which may include birth, child-rearing, relations of emotional dependency and support, generational ties, illness, dying, and death."[15] This book demonstrates that *textual* forms like the *relación,* the petition, and the Indigenous language grammar also inflect dependency. They determine how collaboration, community, and daily life take shape in the Spanish colonial world and "renew" kinship as a "*form* over time, beyond procreation."[16] This book argues that textual forms produce kinship but often escape its study.[17] Consequently, this book defamiliarizes our ideas about the development and meaning of family and kinship bonds, both in the colonial period and today.

The title of this book points to its central contention: textual practice—one type of relations—made and shaped forms of living in the colonial Spanish Americas. Both "relation" and "form" have intersecting meanings in the sixteenth- and seventeenth-century colonial world. "Relation" points to textual forms (i.e., the *relación* and the history) and the act of communicating information about the colonial world (i.e., to relate). This means that a "form of relation" produces social ties: one uses a form to convey something to someone else. Next, "form" also has multiple meanings. It describes the shape that information takes on the page to make legible "content." It also describes the structuring patterns of "relating" in a community: the rhythm and shape of a Christian "form" that aligned with Christian lifeways named the goals of evangelization. By tracing the relational practice of form, *Forms of Relation* shows the inseparable linkages between textual and embodied practice as they intersect with gender, sexuality, kinship, and writing.

I engage Spain's sixteenth- and seventeenth-century transatlantic empire with a focus on the Andean region. This proves a time of flux and uncertainty for colonial subjects—Spaniards, Indigenous peoples, and those of African origin, as well as their descendants. Gonzalo Lamana has posited that the first twenty years of conflict in the Andes was a period of confusion when all peoples competed "to define the new order of things" and "no party managed to have the upper hand."[18] While *Forms of Relation* focuses on later decades that may not have maintained the same level of instability, evangelical and political circumstances did remain unmoored. Various Indigenous groups struggled against their increasing collapse into the categorization of "*indio,*" in part by manipulating Spanish categories of lineage, titles, and blood purity (*limpieza de sangre*); enslaved populations in Lima and the Andes contested their circumstances and composed religious associations that transformed the cultural landscape; Spaniards' pursuit of conversion competed with the devastation wrought by wealth extraction; peoples across the Atlantic and in the Andes continued to debate Spanish and Indigenous rights well after the famous debates at Valladolid (1550); friars' suspicions of religious insurrections made evangelical inroads suspect in the 1580s and 1620s; and Andean writers condemned Spanish violence and undermined claims to Christian supremacy throughout the entire period. These continuous struggles show that the reproduction and renewal of order lived, as David Kazanjian poses of colonial worlds, in the contradictions among discourses and practices.[19] *Forms of Relation* accordingly proposes a shift in its study of kinship: by focusing on *how* bonds of relation took shape in form rather than on *what* relationships count as kinship, it emphasizes the means of making and doing kinship in the sixteenth and seventeenth centuries. Taking kinship as a process and practice that cannot be, as Myra Jehlen argues of history, knowable "before the fact,"[20] we see that different forms of relation keep colonial order unfinished and open—just as it was for the peoples who lived it.

Kinship in Relations

It is difficult to speak of the colonial Spanish Americas without mentioning the *relación* since this form functions as an essential means of documenting and transmitting information about incursions, peoples, trade routes, nature, and other imperial knowledge. Though *relación* can name many textual genres (the *carta de relación* [informative letter], the *relación geográ-fica* [census document], and the *relación de méritos y servicios* [relation of merits and services], for instance),[21] these works always include formal con-ditions: namely, a relational structure. *Relaciones* implicate various interact-ing players such as authors, scribes, interviewees, recipients, and readers. In each case, a *relación* proves to be a practice and product that dictates a rela-tional arrangement of bodies and information. Take the definition offered by the humanist Sebastián de Covarrubias. Curt and matter of fact, his Spanish dictionary, the *Tesoro de la lengua castellana o española* (1611), states that the *relación* is from the "Latine relatio, a referendo, actus referendi."[22] The brevity of this initial entry betrays its semantic plurality. Though *re-lación* begins as a noun, its definition moves immediately to a verb and an intersubjective act of telling ("actus"). Lest we assume that this noun-verb exists in autonomy, the definition shows that the author and text require "relation" to function. To relate is not an intransitive but rather a term in-dicative of content that requires an indirect object. It is relational and de-mands that this "something" be told or given to another. Indeed, when the noun *relación* is used in manifold colonial documents, it is accompanied by the verb *hacer* (to make or to do) and the preposition *a* (to). Made for and given to someone, the information contained in the *relación* accrues value because it builds a tie. In turn, this textual and social form is neither neutral nor established among equals. The relational *relación* is marked by power differentials. When the dictionary continues, it moves to an entry for the legal profession of the *relator* (notary) who serves as a faithful intermedi-ary of a relation in a court of law. These dynamics are combined in the definition of *relación* provided by the *Diccionario de autoridades,* written in 1737. A *relación* is, that entry reads, "a brief and succinct report, made by a respected person in writing or in person to a judge in the course of a trial."[23] This definition brings the report and the relator before the person to whom s/he relates while emphasizing that this *relación* is not accidental but forged between peoples enmeshed in the structures of governance and law. Only after these two definitions do we find a brief evocation of the family that resonates with present-day ideas of kinship. A subsequent entry in the *Dic-cionario de autoridades* shows that the term also means "an attachment or kinship between one person and another," offering the example, "thus, we say Pedro *has a relation* to Juan."[24] This displacement of kinship as we know it—a family tie—from the center of "relation" helps push us to redefine kin-ship in its colonial dimensions. The family is displaced from its dominant position, making formal regulation and performance before the law central.

In concert, I take these three definitions to hold that "relation" can reformulate kinship as a set of overlapping practices that bind people together in acts of information transmission and projects of imperial regulation.

My emphasis on "relation" in its historical and colonial dimensions helps reveal the utility and limitations of kinship as an analytic category. First, attention to relation allows this book to confront kinship study's biologically essentialist legacy. Both anthropological studies and works on the Spanish empire have wrestled with questions of Western universalism and ahistoricism based on genealogy and blood. In anthropology, this interrogation emerged in the emblematic work of anthropologist David Schneider, namely his *A Critique of the Study of Kinship* (1984). He argued that the Western family form based on a genealogical grid of consanguineal relations predetermined kinship study—even when scholars suggested that they focused on ties autonomous to a distinct culture. He contended that even if other classificatory ties were "added" to this schematic, biology and procreation provided the baseline for comparison. Blood and biology were treated as the final arbiters of kinship at the expense of "performance, forms of doing, various codes for conduct, [and] different roles" that bound peoples together.[25] Thus, as Sarah Franklin and Susan McKinnon glossed, Schneider's critique was not simply directed at "biologism" but rather the imposition of European "biologistic" ways of theorizing character, nature, and behavior.[26]

In parallel fashion, studies on Spain and the Spanish Americas have long contended with a similar question of biologistic thinking when addressing the meaning of "blood" relations as metaphor and practice. Since prohibitions against the acquisition of religious and political posts by New Christians (converts with Jewish, Muslim, and apostate ancestry) turned on accusations of *limpieza de sangre* (blood purity), resulting scholarship disputed how historical actors understood the mechanisms of inheritance.[27] Studies on the Spanish Americas have proven equally conflictive since ambivalent and contradictory discourses around *sangre* and inheritance also appeared in descriptions of "Indians," peoples of African descent, and *castas* (the classificatory terms used to describe "mixed" peoples).[28] On the one hand, some scholars' extensive discussion of "miscegenation" insinuated that procreation and biology contributed to identity.[29] However, others critiqued a biologistic formulation as the only means of understanding colonial Spanish American identities and kinship ties.[30] They showed that these "new types" of people were defined by categories that were not biological by instead focusing on *calidad* (quality) and reputation,[31] *vecindad* (belonging to a polity)[32] and identifications based on appearance and performance where to "be" was to "appear" and to "seem like" in the eyes of others.[33] Moreover, scholars who moved against biologistic thinking showed the historiographic consequences of that model. Biologism as kinship could undergird a vision of colonial history predicated on sexual violence,[34] simplistic equations of the biological and the cultural,[35] and an anachronistic projection of the contemporary West's heterosexual norm.[36]

That said, relation shows that kinship need not be jettisoned due to its Western origins and universalism. On the contrary, kinship gains resonance *because* it was (and is) used as a colonial and racializing tool that helps produce and subjugate colonial peoples. Consider that it is no surprise that Schneider's "genealogical grid," condemned as a tool of Western universalization, resonates with Michel Foucault's "grid of intelligibility,"[37] since anthropology worked in concert with imperial projects of knowledge production, as scholars such as Dipesh Chakrabarty have shown.[38] For this reason, while some scholars have asked if kinship retains any purchase, *Forms of Relation* works with a tradition of scholarship that has emphasized kinship's Western origins as a colonial discourse by engaging queer studies, Indigenous studies, critical race studies, and colonial studies.[39] This book contends that to abandon kinship studies altogether is to pretend that its shaping force in the colonial world can be forgotten.

Relations in Form

As a colonial practice, kinship is contingent and inconsistent—it is a tool of empire and a site of its complication. Pierre Bourdieu famously defines kinship as "something people *make,* and with which they *do* something."[40] *Forms of Relation* reveals how people make and do kinship with textual forms, those standardized rubrics that shape knowledge about the colonial world. Textual forms do not simply provide a place to describe. They also mold information according to the conventions of composition, production, and transmission. Forms like the *relación,* the *pedimento* (petition), and the *lexicon* (lexicon) all have ways of organizing knowledge to make "colonial common sense."[41] In turn, as a procedure rather than a product alone, form is defined by its organizational capacity; it extends in spatial and somatic fashion to implicate forms of living in the colonial world. As Pérez Bocanegra's *Ritual formulario* shows, a textual form strives to re-form the lives of others. Forms seek to *make* bodies live differently and conscript people outside the page to regulate—not simply describe—how they should *do* kinship.

To emphasize that form is a site where relations are *composed,* this book first builds upon work by scholars who have looked to writing as a site that produced "rather than merely [reflected]" a set colonial world.[42] Scholars have engaged writing and form to think through the administration of gender, sexuality, and intimate relations.[43] For instance, scholars like Ann Laura Stoler propose that "the nature of imperial rule and the dispositions it engendered [emerged] from the writerly forms through which it was managed, how attentions were trained and selectively cast."[44] As she states elsewhere, "the bureaucratic shuffle of rote formulas, generic plots, and prescriptive asides" help shape—though not fully determine—what could be said and how "and what could not be told, and what could not be said."[45] However, while form could direct imperial authorities' attention to certain kinds of colonial ties, form did not fully restrict *who* could engage the channels of documentation. As scholars of the colonial Spanish Americas have shown, Indigenous subjects,[46] *mestizos,*[47] and peoples of African origin and African descent[48] worked with diverse textual forms to negotiate their religious and political identities in the Spanish Americas. Scholars' investigations have shown that writing was not a unilinear site of dominance as an earlier generation had contended,[49] but rather a complex point of negotiation, collaboration, and contestation.[50]

While those studies of colonial writing provide a point of departure for *Forms of Relation,* this book works with a development in scholarship that focuses on voice and textual standardization, where scholars interrogate the relationship between repetition and subjectivity predicated on form. Against the similarity of formalized documents, scholars foreground traces of individual peoples in documents through a study of deviations in text. We can divide this scholarship into roughly two threads. One reads "against the grain" to find non-Western epistemology and to show how non-Western peoples maintained and inscribed their worldviews in texts that ostensibly meet the demands of imperial forms.[51] Another, newer thread reads language "with the grain" and explores differences in standardized documents as signs of subjects' individual experiences. Specific phrases move to the fore and provide opportunities for scholars to interrogate differential ties of care, obligation, and manipulation between the formerly enslaved and their former enslavers[52] or among servants and their Spanish employers;[53] Andean and African uses of *casta* categories to take control of their own labor;[54] and Indigenous, African, and Spanish women's religious fervor.[55] Among this method's many strengths is its ability to let us read and reconsider how colonialism produces unexpected ties—whether emotional intimacies, collaborations, or new ways of theorizing voice when we have few first-person texts that "speak" about these relationships. In turn, it pushes us to drop preconceived expectations regarding antagonism between colonizer and colonized to reveal the ways that subjects depend on each other, might feel, live in concert, and ultimately renew the colonial world. The deviations in individual cases and voices defy expected oppositions based on predetermined binaries.

Forms of Relation follows many of these studies' points. Their refusal to accept universal and naturalized relations, their desire to expand the social ties that constitute intimacy, and their wish to explore identity construction in a wide body of texts all match the concerns of this book. Yet, *Forms of Relation* adds to this conversation by moving in a distinct direction when it engages form. As this book contends, form shows that subjectivity is in part rooted in standardized discourse and practice. Emphasis on form shows how colonial subjects emerge in what Kathryn Burns names the "productive tension between *teoría* and *práctica*."[56] While *práctica* speaks to the singular case, *teoría* names a formal scaffolding that conditions legibility itself. *Teoría* identifies the manifold dispositions that occasion (or imagine) colonial life as a formal arrangement of bodies and texts: *teoría*—what I call form—points to the ways that life is supposed to be lived and shaped in the colonies, and it names the set of embodied arrangements and textual rules that produce intelligible information and subjects. These regulatory features condition how people can come into contact and make identities in multiple, overlapping, and contradictory ways to gain legibility to a colonial apparatus. The peoples who emerge in forms have identities and positions they enact and at times rework: labels like *indio, criollo,* or *negro* merge with family ties (real, fictive, and allegorical) like father and child, political positions in the community, and bureaucratic roles like translator and testator.[57] As *Forms of Relation* contends, the practices of composition dictated by form also create identities that merit attention and interrogation.[58]

This vision of form is not structuralist and deterministic—that limiting reading inherited from scholar Hayden White. White famously posits that form and content have an inextricable, if not predetermined, link where form conditions content. As he puts it, form "possesses a content prior to any given actualization of it in speech or writing."[59] However, in the colonial world we see a more complex interplay since the content that takes shape in form is affected by what Nancy van Deusen calls "relationality." Any colonial ordering—of information, of community, and of the self—is a conditional actualization determined by a "mutually constitutive self-constitution and constitution by other individuals."[60] Rather than serve as *the* author of determinant content, form becomes a player in the "notion of collective authorship," as writes Alcira Dueñas, that operates "within the trans-cultural space of the 'contact zones.'"[61] Form is embodied and contingent: formal exigencies name the peoples who should be involved, the places where encounters (interrogations, meetings, etc.) can take place, and the organization of "facts" on a page.[62] Form insinuates, but does not predetermine an endpoint. For this reason, form and the relations it occasions are at once openings for colonial regulation and possibility.

Possibility—however small—emerges in these colonial forms of relation. When the Caribbean theorist Édouard Glissant considered the force of poetics and identitary production, he turned to relation as a means of positing how identity operated under the shadow of colonialism. I take inspiration from Glissant to say that the texts studied in this book emerge "in the chaotic network of Relation," where a strict opposition between self and other loses value. Here, in the relations produced in form, we can find different means of "knowing," "becoming," and "being."[63] The sixteenth- and seventeenth-century colonial Spanish Americas, as studied here, present a formation-in-practice where form offers an actualization of relation and not a determinant content of what colonial life, identity, and kinship could look like.

Rhetoric of Relation

As one means of excavating these social practices, scholars have examined many of the defining categories and terms of identity in the colonial Spanish Americas. From *recogimiento* (enclosure)[64] to *honra* (honor);[65] *congregación* (congregation)[66] to *reducción* (reduction);[67] *contra natura* (sins against nature)[68] to *cuiloni* (sodomite)[69] and *huchallicu* (sin),[70] multiple researchers have shown that "familiar" concepts, to again borrow Premo's resonant word, enact the world in "unfamiliar" ways and must be considered in their colonial dimensions.[71] Or to put it differently, as queer studies scholar Valerie Traub writes of the early modern period, words like "'sodomy' might or might not mean 'sodomy.'"[72]

Forms of Relation takes the insights offered by these studies that have defamiliarized "familiar" terms and illustrates how language builds relations in and around form. It focuses on four concepts—use, legitimacy, form, and exemplarity—and considers how they help configure relations and identities among Spanish and Indigenous peoples in the colonial Spanish

Americas. These four terms are not held to be exceptional, nor is the goal to create a new historiography or canon.[73] Instead, these terms offer a means to consider the epistemological and procedural density that exists in colonial texts. They offer an opportunity to better understand the contingent relationships forged among colonial subjects.[74] To that end, no term is hermetically sealed in one chapter. The fourth chapter, dedicated to the study of "forms" made with the rhetoric of "use" in grammars and guidebooks for confessors, cannot be considered without a discussion of doctrinal standardization and the concept of the evangelical "example," the subject of chapter 3. Inevitably, the chapters create a relation of their own.

Forms of Relation features four chapters divided into roughly two parts. The book focuses on the mid-sixteenth to mid-seventeenth centuries, with chapters 1 and 2 addressing high-profile disputes over the methods of conquest and the right to sovereignty. Chapter 1 lays a foundation by studying the rhetoric, transatlantic debates, and terms that cast colonial ruination as a question of kinship relations. The second chapter shows how this rhetoric is applied and used in Andean political conflicts. Chapter 1, "Misuse and Maternity: Infanticide and the Relations of Conquest," considers how the Dominican friar Bartolomé de Las Casas engages the rhetoric of gender, sexuality, and kinship in his scathing critique of conquest. By focusing on the language of "use" and the verb phrase *usar mal* (misuse), this chapter shows how the friar condemns conquistadors for causing infanticide in the *Brevísima relación de la destrucción de las Indias* (1552). He argues that Spanish "misuse" of women leads them to commit child murder. By casting infanticide as a sign of real and allegorical conquest relations gone awry, Las Casas presents distinct relations as a solution: a political and evangelical tie where a patriarchal Father King intervenes through kinship.[75] As a conclusion, this chapter reads the opacity embedded in scenes of infanticide to show where maternal relations cut back against the dictates of use in the organization of colonial order.

Chapter 2 moves to the 1560s and the colonial Andes. "Recomposing Legitimacy: Gender Relations and Indigenous Authorship" interrogates authorial voice and gendered power in the *Instrucción del Inca don Diego de Castro Titu Cusi Yupanqui* (1570), often considered one of the first texts attributed to an Inca author. Contemporary scholarship often engages this text to study a masculine version of resistance that depends upon the "author" Titu Cusi's voice and military might in the rebel stronghold Vilcabamba. In contrast, this chapter shows how relations "compose" the text, evident in the rhetorical calculi of legitimacy, the negotiation of kinship, and the writing of textual forms like the *relación* and the *poder* (power of attorney). By studying the distribution of authority and authorship across gender relations and generic forms, this chapter provides a method to challenge masculinist versions of textual analysis.

Chapter 3 focuses on exemplarity and the idea of the *buen exemplo* (good example) to explain how form creates reproductive relations. "Good Examples: Textual Forms and the Reproduction of Custom" attends to the *Actas* from the Third Lima Council (1582–83), José de Acosta's *De procuranda* (1588), Guaman Poma de Ayala's *El primer nueva corónica* (1615), and sixteenth-century teachers' petitions gathered in the Archbishopric's Archive of Lima. It shows that each work shares a rhetorical conceit: customs are not reproduced via lineage alone but also via exemplarity. Students' customs are reshaped in the mold of an elite example—for good or bad. This chapter emphasizes the utility of this reproductive rhetoric for Indigenous peoples. It argues that Indigenous peoples could condemn Spanish examples to reframe their own identities as relational and learned rather than predicated on an inherent character or lineage. This chapter, therefore, argues that by positing reproduction as a matter of form, Indigenous Andeans could claim to be reproductions of model Christians.

The last chapter, "Form and the Future: Use and the Unfinished Work of Evangelization," builds on the previous one to consider the temporal dimensions of *forma* (form) as an evangelical strategy. This chapter studies the *Grammatica* (1560) and *Lexicon* (1560) by Domingo de Santo Tomás and the *Ritual formulario* (1631) by Juan Pérez de Bocanegra to show how Dominican, Jesuit, and lay clergy believed that Spanish-Quechua grammars and guidebooks for confessors could re-form Indigenous languages and bodies in the sixteenth- and seventeenth-century Andes. However, even though this logic repeats over two centuries, chapter 4 shows that this evangelical project—and the documents needed to carry it out—required revision, supplementation, and reformation. Form, these texts proposed, promised to organize colonial life but constantly proved incapable of doing so. Each text contained a retrospective and pessimistic glance that revealed the limitations of form's evangelical power. They show, as does this book as a whole, that colonial relations prove open to deformation.

The coda addresses Icíar Bollaín's 2010 *También la lluvia,* a film that traces the production of an epic staging the conquest of the Americas. Though *También la lluvia* takes place during the Cochabamba Water War in Bolivia, it uses the conquest to show how the past reverberates in a neo-colonial present. While much of the past is used for these presentist ends, this coda explores why certain scenes remain unreproducible: namely, scenes of maternal infanticide taken from Las Casas's *Brevísima relación*. By using the methods of queer historicism and Indigenous studies, the coda contends that maternal infanticide escapes knowledge and mobilization due to relational opacity and the differential conditions of colonial violence. The coda argues that opacity offers a more ethical engagement for scholars to build relations with the past and better consider the dangers of reproducing the historical violence they seek to redress.

Forms of Relation follows José Esteban Muñoz's call in *Cruising Utopia* to consider how the practice of kinship-in-relation is inextricable from possibility. As he posits, kinship opens up a "vast lifeworld . . . , an encrypted sociality, and a utopian potentiality" that theorizes multiple "*forms* of belonging-in-difference."[76] Muñoz's insight is critical: rather than point to a final synthesis, he describes kinship as a dynamic movement that builds "forms" of living.[77] Relation is not known or static; instead, it takes form in unforeseen ways of being and belonging. Form shows that relation is constantly remade in difference.[78] Of course, remaking happens within and under the shadow of colonialism. This means that form and relation do not offer a liberatory "outside" to the ways that forms were recruited by colonialism to shape what kinship could mean in the past—or today. As María Elena Martínez warned, when scholars work to study or extract imperial subjects from texts, we threaten to duplicate the goals and methods of a colonial apparatus and its agents who used violent methods to discover the "truth" of others.[79] We become parts of a relation made in the colonial dictates of knowledge production. In its standardized rules of relation, however, form is as much a system of occlusion as it is revelation. While form brings subjects into a colonial system, form's standardizing rules keep certain practices and knowledges out of the purview of colonial authorities—and scholars. As Michel-Rolph Trouillot posed, the archive is full of silences.[80] While this book strives to offer new ways of looking at kinship and relations, it also acknowledges the silences occasioned by the interplay between form and relation. These silences can and did frustrate the desires of colonial agents to know and reform the colonial world, carving out spaces of survival for those subjected to colonial power. Hopefully, my emphasis on form can acknowledge the power and value of those silences and leave many of them here.

❦ 1

Misuse and Maternity
Infanticide and the Relations of Conquest

The *Brevísima relación de la destrucción de las Indias,* the Dominican Bartolomé de Las Casas's printed polemic condemning Spanish praxis in the so-called Indies,[1] is a text that has been put to use.[2] By the time it was published in 1552, the Spanish had been granted almost sixty years of authority to convert Indigenous peoples by the papal bull *Inter Caetera* in 1493. Subsequent bulls, the violence of conquest, the failures of conversion, and competition from other imperial powers, however, put that authority in doubt. Pope Paul III issued a bull in 1537, asserting that conversion could not come at the expense of Indigenous property or liberty; likewise, rival empires such as France refused to admit the validity of the early donation altogether. The *Brevísima relación* helped rivals undermine Spanish claims, a fact reflected in the text's extensive translations. By the end of the seventeenth century, twenty-nine editions had appeared in Dutch, thirteen in French, six in English, six in German, three in Italian, and three in Latin. The 1598 Latin edition *Narratio regionum indicarum,* accompanied by Theodor de Bry's engravings of horrific violence, served as many European audiences' first images of Spanish deeds in the Americas and their most authoritative ones. Thus, Las Casas's text and its visceral depiction of violence facilitated the definition of the Spanish on a global stage. For this reason, the *Brevísima relación* is often credited with the foundation of Spain's "Black Legend," a rhetorical strategy by which other imperial powers portrayed Spain's dealings with Indigenous peoples as uniquely cruel.[3]

Yet, while competing imperial powers used the *Brevísima relación* to assert the fixity of Spanish and Indigenous relations, this text was written with a different use in mind. It hoped for change. Las Casas argued for the future transformation of Spanish praxis in the Indies, even though his text was published on the heels of an earlier failure. Las Casas had given an extensive oral presentation (the *Larguísima relación*) ten years earlier to the Crown on the errors of conquest and the excesses of the *encomienda,* a labor system predicated on evangelization under which Indigenous peoples worked for an *encomendero* in exchange for their Christian instruction—a practice that resulted in de facto enslavement.[4] Though the *Larguísima* helped pass the New Laws in 1542, which would abolish the *encomienda,* that section of the laws was repealed only three years later after the viceroy of New Spain refused to enact them, and the viceroy of Peru was killed in return for his attempts. As a partial solution, the *Brevísima relación* thus turns to the relational power of form. Via a *relación,* the author reaches a wider reading public and works to persuade Prince Philip (who would become Philip II) to beseech his father Charles V to abolish this labor system.[5] Though condemnatory, the violence depicted in the *Brevísima relación* is meant to present a distinct political and evangelical possibility—that is, a different relation—to a wide set of interlocutors.

This is, therefore, a text marked by relations. However, not all relations have received the same attention. Among the many scenes that populate the Dominican's polemic against Spanish acts of horror in the Indies, there are moments when the emblematic victims of conquest enact violence as well. Alongside repeating scenes of Spaniards attacking women and children, readers of the *Brevísima relación* confront women—often mothers—who are said to kill children. Since Spanish acts of terror constitute the rhetorical thrust of this text and its polemic charge, scholars have tended to pass over women's alleged acts of violence in the text, perhaps since they function as another sign of horror. However, in diminishing the potential difference of women's violence, we overlook the work of specific relations, as well as the roles of gender, sexuality, and kinship in the text. In this chapter, I take a different approach and engage scenes of infanticide head-on. I focus on infanticide in the *Brevísima relación* to ask, evoking Sara Ahmed, "what's the use" of this specific relation?[6] What relational practices—present and future—do scenes of infanticide occasion in the *Brevísima relación* itself?

"Use" is central to this analysis.[7] While Carlos Jáuregui and David Solodkow contend that a twin economic and religious conception of *usus* and *fructus* helped subtend sovereign right in the Indies,[8] we cannot ignore that production through use is a profoundly gendered relation. In its exercise, *usar* is a transitive verb that defines a hierarchical, male-centered social order whereby women's bodies are engaged to accomplish goals. Gendered land is used for harvest, and women are used to reproduce future laboring ones. If gendered labor occurs, as Faye Ginsburg and Rayna Rapp state, in "events throughout the human and especially female life-cycle related to the ideas and practices surrounding fertility, birth, and childcare, including the ways in which these figure into understandings of social and cultural renewal,"[9] then the misuse of women and the death of children in the world of the *Brevísima relación* forestalls the very relational promise of the Indies and its *evangelical* renewal.

By juxtaposing this text with early modern discussions of kinship, maternity, and child death, I show how intervention on behalf of children served as an imperial practice in Iberia, where royal authorities worked to "save" the children of *moriscos* and *conversos* (Christian converts from Islam and Judaism, respectively) from corporeal and spiritual death. In those cases, however, culpability rested with heretical parents; in the *Brevísima relación,* culpability is rerouted via "misuse" away from Indigenous women and to the Christian actor.[10] Misuse leads away from the mother to the conquistador and, in a striking move, implicates the royal father as well. The textual *relación* works through infanticide to describe the endangerment that Spanish relations pose to the Indies and presents a solution via a change in kinship.

Though I explore the rhetorical "use" of infanticide in the construction of a colonial form of relation, my ultimate question for this chapter is a different one. Is there something outside of the "use" and, thus, the displacement of women? When women are treated as passive mothers *forced* to commit infanticide due to Spanish violence, their acts become easy to resolve—signs of misuse rather than unresolvable moments of confrontation. For this reason, I conclude with a speculative invitation to the reader: I ask how and where we might find the rhetorical relations of infanticide that are managed so tightly in the *Brevísima relación* to be "unuseful." By looking to moments of opacity and differential types of description—in grammar, speech, and silence—I ask if the presentation of infanticide encapsulates small slippages that make relations unwieldy. Of course, I do not attempt to give voice to mothers or women inside or outside of the text's pages since each scene is highly rhetorical, selected, and modified. Yet, even if these scenes are mediated, they should not be taken as one-dimensional. A priority in reading imperial texts will always be an interrogation of why and how certain relational forms might be deemed useful—to whom and to what end. Therefore, we should also ask where, why, and how such useful relations might reach their limits.

Conquest as Kinship

In this study concerned with the mutable relations configured by bodies, gender, sexuality, and text, the form that identifies Las Casas's work—the *relación*—is fruitful. *Relación* is a term that appears in several genres of colonial writing, from *relaciones de méritos y servicios* (letters of merits and services), to *cartas relatorias* (letters relating transpired events), and *relaciones geográficas* (surveys).[11] In each case, the term points to a form of legalese and historical accounting that relies on colonial hierarchies. A *relación* names a relation that creates a mutually affirmative relationship between writer and recipient. This form demands that a witness narrates services rendered to an authority via the faithful vassal-writer's personal experience. The *Brevísima relación* proves no exception in its ascription to this form, as seen when Las Casas introduces passages with the authorizing "one time I saw," "I saw," and "I saw other things."[12] These are not stylistic flourishes. As confirms José Rabasa, these are epistemological conventions that "define who has the authority to speak and what is legitimate knowledge."[13] In that regard, though Cynthia L. Stone, Stephanie Merrim, and Juan Bautista Avalle-Arce all note that the *Brevísima relación* emphasizes history as a "homily" rather than a disconnected series of events focused on Las Casas's embodiment, the experiential convention of form explains how the physicality of relation becomes a means of articulating and building the *relación*.[14] Las Casas serves as the royal interlocutor's eyes since the court "had not seen" the Indies.[15] That said, if the text resonates with certain formal conventions, suggesting that Las Casas has labored as a humble servant who merits recompense from the royal recipient, favors are unique in kind. The demand that Las Casas makes on the royal interlocutor is a change in transatlantic relations writ large. Prince Philip is hailed as a paternal figure who has let his own duties slide, an act that enables the destruction of the Indies. The *relación* demands that the Crown attend to a religious and political promise that has been destroyed by conquest and the *encomienda* system. The *relación* composes a web of kinship in the construction and critique of transatlantic relations.

To understand the operation of the text requires an exegesis of how destruction appears as a matter of kinship, whereby Spanish vassals violate the evangelical goals of discovery (and royal authority) by destroying Indigenous social and family structures, a Spanish political system, and a Christian order, all centered around paternal authority. In each section of the text, Spaniards enter a region, kill Indigenous men, and commit subsequent acts of violence against "exposed" women and children. As a sign of order's deformation in function of this masculine relationality, Indigenous peoples are often identified as parts of a system dependent on able-bodied men. Spaniards separate "fathers from sons and wives from husbands"—terms that cast them in legible family units.[16] By describing Spanish assaults as ones on the family, the *Brevísima relación* locates Indigenous peoples in the inviolate rhetoric of kinship that made a group legible as a polity to Western interlocutors. As Anthony Pagden writes, the family served "as the basis for every social group, as every civil society was created from an aggregation of progressively larger units of which the family was the first, and the city the last stage in the continuum."[17] With an emphasis on the coherent family as part and parcel of all Indigenous peoples' existence, the text casts any negative representation of kinship organization—a commonplace in arguments by apologists of conquests—as a clear consequence of conquistadors, rather than a function of these peoples' inherent "nature, character, or customs," as writes Rolena Adorno.[18]

Indeed, the violation of the Indigenous family by Spaniards opens the text and dictates the initial terms of destruction. The *Brevísima relación* begins "on the island of Hispaniola, which was the first . . . the Christians entered and [where they] began their rampage and ruin of these people whom they first destroyed and depopulated." The inception of the Spanish mission (this is where Christians "entered" and "began") is defined as a devastating practice built around kinship. Violence against the family and population (via depopulation) is inseparable from violence against reproduction/conversion. Indeed, the ironic moniker given to these Spaniards—"Christian"—indicates this fact. However, this violence is not distributed equally. Though the failure of evangelization turns on assaults against the family, women and children face a unique permutation of violence. The text continues to describe how destruction could be seen "beginning with the Christians taking native women and children from the Indian [men] to serve themselves and *to misuse them.*"[19] The "beginning" of destruction emerges from relational violence with women and children "misused."

As noted above, use is central to the expression of conquest as a relational practice. As a noun, *uso* (use) names a subject-object relationship that Sebastián de Covarrubias calls "the act and exercise of using something" in his 1611 dictionary, the *Tesoro de la lengua castellana o española*. Though this relationship is one of using, the options for putting an object into practice are not limitless. The use of something remits to a standard exercise deemed appropriate by a community. As Covarrubias writes of the verb *usar*, using is an action "which is customary," meaning that exercise is predetermined and regulated according to a standard or law.[20] Use is not at liberty to be chosen but rather systematized and ordered. It is dictated by convention.

In the *Brevísima relación,* wherein the object to be used is a gendered one, misuse describes the opposition between destruction and cultivation/ increase. The text notes how Spaniards send "men to the mines to extract gold, which is an intolerable job, and women to the ranches, which are the farms, to till the soil and cultivate the land, work for strong and robust men."[21] With men in the mines, women seed and harvest the earth instead of cultivating the fruit of their own bodies. Las Casas continues, "as the husbands are apart and never saw their wives, generation ceased between them . . . [and] the men perish in the mines due to work and hunger, while women die on the ranches or the farms for the same reason."[22] The present misuse of Indigenous women is figured forward; the cessation of "genera- tion" threatens generations to come due to the recurrent lack of procreation and corporeal harvest. In his section on Cuba, Las Casas records that "with fathers and mothers taken to the mines, more than seven thousand children died of hunger in three or four months in my presence."[23] In each case, labor demands cause the cessation of procreation, with women physically unable to sustain their children and exercise the gendered "labor" of their bodies. As a result, the text states, "The milk of new mothers' breasts dried up [on them], and thus all the little ones died shortly after."[24] The consequence of this act is charged in legal terms; indeed, Emilie Bergmann describes medie- val Iberian legal codes that protected women's breasts "in recognition of the vital role of breast milk in the first two years of an infant's life."[25] However, it is equally important to consider how the grammar of culpability points to the form that colonial relation has taken. Milk dries *on* women, a passive result of conquest acts. When women are put to work for economic ends, their ability to sustain children disappears since misuse has been chosen over proper use.[26] Child death and the misuse of women are expressive of a failed transatlantic relation. Evangelical and political threats take shape in a description of present consequences figured in the bodies of the misused mother *and* the endangered child.

The Use of Misuse

This physical and allegorical focus on the "child" in the *Brevísima relación* resonates with a series of recent developments in queer studies, Indigenous studies, and postcolonial studies that have attended to how children— both real and allegorical—figure in the constitution of colonial programs. In the US context, queer studies has operated under the shadow of Lee Edelman's *No Future* (2004), which emphasized how the idealized "child" becomes a means for conservative policies to justify their implementation, making sure that the proper future exists for the "child" to enjoy. Sharpening this claim, José Esteban Muñoz and others have emphasized that politics focused on the "child" are always colonial in nature. While Edelman focuses on the sexually deviant adult, Muñoz shows that certain youth are marked as "pathological" due to race, ethnicity, or other ideas of pathology.[27] US politics, he poses, do not imagine a universal "child" equally deserving of defense, but rather different children tied to kinship units constituted through racialization.

Such insight is crucial as we begin to consider the *Brevísima relación* since scholars of empire and indigeneity have considered how the "child" often subtended imperial policies and undergirded ideas of racialization. Researchers working on US empire (Laura Briggs) and Dutch East Asia (Ann Laura Stoler) have shown how imperial regimes argued that the education of colonial children was a necessary piece of the white man's burden—a discourse that justified continued dominance and intervention through a practice of racializing infantilization.[28] Indigenous studies scholars reveal similar processes as part of settler colonial projects. Margaret D. Jacobs and Brenda J. Child have shown how the US robbed Indigenous children from their parents and placed them in boarding schools to "reeducate them" in the US,[29] while Enrique Mases has explored similar cases in Argentina.[30] Finally, Mark Rifkin has intertwined these threads by showing how boarding schools worked to transform the kinship practices and sexual identities of Indigenous children through reeducation and racialization.[31]

These studies of imperial management can focus our attention on the place of children in the *Brevísima relación,* but the comparison must be taken with a historical grain of salt. Often, studies focus on the nineteenth through the twenty-first centuries and can thus obscure how a "child" invokes differential types of endangerment in the early modern Spanish world.[32] On the Iberian Peninsula, priests and rhetoricians drew upon narratives that linked infanticide to religious others—namely the Jews and Muslims who populated the Bible and local communities. Indeed, when Spanish humanist Fray Luis de Granada discussed the power of rhetoric in his treatise the *Método de Predicar* (1576), he selected as an exemplary case the "Massacre of the Innocents" from the *Book of Matthew* (2:16). This scene describes the Jewish king Herod murdering all children under two years old and tied Jews to infanticide.[33] In turn, alleged acts of infanticide defined Jews, Muslims, the recently converted *moriscos* (former Muslims), and *conversos* (former Jews) in the flesh via the infamous blood libel.

Cases such as the martyrdom of the "Holy Child of La Guardia" (martirio del Santo niño de la Guardia [dated to either 1490 or 1491]) turned upon the alleged murder of a three-year-old boy known by the charged name of Cristóbal (Christ carrier). The eight Jewish men and one *converso* accused of conducting a sacrificial performance of Christ's passion on this child were captured, subjected to an inquisition trial, and finally hanged in punishment.[34] When reading the *Brevísima relación,* we need to remember that for early modern Iberia, there was no doubt that religious others like Jews and *conversos* were infanticidal criminals.

An ideology of endangerment allowed religious states to proclaim a looming threat of "incapacity" and authorize intervention in Iberia. Even though the regions of the Spanish empire, including Castile and Aragon, did not have a shared or consistent practice regarding the robbery of Jewish, Muslim, or converts' children,[35] they shared a belief in a community's responsibility to the "child." Each polity demanded that a religious and royal state intervene (though we may question the motivations or efficacy of this rhetoric). Intervention on behalf of children stretched across time and space in the sixteenth- and seventeenth-century Iberian territories. While many studies focus on the *morisco* expulsion in 1609, Iberian authorities also forcibly took children and placed them with "Old Christian" families before and after the expulsion of the Jews in 1492, as Mercedes García-Arenal has shown.[36] Mary Elizabeth Perry also reaffirms the long durée of this process, noting that the Archbishop of Granada Pedro Guerrero promoted the removal of *morisco* boys from their homes and their education in Christian schools in 1555–60 (a period that coincides with the publication of the *Brevísima relación*).[37] The transatlantic resonances of this practice were more striking than scholars might know, as the state managed its "reeducation" of *moriscos* in dialogue with the Americas by using the methods of conversion employed in the *encomienda*. *Morisco* children were often subject to labor for their new family in exchange for their religious instruction.[38] For this reason, Georgina Dopico Black posits that these expulsions and child thefts reveal some "of the first instances of *parens patriae,* of a modern state assuming custodial rights over minors of parents deemed unfit."[39]

Therefore, this will be a transatlantic phenomenon, with the *Brevísima relación* serving as one of many rhetorical intertexts. If child murder proved one to be an enemy of Christ, then physical protection of abandoned children showed one to be a "true" Christian and member of a sanctified state. According to Bianca Premo, the discourse of child protection, especially for the "exposed," functioned as powerful rhetoric from the sixteenth through the eighteenth centuries. When parents "orphaned" infants at the doorways of churches, at private residences, and in the streets, officials were hailed to intervene.[40] Though exposure was often little more than a death sentence, as writes Ann Twinam, various communities in the transatlantic Iberian world constructed Casas de Niños Expósitos or foundling homes for these children.[41] Premo notes one case in which a man named Luis Brochero wrote to rally community support to create a foundling hospital in Seville in 1624 by claiming that abandoned children were "yours."[42] Ilder Mendieta Ocampo writes of a similar case in which friars wrote a petition laden with pathos to gain funds for the Hospital de Niños Huérfanos in Lima (1603). There, friars described how they uncovered orphans "eaten by dogs or in rivers or gutters."[43] Similarly, Ondina E. González describes a case from seventeenth-century Cuba where bishop Diego Evelino Hurtado de Compostela wrote Charles II to explain that Cuban mothers would leave children "exposed" in the countryside, in the sea, or in doorways, and thus required support.[44] In these calls for intervention, Spanish authors echoed the same model of the *Brevísima relación*. They suggested that only those readers ignorant of the terrible suffering of children could allow such events to continue and not act. In such calls, the survival of children implicated the entire community. By describing children left "to the dogs," works cast Spanish and *criollo* interlocutors as kin responsible for a child's survival when natal networks lacked means or sought to hide stains on family honor.[45]

When the *Brevísima relación* describes violence against the family, it participates in this staid tradition. To kill children was to be an enemy of Christ. Yet, this text presents an important permutation: the *Brevísima relación* warns that *Spanish* acts of infanticide will make Christian Spaniards appear no different from biblical villains and religious others that the state condemned. The condemnations via infanticide in Las Casas's text are not subtle. As the text notes, these Christians "entered towns, leaving no children or old men, nor pregnant women or new mothers that they did not tear open at the belly or cut to pieces as if they were attacking sheep herded into a pen."[46] It continues to note how this group "took children by the legs from the breasts of their mothers and smashed [the children's] heads against the rocks."[47] In such scenes, women are seemingly all mothers described in terms of their ties to children; they are either currently pregnant or have recently given birth and continue breastfeeding. This alignment between the pregnant woman and child is unsurprising, given that early modern definitions of *madre* cast the mother's existence in function of the child's growth. As Covarrubias wrote, "mother" came "from the Latin noun *mater,* correlate of the child. . . . In women, this is the genitals and the place where the fetus is conceived, *latine matrix, genitale arvum.*"[48] Lest these passages from the *Brevísima relación* be considered only in terms of their descriptions of reproductive death on earth, Las Casas's Christian rhetoric shows that the conceptualization of child death extends to evangelical failure. Bodies and families are torn apart as would be defenseless "lambs" (*corderos*), naming the Christological parallel between the family and the flock. When soldiers enact infanticide, they *become* Spain's religious others from the Iberian Peninsula and attack the Christian state's religious goals in practice.

The condemnation of infanticide in this tract shows how the governmental and spiritual practice of "making live" turns on gender relations and kinship since protection of the "child" focalizes the form of the colonial mission and its relational terms.[49] As pose Jáuregui and Solodkow, "the Lascasian political calculation of sovereignty implies that the king not only 'takes life or lets live,' but also that he *must* 'foster life and prevent death,'" a practice that is at once terrestrial and celestial.[50] The full political equation in this text, however, cannot be understood without attention to gender and kinship. When the text focuses on infanticide and the misuse of women, it condemns a conquest system that cannot make Indigenous peoples live in the political or spiritual body politic. Infanticide reveals an undoing of the religious-political Christian mission, the same one that subtends Spanish legitimacy and its goals in the Indies. In the *Brevísima relación,* the misuse of women and the death of children does not only impinge upon relations here and now but also upon the evangelical making live in the afterlife.

The threat of this current form of relation constituted by misuse and infanticide, however, also contains a resonant response: from the onset of Las Casas's text, the *relación* draws upon a constitution of a paternal relation laid out in the "Prólogo." In an appeal to patriarchal power, the text opens: "Divine providence has ordered of its world, that for the direction and common utility of the human lineage, it shall be ordered in kingdoms and towns. Like fathers and pastors (as Homer names them), kings shall be the noblest and most generous members of the republics. There shall be no doubt of the rectitude of their spirits, and with correct reason, it shall be held that if any defects or ills plague their kingdoms, it shall merely be the cause that the kings are unaware of them."[51] As father to his children and pastor to his flock, Prince Philip is invested with the ultimate responsibility for controlling the social and religious order of the Indies.[52] This organization is cast in patriarchal terms that are at once religious and terrestrial—rhetoric that would be particularly effective in the Hapsburg court, Premo argues, given that this ruling house "thought of themselves as patriarchs who occupied their position, not because of the divine right of kings, but because of the divine right of fathers."[53] With an insinuation of paternal negligence, Las Casas implicates an absentee father who enables destruction by allowing subjects to usurp and thus undermine royal right. In violating royal power across the Atlantic, conquistadors disregard hierarchies in the Indies and divest a political system of its male foundation. Since, according to Las Casas, "war commonly leaves only adolescents and women,"[54] the *Brevísima relación* presents an Indies that meets destruction because it lacks a proper kinship form. The prologue reaches out to its royal recipient through a *relación* that turns on relation, intersecting a textual form with a social-political platform that treats the devastation of the Indies as a struggle in relations. Violence against impotent bodies, signaled through acts like infanticide, lays bare the stakes of the royal interlocuter's intervention or inaction—and presents a viable solution for redemption.

The Unuseful Relation

Spanish acts of infanticide show one way that the *Brevísima relación* brings Indigenous peoples into the text, making kinship a discourse that can condemn current transatlantic relations and offer a method of re-formation. In this final section, I want to address the complexity that emerges in a different relation when Indigenous peoples—namely mothers—kill children in the *Brevísima relación*. These gendered scenes of violence cannot be taken as veridical documentation—each example is selected, if not created, to add weight to the *narratio* and final *peroration* of the *relación*. Yet, to refuse any consideration of these scenes is to accept the passive "use" of women as rhetorical and relational tools *tout court*. Instead, this final section asks how descriptions of maternal infanticide enmeshed in a text that describes the violence of conquest might prove unwieldy and unusable. Might even the strategic, rhetorical presentation of maternal infanticide present an unusable form that is not available for the reformation of transatlantic relations?

The rhetorical use of mothers' infanticidal acts in the *Brevísima relación* is, at first glance, clear. Through no fault of their own, they are incapacitated by conquest violence and led to "expose" a child. In consequence, they permit the text to juxtapose the two models of Spanish relation that have been cast in stark contrast: conquest violence versus political/evangelical reform. Take, for instance, a key example that shows how the text displaces a woman-mother even as she commits this act: "As the wretched Spaniards were travelling with their fierce dogs, searching for and tearing apart the Indians, both men and women, a sick Indian woman, seeing that she would be unable to escape the dogs and thus prevent them from tearing her to pieces as they had done to others, took a rope, tied a one-year-old child that she had to her leg, and hung herself from a beam. She did not do it quickly enough to prevent the dogs from arriving; they tore apart the child, though a friar baptized the infant before it died."[55] Though this passage occurs in a specific chapter on the "Reino de Yucatán," the stage is set in the imperfect tense ("como andaban"), suggesting the systematic nature of Spanish cruelty as opposed to its exceptional singularity. Las Casas moves from the meandering Spaniards into the Indigenous woman's perspective, where he presents her weighing two options. Escape is mentioned only in terms of its impossibility; though Las Casas's comment on illness evinces the place of disease in conquest, it also limits the woman's potential responses to the encroaching Spaniards.[56] Las Casas thus portrays the Indigenous woman as she contemplates the two possible paths of her death. The first is murder by dogs, which repeats similar acts committed "as they had done to others." The second option is cast in opposition to the first one: to avoid the dogs, the woman hangs herself. Ruth Hill reminds scholars to avoid reading such moments as authentic speech or inner thoughts—a topic to which I will return—considering Las Casas's inability to ascertain such motivations or to "witness" interiority.[57] Instead, it proves more fruitful to consider how the text is resolutely relational: though it may begin with the woman, it ends with the child and two contrasting relations.

While the woman opens this tableau, the dogs and priest that conclude it are less concerned with her, suggesting that the child embodies the stakes of the scene. The dogs move with violent intent, but the friar intervenes with baptism. The child, therefore, intersects opposing relations: the form of conquest violence versus religious conversion. Each of these colonial actors poses a distinct relation (and temporal order) with this child: whereas the dogs and conquistadors bring destruction and death, the friar creates an evangelical future through baptism. The text's order emphasizes this point. Though the dogs end this scene chronologically, the narration ends with the friar's baptism of the child. Therefore, against the finality of death, the child's future is ensured by the friar's intervention. If Las Casas had decried the fact that Indigenous peoples die "without religion or the sacraments," here, the friar enables the Indigenous child to "live" as a member of the Christian family in the next world—an evangelical transformation that operates as a "rebirth" in the face of death.[58] The friar does not merely fend off the dogs and soldiers; his baptismal act works as a type of intervention that completes a gendered kinship function: it ensures the (after)life of the child.[59] We must, however, remember that a perverse presence remains: the woman hangs in the background. While this scene might be a case of the church's maternal figuration and salvific intervention,[60] psychoanalytic scholars like Anne McClintock would likely cast it as an example of colonialism's arrogation of women's "power of origins."[61]

Clearly, this intervention is cast as an interruption of the dogs of conquest; it is not an antagonistic response to the potential agency of women or a reflection on the danger of non-Christian parents, as was the case of the *conversos* and the *moriscos*. Rather, this mother is a tragic and impotent victim. This fact merits pause since it provides a contrast to general treatments of infanticide and maternal power that circulated in the Iberian Peninsula. In general terms, mothers could be seen as dangers to patriarchal authority—especially in early life stages.[62] Repeated Iberian legal codes, most importantly, the *Siete Partidas* (1265) upon which much of Spanish American law would be constituted, had treated infanticide and abortion as acts of parricide (the murder of a blood relative) meriting punishment by death or life imprisonment. In Iberia, the idea that a mother had committed infanticide was a grave accusation.[63] In turn, in the specific case of the Americas, multiple extirpators of idolatry would engage the idea of infanticide as a way of imagining the Indigenous collective in difference.[64] By contrast, the attribution of maternal threat has no apparent presence in Las Casas's text. Instead, Indigenous infanticide always follows from Spanish violence, i.e., misuse. Las Casas answers the question of "why" this act has been committed before it can be asked by letting a reader see the motivation of a woman who "sees [herself]," making salvation an efficacious solution to a scene of maternal desperation. She does not act. She reacts. In the process, Las Casas's text evacuates ambiguity. The desired escape for the self and the child is explained, making sense of the senseless.

This pattern of making sense through causality does not exist only in the *Brevísima relación*. It also appears in a "Carta" written by the Dominicans of Santo Domingo on June 4, 1518, to William II of Croÿ, an advisor and tutor of the young Charles V. This letter is a probable source for many of the *Brevísima relación*'s scenes—including the one described above.[65] Yet, many of the "Carta's" scenes present important differences. In one case of maternal infanticide, there is again a promise of interior motivation even though the "Carta" presents a crucial difference: there is no religious intervention. One passage is worth quoting at length to show this resonance and divergence between the two texts:

> Given that these mothers saw that they could not have or raise children without suffering intolerable labors and cruelties for having done it, they were forced to avoid conception, or, if already pregnant, to abort, or, if they gave birth, to kill the child to keep him from such terrible afflictions and the captivity they lived under. And this reason has brought them to cease multiplying in the Indies. Like beasts, they kill their children, an act impossible to say of any peoples or even any wild beast, be it tiger or serpent. Certainly, every animal seeks to raise its child. But these women, as stated, unable to suffer the cruelties of the Spaniards, wanted to be free to serve the Christians according to their desires.[66]

This passage casts maternal infanticide as an impossible act that comes to fruition; it states that no mother could kill her child. Yet, these mothers *do* kill their children; they avoid conception, abort pregnancies, and murder their newborns. Mothers go against a "natural function" to reproduce—a symptom and a sign of Spain's transatlantic errors.

The quote is ambivalent regarding a *human* mother's unique affective relationship with her child. Rather, the maternal tie is defined by an impulse that turns on the desire (*querer*) of *all* creatures/beasts (*bestias*) to raise (*criar*) children and produce kinship. Such universality can be seen in Covarrubias's definition of the operative verb *criar*. For the humanist, *criar* links utility to procreation, growth, and production. As he defines *criar*, "It is often taken to mean to raise/to give rise. That is to say: This land gives rise to brave and robust men. In Sicily, one raises (*se cría*) a good deal of saffron; in Cordoba, one raises (*se crían*) good horses, etc. This regimen gives rise (*cría*) to cholera, this other, melancholy. Raise (*criar*) birds, to fatten them [for eating]; raise (*criar*) rabbits, to domesticate them. Contentment gives rise (*cría*) to healthy blood."[67] *Criar,* more than an affective relationship, promises a future result achieved through present practice. Just as in the case of *usar, criar* insinuates value and exercise—each place or person has a "use" to maximize returns. The primary thrust of this definition is (male) power and error regarding the employ of objects. In that regard, infanticide becomes, in part, a reflexive misuse—a disturbed primary function. By quickly sliding infanticide away from human specificity into the realm of the "beast" in the animal kingdom, the passage moves away from the autonomy of the mother's actions. Instead, it highlights male practice as a source of devastating consequence. Though women act, the "Carta" insinuates the same attribution of culpability and causality where men subvert the proper use of Indigenous women we saw in the *Brevísima relación*. These women "were forced" (*eran compelidas*) to kill their children because of what they saw; even though these acts and their motivation are partially explained, the trauma and disruption remain attributed to another. Yet, against a possibility of future change, these are moments that persist in a present that forecloses a redemptive future. Women are said to remove themselves and their children from the captivity in which they live. This scene asks if infanticide troubles a redemptive narrative when *women* perform the act.

While a similar example of the temporal predicament that inheres in maternal infanticide does appear in printed editions of the *Brevísima relación,* it is not quite inside the text. Instead, an explicit scene of unresolved infanticide surfaces in an "epistolary fragment and relation" appended to the *Brevísima relación* and attributed to an "unnamed writer."[68] It is fitting that this fragmented *relación* extends beyond the *Brevísima relación*'s more familiar relational logic, given that this passage questions the "use" of the maternal relation. As it notes:

> And when the said captain left Quito, taking with him a large number of its inhabitants and separating couples . . . , a woman with a small child in her arms went after him, shouting and telling him not to take her husband since she had three small children that she would be unable to raise (*criar*) and they would die out of hunger. And seeing that she was ignored, she spoke a second time even louder, yelling that her children would certainly die (*on her*) out of hunger; and seeing that she was to be dismissed and that they would not return her husband, she threw the child against some rocks and killed him.[69]

Here, the text consolidates multiple forms of violence into one passage: the *encomienda* system, predicated on Spanish power and male labor, leads to a mother's incapacity and the cessation of reproduction. Though this scene appears in the voice of the witness-author, it explains the relational logic of a disrupted kinship form from the mother's point of view. She asserts that Spanish action eliminates her husband's presence and will lead to the death of her "three small children" (*tres niños chiquitos*), a future event that the text articulates through a passive construction that attributes culpability to exterior force "would die *on her* out of hunger" (*se le moririan de hambre*). This scene thus makes explicit the relational claim that Las Casas poses throughout the *Brevísima relación:* a stable patriarchal structure undergirds the family form, and the death of children remits to Spanish acts. However, in the final sentence, the woman's violent action inverts her powerlessness and mirrors Las Casas's earlier condemnation of active Spaniards who "smashed [the children's] heads against the rocks."[70] Though this scene includes the same pieces of the *Brevísima relación,* it puts them together in a different and troubling way. While there is the same articulation of misuse, the mother's act renders her useless in this economy predicated on male power and reproduction. This act forestalls the possibility of future change. Instead, it enforces a relation that exists in the present and cannot be re-formed in the shape of intervention to come. This open-ended relation in the epistolary "fragment" creates a *relación* without closure; it is a kinship form in the present that does not relace a possible resolution or horizon of reformation. This returns us to the friars' "Carta." That letter shows how the undefined and uncaptured physical and affective "labors" in the present always undermine the passivity of *criar.* Infanticide doubles back as a foreclosure of new relations or forms of colonial kinship that depend upon maternal labor.[71] The opacity surrounding maternal infanticide is too dense to be used or reformed in a facile way. It is *unuseful.*

If use and misuse help build the relations that bind the *relación* together, then the unuseful is dissimilar. The unuseful relation cannot be corrected in a future moment because it cannot be reversed, recuperated, or repaired. To that end, I conclude with a final example of infanticide that is easily overlooked in the *Brevísima relación* to show how the unuseful can disappear from a text when it exits from the system of relation named by the *Brevísima relación*'s kinship forms—whether those be conditioned by destruction or repair. In its unusability, this scene of infanticide refuses the dialectic between use and misuse and instead turns away from relation. Here, Las Casas describes the Spanish robbery of Indigenous foodstuffs, a practice that led to widespread starvation. After a description of this devastation, he concludes, "It occurred that a mother killed her child out of hunger to eat him."[72] In the ultimate disruption of reproductive logic, a woman is said to kill and consume her child.[73] The stakes of this passage are, of course, the horror of the event, one caused by the violence of Spaniards and conquest. Yet, a differential presentation makes this scene of maternal violence unusable. Though the inclusion of this passage in the text lets it be "seen" by readers, it has not been seen by the writer. The passage is introduced by the agent-less "it happened" (*acaeció*).

Alongside *usar, acaecer* helps define the relational terms of violence in the *Brevísima relación*. However, given the verb's removal of an explicit agent, it provides a different structural frame that extracts responsibility for the form of relations that Spanish praxis has taken. *Acaecer* shows that the Indies have an immanent use that has been undermined systematically. Indeed, this verb opens the "Argumento del presente epitome" to explain that the providential possibility of the Indies and the subsequent violence— "all things that *have happened*" (*han acaecido*)—have not been seen by those who remain in Spain.[74] In his treatment of this verb, Obed Omar Lira posits that *acaecer* draws from a common biblical tradition of the *sermo humilis; acaecer* is an introductory phrase to a staged tableau that lifts human struggle toward the divine.[75] It is a rhetorical conceit that converts the terrestrial into the holy. Yet, lest we forget, the *relación* also insists on the visual; it is a transatlantic transit of information in and as a composition of relations that is both rhetorical *and* sensorial. Though this moment may be unseen, it makes a claim on the embodied. It is this visceral employ of *acaecer* in the description of an unthinkable, physical act that makes it so out of place and time—so *unuseful*—for a narration of repair and redemption. Unlike other moments of women's infanticide that exist in proximity to male actors, the woman's action turns against presence and intervention. The "familiar" act operates in an unfamiliar way, refusing the logic of maternal infanticide's binary of use-misuse as deployed by the text. The mother does not take presence, and she forestalls relation. Even the verb that puts her in relation is at once transitive and intransitive: "to eat" (*comer*) can make relation and take an object but also refuse relation altogether.

This scene does not offer itself to be viewed but rather looks away—even as it demands to be recognized. Of course, the historical "event" of maternal infanticide is presented in the *Brevísima relación* for external consumption as a relation that builds the *relación*. These acts of violence are part of the textual form that occasions relations between the writer and the reading public. This means that, as Avery Gordon writes after Hortense Spillers, we see violent acts put into use.[76] These are events that "*do* occur, to be sure" and repeat their violence (if differently) in "the conventions dictating how we receive, imagine, and pass them on."[77] The mobilization of infanticide for "use" in Las Casas's text—and here—is a violent form of relation in reproduction. Yet, this scene reminds us that such acts also contain an opacity that remains. Infanticide is seen but obliquely; it is related to other acts of violence that are described but unresolved. Just as Kimberly Juanita Brown writes of mothers who commit infanticide under the impossible conditions of enslavement, this act in the *Brevísima relación* shows that all described scenes exist "outside the realm of racial and corporeal familiarity and 'knowing.'" Each scene shows a moment and a tableau where a mother "turn[s] [her] back (refusing a full entrance into the frame) on those who would propose to know [*her*], to put mystery in the place of that *knowing*."[78] While comparison is, by nature, vexed, Brown's statement suggests a resonant "kinship" with Las Casas's text.[79] Maternal infanticide presents a specific turning away that is at once discursively employed and outside the logic of representability and use.

A relation made in form depends upon the intersection of multiple constituents and their arrangements in body and text. In its ascription to these rules, the *Brevísima relación* proves no different: its explicit hail and rhetorical conventions make the textual relationships built outside and within the text part and parcel of a *relación*. Just as Las Casas ties himself to Prince Philip, he brings both himself and the prince into contact and obligation with Spanish Christians (in name only) as well as Indigenous men, women, and children. These overlapping relations constituted in and as form make the *relación* a site that forges kinship: it is not a description but a constitution of a transatlantic polity that defines relations in physicality, rhetoric, and text. There is an urgent and ethical function in this construct. On the one hand, descriptions of infanticide do affirmative, transformative labor. They add urgency to the text and demand intervention from an authority who can and must transform the very real violence and enslavement that constitutes a relational form outside the page. Yet, there is also a need to focus on the differential acts—even those of violence—described in this text, lest we reduce action to Spanish and Indigenous male subjects alone. By considering the mobilization of use, misuse, and uselessness as I have done here, we reveal additional relations that exist in excess of one privileged form. Transatlantic praxis takes on valences that speak to an "Indies" that escapes formal control. We find the opacity of Indigenous motivation, the failures of redemption, and a future that remains out of reach. As has been well studied, the *Brevísima relación* is not representative of Las Casas's greater textual body of work or later political platform; the culmination of his disputations led to an argument for the full restoration of Indigenous sovereignty in his *Doce dudas* (1564) and a proposition that Spaniards could only evangelize, not invade.[80]

Even if the *Brevísima relación* is neither representative nor final in its presentation of Las Casas's work, the gendered logic of "use" continues to appear in colonial texts. Gendered use relations not only refer to mobilizations of human bodies but also land, mines, and souls as the following chapters show.[81] While we may want to decry the use of gendered relations and move on, we must continue to confront these texts head-on—even as we open new archives and supplement well-worn documents. As we trace the use of gendering rhetoric in the canonical works of early colonialism, we must also ask where and how these forms unravel or reach their limits—lest we allow these relations and the forms they take to become settled.

❧ 2

Recomposing Legitimacy
Gender Relations and Indigenous Authorship

Though the *Instrucción del Inca don Diego de Castro Titu Cusi Yupanqui* (1570)[1] is often held to be one of the first Inca-authored histories of Spanish conquest, it does not, strictly speaking, have only one author. Instead, it is a relational text produced in muddled encounters: of speakers, translators, and scribes; of languages and epistemologies; and of textual and rhetorical forms. The notary who concludes the *Instrucción* explains this confusion best. While Titu Cusi presents his words orally to an Augustinian friar, the notary writes down the narrative as the friar "related and organized it."[2] We must, therefore, ask who speaks when Titu Cusi's "I" states—via this translator's "ordered" words and a scribe's pen—that collaboration proves useful since "*I* do not know how Spaniards phrase such matters."[3]

Perhaps, in consequence of this scriptural relationality, the text is marked by discordant commitments. The *Instrucción* condemns Spanish violence against Atahualpa (Titu Cusi's uncle) and Manco Inca (Titu Cusi's father) as illegitimate acts against superior lords to reaffirm Inca political legitimacy. Yet, it also asserts Philip II's authority in the Andes. In turn, it posits Titu Cusi's political merit in the language of kinship, asserting that Titu Cusi is a legitimate heir in the Andes. However, each time the text returns to this assertion, it uses multiple, incompatible proofs. Finally, the projected use of this document undermines the ethnic antagonism that it purports to map. The *relación* (history) is bound to a *poder* (power of attorney) that affords then Viceroy Licentiate Lope García de Castro with the authority to negotiate on Titu Cusi's behalf before the crown.[4] When the *Instrucción* crosses the ocean with García de Castro and "speaks" to the king, it will be in the hands of a Spaniard: García de Castro will embody Titu Cusi before the king and speak as/for the Inca. For this reason, scholars such as Gonzalo Lamana classify texts like the *Instrucción* as "native-like," a category that includes documents and genres from the first decades after the conquest of Peru that were written with the support (coerced or intentioned) of kin, interviewees, scribes, and friars.[5]

As discussed in the last chapter, colonial documents are relational works. Though a text may "speak" with an individual "I," compositional practice and the prescriptions that encourage felicitous reception draw other subjects into what I call colonial "forms of relation." Attention to relation may not prove as contentious in an analysis of western texts such as Las Casas's *Brevísima relación*. However, a focus on relation in the case of "native-like" texts proves more vexed since decolonial studies of Indigenous works often have different priorities. Relation can be an obstacle to one method of studying authorial autonomy, Indigenous epistemology, and agential opposition. However, in this chapter, I contend that a study of relation in the *Instrucción* can support these reading practices and still preserve decolonial commitments: first, it can help foreground instability and uncertainty as a condition of colonial politics and second, it can recenter feminist approaches to texts that are often attributed to male authors and marked by masculinist historiography.

This chapter focuses on form and relations to show how gender rests at the center of a document that works to re-compose an Andean polity in dispute and flux. To illustrate this point, I discuss the discordant deployments of the concept of "legitimacy" in the *Instrucción*. Legitimacy proves particularly useful since, as scholars have noted, gender relations and politics intersect at the core of this concept.[6] While the concept conditioned one's racialized identity,[7] determined the ability to gain Church positions, government posts, and to earn respect in a community,[8] it also served as common parlance to describe political right in the Americas.[9] All of these dimensions are central to the *Instrucción*. Legitimacy will identify sex/gender ties, royal inheritance, and political authority—relations that depend upon the management of social, rhetorical, and textual forms. While scholars have studied the appearance of the concept of legitimacy in the *Instrucción*, they have often engaged this idea to consider the possible authorial influence of Titu Cusi. By addressing this concept's plurality, I foreground how it brings the compositional presence of multiple gendered actors who are not "writers" into view.

When these multiple and discordant attempts to give legitimacy shape surface in the *Instrucción*, they show that this concept provides a point of dispute and relation. Legitimacy reveals how, as Lamana puts it, colonial "practices often ran ahead of discourses."[10] By bringing the appearances of legitimacy to the foreground, we move away from an oppositional narrative where Titu Cusi fights inevitable Spanish dominance.[11] Instead, we recenter gender ties and the historical uncertainty that mark Andean politics.

By no means does a focus on relational composition ignore unequal hierarchies or obviate gendered violence; rather, this focus demands that we conceptualize resistance as less clear-cut in political, epistemological, and gendered terms. Attending to the overlapping and provisional meanings of legitimacy in the *Instrucción* and the relations that their different forms demand show how texts are composed in the uncertainty that surrounds them. Contested forms of relation demonstrate that political order remains unfinished and highlight the intersections of gender and power that define a text made in the fissures of colonial dispute.

Formal Collaborations

The *Instrucción* lends itself to a masculine version of resistance, given its focus on Manco Inca and Vilcabamba—a man and region studied for their opposition to Spanish incursions into the Andes. This narrative focuses on Manco Inca, who, after ending his alliance with Spaniards, led a devastating nine-month siege of Spanish-held Cuzco (the former center of the Inca Empire) between 1535 and 1536. Though he did not retake the city, he managed to entrench himself in the mountainous region of Vilcabamba. Spaniards attempted to destroy Vilcabamba through military incursions over the next thirty years (with the support of Indigenous Andean allies–both Inca who had not joined Manco Inca and other groups).[12] Though at times these battles had destructive effects on the Incas of Vilcabamba, the Spaniards and their Andean allies were unable to capture Manco Inca. Instead, Manco Inca's death came at the hands of Spaniards who had been admitted into Vilcabamba against the advice of Manco Inca's generals, narrative details all recounted in the *Instrucción*. These Spaniards had chosen the losing side of the civil conflicts in Peru by supporting Diego de Almagro (Francisco Pizarro's erstwhile partner turned foe) and had fled Pizarro's forces. As the *Instrucción* would have it, these Almagristas sought to regain a place for themselves in the Spanish polity by murdering Manco Inca, confirming Spanish treachery (and Manco Inca's magnanimity) in the process. For Titu Cusi, such a story suggests that Spaniards could only achieve power through duplicitous means. For scholars, the masculine tenor of this narrative is most convincing. Since, as Lamana puts it, bellicose masculinity proves a familiar and legible form of antagonism that consolidates two oppositional sides, Spanish versus Inca,[13] military "rebellion" provides historiographic fodder for a triumphant representation of Manco Inca as a true insurgent, one who takes up arms in defense of his territory and people. Likewise, Vilcabamba serves as a place of masculine—if futile—resistance, where Manco Inca and his followers perform heroic acts against Spanish power, leading scholars to call "the Vilcabamba region . . . the final bastion of indigenous resistance against European hegemony"[14] and Manco Inca's struggle "the most significant act of resistance of the period of conquest and colonization."[15]

Titu Cusi can offer continuity in this oppositional story. The Crown had already engaged Titu Cusi's brother, Sayri Túpac, a former ruler of Vilcabamba and encouraged that man to leave Vilcabamba in 1557 by granting him the wealthy estate of Yucay. This did not solve the Spanish Crown's difficulties. Titu Cusi remained in Vilcabamba, and Spanish authorities were forced to continue negotiations with letters passing back and forth again, starting in 1561. As the *Instrucción* notes, Titu Cusi signed a partial treaty in the 1566 *Capitulaciones de Acobamba*,[16] where he promised to admit friars into his region (which he did in 1567) and to accept baptism (which he did in 1568). However, colonial negotiators complained that he did not accept the tenets of faith and refused to abandon polygamy. In turn, Titu Cusi promised to leave Vilcabamba and accept Spanish rule (which he did not)—assurances repeated in the *Instrucción*. Given that Titu Cusi never left Vilcabamba, these promises remain circumspect.[17] Thus, he seems to continue in the tradition of his father, even if his weapons are words. Continuing the legacy of his father, Titu Cusi embodies masculine resistance against Spanish assaults on Inca sovereignty in text.

However, if masculine autonomy and binary opposition define discourses of resistance, multiple elements of the text require explanation: its relational composition, the overlap between Titu Cusi's and others' voices, its engagement with Spanish forms, and its performance of supplication and deference. For instance, while the text often uses a first–person "I" that remits to Titu Cusi, the *Instrucción* makes clear that its composition passes through a translator, the Augustinian friar Marcos García, and a *mestizo* scribe, Martín de Pando. Both degrees of separation make Titu Cusi's control over the message in Spanish uncertain.[18] According to the notary, veracity not only depends on the representation of Titu Cusi's voice but also on the structuring force of the friar. The notary must certify that the friar's narrative form (order) and words are represented on the page. As the notary writes at the end of the *Instrucción*, "I, Martín de Pando, notary commissioned by the very illustrious Licentiate Lope García de Castro who was governor of these kingdoms, swear that the above was written as it was related and ordered by said father at the insistence of don Diego de Castro [Titu Cusi]."[19] Form is also consequential. As noted in the introduction and chapter 1, a *relación* has an explicit recipient for whom the information is shaped to persuade, meaning that the Spanish form has a determinant influence on the manner in which information is presented and the way that Andean peoples and Spaniards relate in and around the text to convey a politically salient message. Beyond the collaboration implicated by this writing process and its possible displacement of Titu Cusi's authority, the text is structured by Spanish forms that are cooperative, if not deferential. While a *relación* (history) is by nature a relational form that creates a tie between a writer and recipient, often to procure favors from the latter, it is important to recall that the text is not only a *relación*. It also contains a *poder* (power of attorney).[20] In the *poder,* the text enables García de Castro to speak on Titu Cusi's behalf and in his interest on the other side of the Atlantic. It lets García de Castro speak *as* Titu Cusi. As the final *poder* states in an "I" attributed to Titu Cusi, García de Castro is authorized to speak "in the same way *as I would say and declare everything*" with all petitions and affairs before civil and ecclesiastical courts.[21] In a collapse of Inca self and Spanish other, Titu Cusi becomes García de Castro in this representation, and vice versa, a displacement that emphasizes how the relational frame binds "yo, don Diego de Castro Titu Cusi Yupanqui" to the governor of the Viceroyalty, from whom Titu Cusi had "received many grants and favor."[22] According to the text's introductory frame, Titu Cusi and García de Castro have and will work together with Titu Cusi humbly accepting the authority of the Spanish Crown, "under whose protection I have placed myself."[23] Thus, masculine first-person power rubs against the relational form.

Relation and form, therefore, provide a source of tension in scholarship that interrogates—if not desires—masculinity and authority. While studies of the *Instrucción* recognize the relationships that drive the text's production, they often analyze particular forms and discourses as contributions from different individuals.[24] For instance, by noting the frequent praise of García de Castro in the opening and the *poder,* Marguerite Cattan considers sections of the *Instrucción* to be a self-authored *relación de méritos y servicios* that point back to García de Castro and his own political goals.[25] In contrast, scholars attuned to Titu Cusi's authorial presence have focused on the extensive soliloquies in the *relación* as signs of Inca rhetoric and, in turn, Titu Cusi himself embedded in the Spanish form. Martín Lienhard considers these soliloquies to be "homenajes ritual al Inca" (ritual homages to the Inca), an Inca rhetorical form whereby a new leader would consolidate his rule by casting himself in his father's image while reshaping history.[26] While the soliloquies are many, as the *relación* nears its end, they do function in this manner: Manco Inca "speaks" to the need for Incas to support Titu Cusi's rule. In fact, the "biography" ends with a speech that confirms the passage of Manco Inca's rulership to Titu Cusi and recommends him to his people as their new leader. Yet, while Catherine Julien acknowledges that there is Inca precedent for "dialogic forms," she also notes the prevalence of similar structures "in European colonial texts" like Juan Ginés de Sepúlveda's *Democrates secundus* (1550) and Pedro de Quiroga's *Coloquios de la Verdad* (ca. 1563). In turn, she suggests that these "speeches" in the *Instrucción* present divergences from traditional Inca features, such as the absence of Manco Inca's lineage.[27] Such cacophony makes the text's forms a site of conflict and not resolution or differentiation. These multiple textual forms show why scholars like José Antonio Mazzotti have located the text in the cross between orality and writing and explain why Frank Salomon has cast the text at the brink of intelligibility—stating that it is a "chronicle of the impossible."[28]

I want to ask, however, if this very semantic density, epistemological tensions, and unclear production—the impossible separation of its relations into constituent parts—undergird its political prospects. Possibility happens in uncertainty. Take, for instance, the concept of the *señor natural* (natural lord), a polemical one that Spanish *and* Indigenous actors employed in the sixteenth century to pose competing claims to legitimacy in the Americas.[29] The *Instrucción* deploys this concept with almost casual yet devastating effect in the first pages of the text two times and in two interlocking ways. The text posits (in first person) that it will write a genealogy of "I, Don Diego de Castro Titu Cusi Yupanqui, grandson of Huayna Capac and son of Manco Inca Yupanqui, who were *natural lords* of these kingdoms and provinces of Peru."[30] It also states that "I am certain that many people have already made public (*se habrá publicado*) who the *natural lords* of this land were, as well as from where and how they came [here]. For this reason, I do not want to linger on those matters."[31] Both cases remit to Titu Cusi's first-person "yo," and yet they reach beyond him. They invoke ideas of lineage and competition that are in circulation and speak to an unnamed method of "making public" to an unspecified audience.

Since the phrase *natural lord* conjures a polemical discourse that had purchase in the region and direct relevance to Titu Cusi at the time of this text's composition, the pithy claim made in this statement belies its importance. With this proclamation, the text presents Titu Cusi as part of the group of natural lords, a designation for a ruling class that gained legitimacy through longstanding precedent rather than recent events. This formulation leaned on Iberia's medieval legal code, the *Siete Partidas,* designating, as writes Robert Chamberlain, one who "attains [political] power *legitimately* and exercises dominion over all within his lands *justly and in accord with divine, natural, and human law*" while being recognized by those under him.[32] Friars like Las Casas engaged this concept to support Indigenous sovereignty and, by the time of the composition of the *Instrucción,* Titu Cusi. In his *Doce dudas* (1564), Las Casas made the damning assertion that "for his salvation, the Catholic king of Castille, our lord, must restore the kingdom or kingdoms of Peru to the aforementioned King Titu [Cusi Yupanqui] and to those other lord Incas that which was theirs."[33] And while Las Casas's logic of natural lords, as Rolena Adorno writes, might have been "visionary and quixotic, [it] was not illogical"[34]—evinced by the fact that colonial administrators in Peru still felt the need to combat it. As David T. Garrett explains, the question of "how to deal with these imperial heirs remained at the heart of viceregal politics until the 1570s[, and] Manco Inca's inheritors loomed largest in royal attention, with their ongoing kingdom at Vilcabamba."[35] To that end, Viceroy Francisco de Toledo, who arrived in 1569, worked to gather and eliminate documents that employed the concept of the natural lord, especially those printed without a license,[36] and sponsored new historiography designed to contravene the ability of Incas to claim legitimacy[37] by emphasizing king lists and genealogies that delegitimized Titu Cusi among others.[38] New works written before the viceroy's arrival such as Juan de Matienzo's *Gobierno del Perú* (1567) and those written under his patronage like Pedro Sarmiento de Gamboa's *Historia de los Incas* (1572) described the Incas in direct contradiction to the terms of the natural lord and "legitimate natural law."[39]

Though this engagement with the theory of the natural lord in the *Instrucción* could again lead us to an interrogation of authorial origin, it is as interesting to consider how this concept expands the field of relations in the text. When Sarmiento contests the idea of the natural lord, he shows that he is speaking of "law" in terms of a *gendered* lineage. To recall, this text had opened not only with the discourse of the natural lord but also with Titu Cusi's genealogy—with a naming of his grandfather and father. And though cast as a male line, lineage raises the question of gender relations that now emerge as part of this text's composition in rhetoric and practice.

Gendered Evidence

While this first invocation of legitimacy in the *Instrucción* suggests a po-litical conception of the term, Sebastián de Covarrubias's definition of "legitimate" shows that the "vulgar" understanding of the word is insepa-rable from sexual and gendered relations. In his dictionary of the Spanish language, the *Tesoro de la lengua castellana o española* (1611), Covarrubias writes that "legitimate" is first and "ordinarily" understood to mean the child born of a "legitimate marriage."[40] This definition, however, also re-quires a legal understanding. "Legitimate is all that which is done in agree-ment with the law. Latin, legitimate, that which is just, fair, befitting, laws, mores, and that established by ancestors."[41] This inscription of legitimacy as a political/legal concept tangled with sex and gender relations and fixed over time (by ancestors) has important consequences for the *Instrucción*. The logic that determined the legitimacy of an Indigenous group was set by the legal phrase "usos y costumbres," which codified conventions. These were to be respected and systematized by the Spanish as long as they did not conflict with the Spaniards' own laws.[42] To fully undermine Titu Cusi's authority as a natural lord, writers like Sarmiento had to dispute legitimacy according to the Incas' "own laws," as the Spaniard (strategically) presented them. As Luis Millones Figueroa summarizes, Sarmiento could not rest his condemnation of the Incas on Spanish law but rather had to couch part of his disputation in the Incas' own legal logic. To do so, Sarmiento had to re-cur to gender and sexuality, rules of succession, and lineage. He posited that the Incas themselves would not recognize Titu Cusi by stating that "it is known that no person in these kingdoms could rightfully or lawfully claim the right of succession to the Incaship by lineage in the kingdom of Peru either by being natural lords or by being legitimate, since they were not, nor are any even according to their own laws." He then, in terms that will resonate with the *Instrucción,* claimed that the remaining Incas—including Titu Cusi—were publicly known to be *bastards* and apostates who could not be inheritors of the land since their fathers, and thus their lineage, were also illegitimate.[43] As notes Tom Zuidema, authors like Juan de Betanzos in the *Suma y narración de los Incas* (1551) explained and understood the transition of Inca political power in terms of polygamy and competition among kin groups. Thus, Sarmiento's emphasis on linear descent some twenty years later seems suspect, if not strategic. (Zuidema calls it directly falsified.)[44] This might, therefore, point us to Tamar Herzog's assertion that "Spaniards often supported a somewhat fictitious continuity with the past, while at the same time attempting to modify and control its recollection" via the legal language of custom that confirmed legitimacy.[45] Falsity aside, the condemnation of legitimacy in the language of descent points to the discourses and subjects that these claims draw together. If to be a "lord" suggests a polity, to be a "son" reminds us of the centrality of kinship.

Like Sarmiento's text, the *Instrucción* promises to "tell the king how I am the *legitimate son,*" a claim of descent that intersects the logic of the natural lord with a formation of law based on rules of succession that are rooted in kinship.[46] According to the *Instrucción,* Titu Cusi's legitimacy arrives through a patrilineal model of primogeniture where he is the grandson of Huayna Capac and the son of Manco Inca, as well as "the firstborn and the son with the right of succession of the many children left by my father."[47] With such a statement, the text affirms a European logic of inheritance and the strategy of linear genealogy or "king lists" that had been—and would continue to be—increasingly codified in Spanish texts designed to disavow Inca claims.[48] Yet, despite the simplicity of this statement, its logic is not, in fact, straightforward. As scholars have noted, Titu Cusi and his father, Manco Inca, are not presented as "legitimate" according to the same rubrics. While Titu Cusi is legitimate according to primogeniture, Manco Inca, the text notes soon after, is legitimate because his brothers are illegitimate *bastards* with bad *maternal blood.* Though Manco Inca is the rightful heir, he is not the firstborn. Manco Inca was the "son of Huayna Capac and grandson of Tupa Inca Yupanqui—and descended from this lineage *in a straight line*—as were his ancestors [and thus he] was the principal lord of these kingdoms of Peru as proclaimed by his father and recognized and obeyed as such."[49] Here, notably, primogeniture falls out of the frame. Instead, mothers, blood, bastardy, and recognition become central to an assertion of Manco Inca's legitimacy. As the text notes, Manco Inca had received "all the power and authority that his father Huayna Capac had conferred," not Atahualpa who, "although an *older* brother," was *"a bastard."*[50] Recalling Covarrubias's definition, the *illegitimacy* implicated by "bastard" invokes a legal code where the child of a union is not certified by a particular legal regime. However, while bastard in the Christian frame implicates marriage, this sacrament does not appear in the *Instrucción.* Instead, the text only asserts the bastard status of Manco Incas' brothers in function of "maternal blood." According to the text, these men, Atahualpa (and also Huáscar), "although children of Huayna Capac, [were] of mothers with low and common blood, and my father was the *legitimate* son of royal blood as was Pachacuti Inca, grandfather of Huayna Capac."[51]

Legitimacy, according to this passage, is a matter of bloodlines—namely maternal ones in the case of "bastard brothers"—since all share the blood of Huayna Capac. To talk about legitimacy in the *Instrucción* via kinship is to talk about gender relations and women—even if they appear to be marginal topics, briefly mentioned and then abandoned.

Anthropologist María Rostworowski de Diez Canseco offers contextualization for these condemnations of maternal blood. Given that an Inca ruler had several wives, claims to legitimacy depended on the status of an Inca's mother, her lineage, and her hierarchical descent group (called a *panaca*)[52] in relation to the genealogical founder of the Incas—Manco Capac.[53] Though, as write Rostworowski de Diez Canseco and John Murra, partisanship, intrigue, and assassination led to the declaration of a new ruler,[54] official determination of legitimacy required, Julien writes, "a genealogical calculation. . . . [I]t was the bloodline of the mother, not the father, that would determine a greater or lesser degree of *capac* [hierarchical] status" and political possibility.[55] Spanish authorities at the time had partial awareness of this model of legitimacy and used the term "bastard" to explain which children were less likely to claim legitimacy in succession. For instance, Zuidema notes that the term "bastard" appears in the *Suma y narración de los Incas* (1551) by Betanzos and the *Apologética historia* (1560) by Las Casas, who used Domingo de Santo Tomás as his primary source to describe these children of secondary wives.[56] Sarmiento acknowledges the role of maternity in struggles over legitimacy as well, though he casts the true law of the Incas as that of primogeniture. "Though the custom of these tyrants was that the first and oldest legitimate son inherit the state, they rarely kept this, and instead selected the most beloved [son] or that of the most loved wife, or the most capable of his brothers and he ended up with everything."[57] Sarmiento posits that succession through intrigue, love, or family power undermines the law (*costumbre*) where the "oldest legitimate son" should inherit power. Evoking the legal expression of "usos y costumbres," Sarmiento again points to the intersection of law, gender, sexuality, and legitimacy as a means of contesting Inca authority. To know and assert who "inherits" (*heredase*) legitimacy is a means to accept or discredit political rule.

For this reason, scholars who attend to gender in the *Instrucción* have noted the marked absence of Manco Inca's maternal lineage. While Manco Inca's brothers Atahualpa and Huáscar are both labeled "bastards" due to their mothers' "low and common blood," no mention is made of Manco Inca's own mother. Instead, the text only states that Manco Inca shares royal and legitimate blood with his father Huayna Capac and his grandfather Pachacuti Inca. While a reader could assume that Manco Inca's mother is of high status, no information is provided to prove this fact. Instead, Manco Inca is only legitimated through vertical, male lineage—a pattern that would apply to Atahualpa and Huáscar as well (given that they, too, are sons of Huayna Capac). In their readings of this text, Nicole Legnani, Ralph Bauer, and Catherine Julien all provide careful comparisons to studies to consider the potential strategy that subtends this absence. By referencing anthropological studies of descent and the role of maternal bloodlines in the calculus of legitimacy, for instance, Legnani considers the likely low origin of Manco Inca's mother in the Inca royal hierarchy.[58] Bauer, after Julien, also notes that "in light of Titu Cusi's claims about the illegitimacy of Atahuallpa and Huascar as rulers based on their mothers' hereditary identity, it is significant that he provides no specifics about Manco Inca's mother"—a statement that references Julien's similar point that Manco Inca's pedigree was most likely "less than ideal."[59]

At the same time, both Bauer and Julien reaffirm the disruptive impact of colonialism on the regulations of succession. The consecutive deaths of Inca rulers make a reaffirmation of the "normal" difficult to subtend. Bauer helpfully posits that "it is possible that Titu Cusi's pragmatist arguments were a more or less realistic reflection of the historical impact of the cataclysmic events just before and during the Conquest upon Inca logic of succession. As Julien points out, the combined impacts of the pre-Hispanic civil war in Peru (in which Huascar and scores of his descent group died), European diseases (killing both Huayna Capac and his heir), as well as Atahuallpa's murder by the Spaniards left a tremendous stress on the traditional Inca logic of succession resumed by Huayna Capac's father."[60] As both scholars suggest, the upheaval of colonialism makes the expectation of static Inca codes illogical. By presenting the text as a production that negotiates a new and uncertain colonial environment, these scholars suggest that Titu Cusi's "pragmatism" may respond to an unfolding and uncertain situation. However, should we focus on stratagem alone, there remains a threat of moving away from the relation implicated in this colonial circumstance. This has a consequence for our readings of gender relations and women, which are so central to the text. Sexuality, gender, and the ways that women are tied into the production of the *Instrucción* threaten to be displaced and become codes to be read—occluded by intention and/or necessity. Reading for intent can obscure the epistemological density and relational production that marks the text's "doing" legitimacy. Yet, "stress," as Bauer puts it, points to the pressure that colonial relations put on a system. Stress suggests that the composition of colonial politics is taking place in and through relations—evident in the way that legitimacy is being articulated as a concept and practice. As is clear from the incommensurate rubrics deployed in the text, no organizational practice consolidates into a final form. I now turn to a scene that shows how the composition of legitimacy incorporates and implicates sex/gender relations and women as an active and uncertain practice in relation.

The Coya That Is Not One

Reading for Titu Cusi's voice and resistance may bring gender into view, but it does not necessarily produce a gender analysis. This appears most clearly in analyses of a famous scene of an attempted Spanish-Inca marriage detailed in the *Instrucción*. This scene does not occur at the time of the text's writing. Instead, it takes place in the past and is described in the extensive section dedicated to Spanish assaults on Manco Inca that help explain why Manco Inca "rebelled" and fled to Vilcabamba—leading to the composition of the document. At this juncture of the text, Spaniards have imprisoned Manco Inca and demanded a ransom of gold and other precious items in exchange for his freedom. Ostensibly, the Spaniards shackle Manco Inca due to rumors of rebellion. His release depends upon a show of friendship to be signaled by the payment of gold and silver. However, the text makes patent that precious metals are not the only item that Spanish soldiers desire. Under the guidance of three Pizarro brothers—Gonzalo, Hernán, and Juan—they also require Manco Inca's sister, the Coya Cura Ocllo. This pattern of imprisonment and ransom repeats two times. When the brothers first imprison Manco Inca, Hernán Pizarro proclaims in an embedded quotation, "Even if the rest of you let him go, and even if he gives you more gold and silver than would fill four rooms, I will not consent unless he first gives me the Coya, his sister named Cura Ocllo, as my wife."[61] Despite this ultimatum, the brothers accept Manco Inca's refusal and take the treasure instead. Upon Manco Inca's second imprisonment, however, the brothers insist, and Manco Inca must finally acquiesce.

In the aptly named section "How the Coya was Given" ("La manera de dar la coya"), the *Instrucción* focuses on the way in which an imprisoned Manco Inca manipulates this scene of "giving." While the Pizarro brothers believe they will get the Coya, Manco Inca disguises a series of other women to offer them in the Coya's place.[62] The text describes how Manco

Inca relies on strategic dissimulation and presents various women to hide the Coya from the Spaniards. As the text posits, Manco Inca orders that a "young, beautiful Indian woman, well-arrayed and adorned, be given to the Spaniards in place of the Coya for whom they had asked."[63] The Spaniards, skeptical, refuse and state that she does "not *seem/look*" like her to them.[64] However, they do not know who the real Coya is, nor are they in control of the scene. Manco Inca continues this process with more women from his retinue. "To tempt [the Spaniards] he had more than twenty other young women of that sort, some good and others better, brought out."[65] No one can put a stop to this game but him. Finally, once Manco Inca—or as the text calls him here, my father (a statement which remits back to the compositional present and Titu Cusi)—decides upon its conclusion, he orders that a final woman be brought out. "Once it seemed to my father to be time, he commanded that the principal woman in his household come out and be given to [the Spaniards]. She was the companion of his sister, the Coya, and looked like her in almost all aspects, especially if she was dressed like her. She was named Ynguill, which means 'flower,' and she entered in front of everyone, dressed and adorned just as would be the Coya, which means 'queen.'"[66] By wearing the clothes and adornments of the Coya, Ynguill—this Coya who is not one—can be presented in the form of an Inca reality as the Spanish want to see it, showing that Manco Inca understands what Spaniards desire and can give them a false version of it. But what, exactly, do the Spaniards desire?

Desire in this passage is equivocal. At first, according to the text, Gonzalo Pizarro[67] wants the Coya out of love. "He *had seen* her"—*the* Coya—and "her beauty, and thus fallen in love with her."[68] However, when Manco Inca offers the Spaniards this series of women dressed as the Coya, it becomes clear that Pizarro and his fellow soldiers do not in fact "know" her. The text notes that the Spaniards rejected each possible Coya with suspicion rather than certainty since "they did not *know* the Coya, [and thus] they stated that it did not *appear* to be her."[69] Such unfamiliarity suggests that the prior assertion of desire predicated on visual identification holds little weight. Instead, it presents desire of a different sort. As noted above, political legitimacy among the Incas implicated maternal bloodlines, so marriage with the Coya would be no small matter. Anthropologists have shown that the term "Coya" designates the woman who is both the sister and the principal wife of an Inca ruler. This matrimonial practice, known as "royal incest," consolidated the royal bloodline and supported future authority by limiting possible pretenders to the throne.[70] The Coya was, thus, the woman with the greatest status and the one whose children could make the strongest claim to succession. Desire for the Coya is at once gendered, sexual, and political. As Julien puts it succinctly, "This incident indicates how the Spaniards were trying to take women who were important in the reproduction of the dynastic line."[71] However, though the Spanish may be *trying* to take women as a strategy to interrupt Inca dynastic lines, the *Instrucción* emphasizes the illegitimacy of this manipulation. As the text notes, Pizarro embraces Ynguill "as if she were his *legitimate* wife"—a term that evokes both the falsity of the woman's identity in an Inca political realm and a Christian matrimonial system.[72] As if to confirm the failure of this marriage and its ultimate political illegitimacy in function of its falsified kinship, only a few pages later, Pizarro will tell Manco Inca erroneously that their "friendship will last for a long time between the two given that they are brothers-in-law."[73] Pizarro gives voice to his failure since the scene shows that he is not kin—in either a Spanish or Inca sense. As Kathryn Burns notes, Spaniards "were quick to grasp the benefits of [cohabitation]: the Inca nobility regarded those living with elite native women as kin and assisted them accordingly."[74] This scene posits that Manco Inca understands this logic and its attempted manipulation. In response, he thwarts it.

On the one hand, this scene can be read as another assertion of Titu Cusi's presence and Inca resistance voiced through a recollection of Manco Inca's answer to Spanish violence. Manco Inca inverts power relations, switching from an imprisoned subordinate to an authoritative master when Spaniards like Pizarro are beholden to an Inca system where maternal bloodlines and ties to the Coya afford political power. Along these lines, the Coya again appears and shows Spanish failure and, perhaps, impotence in gendered terms even though they finally capture and attempt to violate her in a future section, "The Arrival of the Inca at Vitcos" (Llegada del Ynga a Vitcos). There, the Coya condemns the Spaniards for their cowardice and commands them to kill her quickly. Though not a soliloquy, the text gives the Coya a direct quote as if to confirm her unique status: "You take revenge on a woman? What more would another woman like me do? Hurry up and get rid of me. The deed expresses your nature in every way."[75] While this condemnation undermines Spanish power in function of gender since they take out their revenge and impotence on a woman, it also foregrounds the way that gendered violence and power appear in unequal terms. The Coya asks, "What would another woman like me do?" However, the text has already suggested that no other woman is like her.

It is, therefore, crucial to note how a focus on the triumph of the Coya can present a model of resistance that obscures the rhetorical use of women (including the Coya herself) in the *Instrucción*. As writes Jane Mangan, "until the fall of Vilcabamba, native elites still might use marriages as a way to stem the tide of physical or cultural violence but the negotiations entailed risks and women, particularly, might suffer."[76] This violence can be displaced should we foreground Manco Inca and his "heroics," since prowess depends on an ability to trick the Spaniards and sacrifice the *right* woman. Focus on the Coya's specificity can displace other moments of violence. Her speech and its moving pathos can overshadow the silence cast on Ynguill and the other women paraded across the page. Manco Inca's attempt to save the Coya depends on the sacrifice of others;[77] his *use* of Ynguill and the other women become justifiable casualties. Recall: When Pizarro runs toward Ynguill, Manco Inca gives a perverse blessing, "Many congratulations; do what you would like," and is said to "laugh a great deal."[78] Therefore, in the description of masculine resistance, there is an uncomfortable attribution of differential value and utility to women's lives. Chang-Rodríguez points to this dissonance. As she notes, Manco Inca's purported heroism and rebellion make one woman's survival come at another's expense.[79] For Manco Inca to triumph, Ynguill must lose. In turn, the Coya's ultimate death becomes a sign of Manco Inca's failure. His masculine attempt to save her (from usurpation) becomes a reflection of his own fate and value. Women enable narratives of male opposition and fights for legitimacy, first in scenes of success and later failure. Women cease to become relational participants. Instead, they become signs of masculine prowess and narrative plot points in a historical account of resistance achieved and lost.

What might be another way to conceive of this composition that does not take women as "evidence" or power? We might begin this project by reconsidering the relational content and context that make up the density of scenes such as "How the Coya was Given." This scene does not present a binary struggle between Pizarro and Manco Inca but rather an event that involves various participants who show that legitimacy is unstable and composed in a moment that exceeds one "author's" control. Even though one Pizarro brother demands the Coya for himself, the text makes clear that it is a collective who does the demanding (*pedian*), seeing (*vieron*), speaking (*dixieron*), and (mis)recognizing (*desconoçiendo*). Pizarro's push for legitimacy can only accrue meaning—a meaning the text shows to be unclear—because it is enacted *in front of everyone* (*delante de todos*), a conglomeration of Incas and Spaniards who look on in unmoored and undefined awe (*en admirasçion*).

If anything, relational awe composes this disputed legitimacy. The sounds and sights of others bring it into a precarious state of being. Among these people joined in awe is Ynguill who is not, in fact, silent. Instead, she screams. When Pizarro runs toward her, Ynguill does not go. At the moment of her embrace by Pizarro, the text states that she "screamed like a madwoman" and claimed with "terror and dread" that "she did not wish to face such people."[80] While this interruption is brief and traumatic, it is destabilizing to any one subject's unidirectional management of the scene. It contravenes the fiction of absolute, autonomous male power and shows that gender relations are present and active, rather than manipulated and inert. The text notes that relations determine the fate of all in the room. Manco Inca's release is contingent since, as the text states, Manco Inca "knew that his freedom [rested on Ynguill]," a freedom that her scream conditions.[81] Even if Manco Inca does silence Ynguill and force her to leave with the Spaniards, this scream ruptures the narrative *and* helps constitute the relations that bring it into being. A brief exclamation of (indirect) speech shows that Ynguill is an active part of this relational composition—not "evidence" of authorship. Though Ynguill is clearly enmeshed in colonial violence that is distributed unequally, it would be a mistake to suggest that she is passive and silent.

Composing Relations

By reading how gender relations proved central to the composition of Manco Inca's legitimacy in this text, we can better see that gender relations are equally important to the terms of the text's composition in 1570. Gender relations in the *Instrucción* are not an "internal matter" discussed and solved but a concern that is ever-present and evolving. While the *Instrucción* may describe the historical intersections of gender and politics, it continues to contend with the same questions in its present.

Once the text turns away from Manco Inca's experiences to Titu Cusi's, the document presents the familiar paradoxes of control and collaboration, where Spaniards and Incas live in tense proximity. The work reviews a series of negotiations that occurred at Acobamba[82] and Chuquichaca[83] and describes how battling parties reached a series of agreements: "After this, the treasurer García de Melo returned with the dispatches from Your Lordship which advised me regarding what I had told him, that we marry my son Don Felipe Quispe Titu to his cousin Doña Beatriz, and we agreed to this and made peace in Acobamba by order of your Lordship, he and I bringing the witnesses your Lordship indicated. Present were Diego Rodríguez, as *corregidor,* and Martín de Pando, as secretary."[84] Again, while these flourishes of rhetoric are commonplace features in colonial forms, they ask us to think through the constant reconfigurations of obligation and allegiance that colonialism occasions. Even though the text speaks through Titu Cusi's first-person singular, authorship as causality is given to the king. According to the document, the king is the active agent who wields relational power: he brought the treasurer García de Melo and the Judge Juan de Matienzo[85] into contact with Titu Cusi in both Chuquichaca and Acobamba; the king encourages Titu Cusi's baptism—an act that will redefine Spanish and Inca religious politics—and the king dictates procedure.

Emphasis on men, however, would be parochial. Gender relations are central to this passage. Though it is only a clause, the middle of the quote reiterates an agreement regarding a marriage between Titu Cusi's son, Quispe Titu, and niece, Beatriz, around which earlier meetings had turned. As scholars have noted, the marriage between this woman and Titu Cusi's son had been a "linchpin" of each prior agreement.[86] The daughter of Sayri Túpac, Beatriz was a high-ranking Inca woman in the Andean region at the time of the *Instrucción*'s composition, and this marriage would have resonance in Inca terms. Beatriz had a stronger lineage than Titu Cusi and Quispe Titu,[87] and she had also inherited the immense *repartimiento* of Yucay that had been given to Sayri Túpac as part of the terms of his exit from Vilcabamba. Yucay was resonant with symbolism, given that it had been reserved for the royalty in pre-colonial times.[88] Despite these potential Inca meanings, Spaniards proved willing to assent to such an "idolatrous" and "incestuous" union because it could portend a Christian future. As wrote Titu Cusi's future "advocate," García de Castro, in a missive to the Crown, "I presented to your majesty testimony regarding the baptism of the Inca's son and explained why one of the chapters made with the Inca specifies that this child marry Sayri Túpac's daughter, even though they are cousins twice over. Here in their infidelity, [the Incas] marry brothers and sisters to each other."[89] Though García de Castro casts marriage, a Christian sacrament, as a sign of idolatry, he posits that the union must proceed as a strategy of Christianization. As he concludes, "Your majesty must send for authorization from Rome. The matter is of such importance that His Holiness must give dispensation [for this marriage] to convert these two and [thus] bring peace and tranquility to this kingdom."[90] Like the uncertain terms of legitimacy inscribed in the *Instrucción,* these terms of negotiation made in and around the text remain unsettled. Could a legitimating papal bull overwrite the illegitimacy of an "incestuous" marriage and facilitate peace (and Christianity)?[91] Would Spaniards and Incas see the exchange of

Yucay in the same light? Perhaps not. As Mangan writes, Yucay was "land viewed by Spanish as their gift, but most likely understood by the Incas as theirs since the Spanish had taken it from them."[92] Even if multiple parties agreed upon the conditions of this union, it might have different meanings and outcomes.

Recentering Beatriz in this relational composition does not resolve the problematic gender politics that inhere in and around the text's "present." There is a clear and familiar equation of land and women, not only as metaphor but as reality. Marriage to Beatriz determined access to territory, material wealth, and legitimacy via Yucay. However, while the impact of this gendered reality cannot be disavowed, scholars such as Jeremy Ravi Mumford and Sara Vicuña Guengerich have studied this case and shown how deeply the relations composed with Beatriz muddy the lines of gendered power and authority. Though too extensive to be treated in full, Beatriz's mother Kusi Warkay (baptized as Doña María) and two wealthy *encomenderos,* Arias and Cristóbal Maldonado, prove famous for throwing a potential wrench in the terms of the *Instrucción* and its historical accounting. Beatriz was placed in the convent after her father's death—a location where Indigenous and *mestiza* women were expected to learn "good customs."[93] In 1565, when Beatriz was somewhere between the ages of seven and nine, Kusi Warkay removed her daughter from the convent. At the Maldonado estate, Beatriz was allegedly betrothed to Cristóbal and reportedly raped, a violation that would force a union and give the Maldonados (and Beatriz's mother) access to Yucay and Beatriz's fortunes. García de Castro quickly reacted, given that this marriage would prevent any agreement with Titu Cusi. He returned Beatriz to the convent and exiled Maldonado in 1567 under accusations of rebellion.[94]

With this theft, Beatriz's biography echoes the scene of violence described in the *Instrucción,* where Ynguill (and the other unnamed women) bear the brunt of dispute and sexual violence. She appears to be a conduit for male struggles and power rather than a party to it. However, as Mumford and Guengerich show, Beatriz does not name gendered impotence but a cluster of relations that defy the imposition and stabilization of male power. News of Quispe Titu and Beatriz's potential marriage could have incentivized Kusi Warkay to remove her daughter from the convent—a reminder to the crown that Kusi Warkay was also a leader who merited greater attention and financial support.[95] In turn, there may be a cultural precedent for Kusi Warkay's act. As notes Rocío Quispe Agnoli, the arrangement of elite women's marriages was also the purview of Coyas, meaning that "although these women appear in the first place to have been objects of Spanish sexual conquest, we need to look at their roles within pre-colonial Inca terms and how these roles adapted to the Spanish colonial order."[96] In the case of Kusi Warkay, such adaptation, allegiances, and obligations are complex. In the Cuzco region after the death of her husband Sayri Túpac, she was at once an "outsider"[97] and also linked to local networks formed by Inca factions, the *mestizo* children of her own kin, and Spaniards who understood how to navigate the legal channels of empire.[98] She shows, as much or perhaps more than the *Instrucción,* that colonial power and legitimacy were negotiated in gender relations that engaged a violent *colonial* realm that was not determined by a consolidated Western logic.

We need to stay with these struggles in and around texts like the *Instrucción,* moments that bleed into disputes across the colonial landscape and the Atlantic, in order to understand how colonial politics are not "settled" sites of consolidated Spanish power that operate *through* gender. Indeed, Beatriz could be used to narrate the fall of Vilcabamba and the gendered transition of colonial power because of her "ends." She does not marry Quispe Titu, but instead Martín García Óñez de Loyola. Against the negotiations pursued by García de Castro, his successor Viceroy Francisco de Toledo refused to continue antiwar tactics and pushed for a military incursion into Vilcabamba. Yet, by the time Toledo's forces arrived, Titu Cusi had died. His brother, Túpac Amaru (now more famous in historiography), was captured and led back to Cuzco. There, he was garroted in the city square—a fact that horrified Philip II when he learned of this event, given its striking resonance with regicide. Adding insult to injury, Beatriz married Loyola, the nephew of the founder of the Jesuits and the man who had captured Túpac Amaru in Vilcabamba. Though Loyola had not originally assented to the marriage, he changed his mind upon learning of the Coya's vast fortunes.[99] Tied to a man who emblematized both Christianity and Spain's military might, Beatriz can figure as another allegory of Spanish consolidation via women, a smooth narration of historical transition captured in the heterosexual and Christian family form.[100] Indeed, unlike the relational complexity that composes the *Instrucción,* another document—Beatriz's convent registry at Santa Clara de Cuzco—presents a smooth passage from Sayri Túpac to Loyola. There, it records: "Doña Beatriz Yupanqui, daughter of Sayri Túpac Inca. Entered the Convent as a *donada* on the twelfth of August 1563. She was brought by Father Melchor de los Reyes of the Order of Our Lord Santo Domingo so that she could be raised and learn good customs in said house. No agreement was made regarding what should be given for her room and board. She was married to Martín de Loyola, Knight Commander of the Order of Calatrava, Captain of Viceroy Francisco de Toledo's guard."[101] From Sayri Túpac's arms to the convent to Loyola's hand in marriage, the complications of the *Instrucción* are scrubbed out of the narrative. Yet, the relations traced in this chapter that are composed in and around the *Instrucción* defy this neat historical timeline. On the contrary, the composition of the *Instrucción* shows the uncertainty of the Andean landscape via its negotiation of gender relations. Spaniards seek—and receive—special dispensation from papal authorities to enable the "incestuous" marriage between Titu Cusi's son and niece. Spaniards make concessions and prove willing to "overlook" polygamy. In turn, Titu Cusi allows friars into Vilcabamba and works with them against Inca antagonists who have allied with Spaniards in Cuzco. The possibility embedded in these relations depend on the unknowability of a final form of living in the colonial Andes, as evidenced by the collaboration and antagonism that saturates the *Instrucción*'s account of the past and imagination of the future. Legitimacy—its terms, at least for that time being—remained uncertain. To that end, emphasis on the *Instrucción*'s location in a set of relations shows how the document is authored by colonial practices. It is, as Michael Horswell has posed, a work that lives on the *chaupi,* a Quechua term designating "the conflicted contact zone of coloniality."[102] The *Instrucción* does not point to finality and closure, but instead creates forms of relating that open up spaces of *chaupi* as "knowing, being, and telling" *in* and *as* conflict.[103] By no means does this fact reduce the weight of violence in this text or present a utopian horizon of possibility. But in this attention to the *Instrucción* as one of many moving parts, as a work that builds relations, we not only ask who puts pen to paper or sends this missive across the Atlantic. We also see the wider conditions that bring subjects into cooperation, contention, and confusion—and we interrogate the ways that relation distributes survival and possibility, if unequally.

❧ 3

Good Examples
Textual Forms and the Reproduction of Custom

When the papal bull *Inter caetera* (1493) stamped a seal of approval on the Spanish imperial project, it employed terms by which the evangelical mission would be defined and measured: Pope Alexander VI summarized that Spaniards had to "instruct said native peoples and inhabitants in the Catholic faith and instill them with good customs."[1] The latter concept, uses or customs (*usu et moribus*), constituted the practices of a people; indeed, customs defined a group of people itself, for these acts (*costumbre; consuetudo*) provided language to circumscribe a socio-political group in both practice and law.[2] In the eyes of Spaniards, customs forged Indigenous peoples—the *indios*—and established their distance from Christian norms. Thus, the obligation demanded by this pithy requirement to instruct good customs contained a question and challenge from the outset of the colonial mission: it asked how and if customs could be changed if "bad customs" defined the *indios* as such.

As the so-called failures of evangelization became evident by the second half of the sixteenth century in both the Viceroyalties of New Spain and Peru, many friars began to insist that Indigenous peoples remained unchanged due to the immutable difference of their bad customs. Peninsular religious ideology helped subtend this belief. One prevalent strain of religious thought in Iberia stated that only those who could be designated Old Christians (persons without Jewish, Muslim, apostate, or newly converted forefathers) could reliably maintain the true faith and its good customs. The "tainted blood" of New Christians amounted to an indelible stain that corrupted converts and passed on to their children. Regarding the Spanish Americas, María Elena Martínez has noted that jurists and friars initially remained undecided regarding Indigenous peoples' Old or New Christian status, given that American subjects had no prior knowledge of Christianity. The recency of Indigenous peoples' exposure to the faith challenged their designation as New Christians; at the same time, their customs—especially by the late sixteenth century—were increasingly considered ingrained by lineage.³ Imperial officials thus began to see evangelization as an eternal task, for they viewed Indigenous customs as a deviant inheritance that defined *indios.*⁴

There is, however, another "form of relation" that interrupts lineage and the genealogical inheritance of custom. In this chapter, I argue that religious officials of Spanish background in the sixteenth and seventeenth centuries wrote of a reproductive and relational strategy that fell under their control: exemplarity. According to evangelical tracts, a friar's "good example" would create a kinship tie with Indigenous catechumens and reshape these pupils' customs according to a religious model's form. This theory of kinship and reproduction was an evangelical strategy that appeared in early Christian texts and held that the mere presence of religious models and the example that they provided would transform the customs of the unconverted into those of the good Christian. I focus on documents from colonial Peru to show how this theory and its implementation of exemplarity focused on standardization in two ways. First, via the use print technology that would create an *exemplar* (a term meaning the standard) of doctrine that would prevent any distorted copies of doctrinal text. Second, via the control of the embodied example that would circulate, present doctrine, and reform Indigenous peoples. The circulation of these two standardized *exemplars* would ensure the standardized reproduction of those exemplary *"bonis et moribus"* of the Christian subject.

However, this need to standardize friars' performances raised a dangerous question regarding inheritance. Why should friars require regulation if their Old Christian lineage guaranteed custom? The need to police friars, scrutinize their behaviors, and ensure that they reproduced a template suggested that genealogy and bloodlines were themselves insufficient to ensure Christian custom. No material substance that traveled from the Old World could assure the possession of good customs. As a damning corollary, then, Indigenous lineage alone could not be blamed for bad customs. Bad customs might simply be reproduced from a bad (Spanish) mold. A theory of "relation" and identity based on exemplarity thus presents a site of possibility, one that allows Indigenous peoples to challenge the idea that only Spaniards could inherit good customs based on their Old Christian lineage.

The chapter proceeds in four parts. The first focuses on the definition of the *indio* and the question of his or her conversion in early evangelization. Given that customs helped define Christians, the early evangelical mission worked to determine the quality of Indigenous behaviors and their compatibility with Christian practice—termed *policía.* A critical corollary to this scrutiny of Indigenous custom was the theorization of its transmission. This was no trivial matter—the method by which Indigenous peoples would inherit customs helped define their racialization. This led to an unresolved tension between those authorities who placed the inheritance of custom in material processes and those who theorized the inheritance of custom as a matter of education.

The second section explores exemplarity and its promise to transform Indigenous customs in the second half of the sixteenth century in Peru. It reads the Acts of the Third Lima Council and *De procuranda Indorum salute* (1588), a text published by a central figure in this meeting, the Jesuit José de Acosta. While these Acts emphasize the power of print and the creation of a *textual* exemplar, the reproduction of custom by an Indigenous catechumen also depends upon his or her vision of a *human* exemplar. Indigenous peoples were destined to observe and reproduce a friar's performance. Therefore, what bodies do and how they are perceived always threaten to undermine print's fixity; bodies must always be put into practice and seen. The customs of a friar had to remain consistent and unchanged in their corporeal circulation, lest their divergent examples undermine the ability of an exemplar to reproduce his correct customs and transform Indigenous ones accordingly.

The third section shows that these anxieties were not unfounded. The Indigenous subjects of the Spanish empire could highlight friars' bad example to refuse the hierarchical difference between Spaniard and *indio* based on lineage while suggesting that the reproduction of bad customs by Indigenous peoples remitted to the example of Spaniards and not to an inherent Indigenous character. Felipe Guaman Poma de Ayala's *Nueva corónica y buen gobierno,* a 1,189-page petition sent to King Philip II, illustrates this fact. This Andean *indio ladino*[5] engages the rhetoric of exemplarity to posit that bad customs arrive with Spaniards' bad example.[6] Alongside the use of religious rhetoric, Guaman Poma engages the language of exemplarity to suggest that Andean peoples and others in the Andes have seen and reproduced friars' bad examples. He condemns friars for their actions and casts bad examples as a biopolitical disaster: a scourge of his text is the "mixing" across races and the illicit sexual relations between friars and Andean women that *follows* from the bad example: men and women are led astray because they see and reproduce the customs of a bad Spanish model.

I conclude with a proposition: the tautological relationship between sight and surface in the reproduction of an exemplary identity produces another possibility for Indigenous peoples. As the chapter shows, one's exemplary identity is a matter of its perception by others rather than its autonomous assertion. This fact is no clearer than in a series of nineteen petitions housed in the Archbishopric's Archive of Lima, submitted by teachers who were required to be good examples capable of reproducing their customs in pupils as a condition of their profession. Proof of this quality depends on the fact that the petitioner can be "seen" to be a good example by others, showing that exemplarity exists on the surface according to regulated practice. This regulation provides a possibility for Indigenous peoples: a final petition submitted by an Indigenous teacher that follows the same procedure shows that the reproduction of a standard form enabled this Indigenous teacher to lay claim to good customs by being seen to be a good example on the surface. As he shows, forms can make Christian identity and its concomitant customs true.

Customs: Small Errors and Single Syllables

A central question for the evangelical mission would be the origin and transformation of Indigenous customs: the laws and practices that defined this group of peoples (*ius gentium* or *ius naturale gentium*). In part, the evangelical mission borrowed from a classical tradition that found custom to define a people. As Donald R. Kelley summarizes, custom referred to "regular social patterns" that guided the legal and what we would now call "cultural" practices of the inhabitants of a territorial region.[7] However, early modern theorists believed that customs were not necessarily "inborn"; rather, customs had a temporal relationship to an inhabitant's duration in a community. Tamar Herzog notes that while jurists held "native citizens" to have a "natural inclination" for their community of origin, "newcomers could also acquire this habitus once they lived in the city for a sufficient period with the intention of integrating into it."[8] And if early modern scholars held, as Aristotle had claimed, that custom depended upon repetition (over a long period of time), then practices were malleable based upon their continual enactment. Thus, while customs made a people recognizable as a group, people were not trapped by the customs of their forebearers.

However, it is difficult to think of Iberia's early modern classifications without considering the reification of difference that related the customs of a people to their lineages. The well-studied purity of blood statutes that gained strength throughout the early modern period held a relationship between lineage and intractable difference, one that could not resolve the tension between conversion's stated ability to wash away the sins of ancestry and a belief that the stains lingered. Though ideological motivations for these discourses of "difference" may have been in part economic or political, assumptions that *conversos* (Jewish converts and their descendants), *moriscos* (Muslim converts and their descendants), and children of apostates were considered indelibly "stained" and different from Old Christians led to suspicion and the expulsion of the *moriscos* in 1609. Conversion could not remove the threat that lineage and "crypto" religious practice posed to the Christian polity. Meanwhile, even if philosophical discourse insinuated that inheritance was mutable, in early modern Iberia's hierarchical environment, fictions of immutable lineage afforded political power and privileges. The Castilian crown extended *hidalgo* (petty noble) status to entire populations (such as the Basques) considered free of "Semitic" blood due to the (fictional) proposition that no Muslims had entered their territory and compromised the inhabitants' purity. Therefore, "custom" in early modern Iberia posed a marker of uncertain permanence, one that offered different outcomes based on assumed origins and trajectories of ancestry.

The contradictions embedded in the term "custom" extended to the governance and evangelical project of the New World and the constitution of the term *indio*. José Rabasa, for instance, notes that Law XIX in the New Laws of 1542, developed via the lobbying of Bartolomé de Las Casas, required that litigants follow the "customary law" (*usos y costumbres*) of Indigenous peoples—that is, Indigenous peoples' own "customs"—ideally to prevent abuse by Spanish colonials[9] and to diminish the violence occasioned by friars who responded to "idolatry."[10] Ironically, this condition bound Indigenous peoples together as a legal and political entity (in theory if not always practice) in custom in the *República de indios.* And like the *conversos* and *moriscos,* this legal category carried a relationship between lineage and custom, though it would be articulated in difference from these two Iberian groups since, as new converts who had no exposure to the faith before the conquest, Indigenous peoples did not have the same opportunity to accept or reject Christianity and were thus extracted from the legal and religious thumb of the Inquisition. However, as Martínez highlights in her reading of Mexico's Third Provincial Council (1585), where the friars of New Spain designated Indigenous peoples as "tender plants in the faith," such "claims enabled the exclusion of native people from the priesthood and certain religious offices and institutions without necessarily contradicting the official discourse regarding their 'purity of blood.' In other words, it allowed for their construction as not quite 'impure,' but also as not quite 'Old Christians.'"[11] Trapped between Old and New, Indigenous peoples were held in a state of perpetual infantilism whereby it was not clear how or if the Indigenous person could "grow" into a full Christian, by what means, and after how long.

In part, Indigenous separation from Christian custom rested on those unspeakable, yet highly spoken about, types of relation that fed the European imaginary: cannibalism, polygamy, and sodomy.[12] However, it would be a mistake to think that those customs in need of modification were only these spectacular and often imagined practices. Throughout the sixteenth and seventeenth centuries, the customs that required reformation intersected the spectacular with the banal. It was not only mythical deviance that needed to change but also the practices of daily life called *policía*. The 1573 "Ordenanzas de Su Magestad hechas para los nuevos descubrimientos, conquistas y pacificaciones," for instance, presents such a juxtaposition when it states that in the case of new "pacifications," Spaniards could avoid that Indigenous peoples "kill, sacrifice, or eat [each other] as they once did in other parts" by "instructing *policía*" (*enseñado pulicia*) in its pedestrian—but regulatory—terms. Spaniards would show that conversion accompanied education in "the use of bread, wine, oil, and other goods; cloth, silk, linen, horses, cattle, tools, arms, and everything else that Spain has . . . to live well." And all this, they claimed, "could be enjoyed by those who would come to obey us and our Holy Faith"—that is, learn *policía*.[13] Though non-elite Indigenous peoples were later prohibited from accessing several of these "recommended" goods (for instance, arms, horses, and sartorial finery), this articulation of *policía* as the instruction of a regulated colonial and Christian life rhythm continued through the seventeenth century. In colonial Peru, the founding constitutions of Jesuit *colegios* for the Indigenous elite included among their bylaws quotidian dictates on what and how children should eat as well as where and with whom they should sleep.[14] Christian *policía* depended upon the modification of customs that determined what a Christian community looked like in practice. *Policía* dictated forms of life.

The repeated insistence on these educational dictates indicates fears of evangelical failure, with utopian aspirations giving way to frustration and suspicion in the latter half of the sixteenth century.[15] This reassessment of the evangelical project focused on two intersecting concerns: Indigenous capacity and evangelical strategy. Regarding the former, Indigenous custom appeared increasingly calcified and opposed to Christian *policía*. Perhaps one of the most cited examples of this condemnation of custom as a condition of Indianness in colonial Peru is the *De las costumbres y conversión de los indios del Perú: Memorial a Felipe II* (1588), composed by Bartolomé Álvarez, the parish priest of Charcas.[16] In this text, Álvarez presents a paradox: "Indian" custom is the impediment to its own transformation. He summarizes, "Of the customs of the Indians, one must understand how inexperienced and clumsy they are for all things that one intends to plant in them. And since for what matters—being Christian—it remains necessary to be granted good and politic customs (*políticas costumbres*), both human and honorable, and in them (*en ellos*) there is no such thing, how will they become Christians?"[17] While unspectacular in his condescension, Álvarez presents a twist: he makes the customs of policía not only the end goal but also the precondition of Christianity. To *become* a Christian with good customs, one must already *possess* them. This temporal play makes conversion an affirmation rather than a transformation. It can only confirm what was already present, making custom the hard boundary between Christian and Indian that cannot be traversed. Against the dictates of the papal bull that present custom as an end of instruction, Álvarez suggests that Christian practice cannot be implanted because it is not "native" to Andean soil.

Other friars proved more amenable to the possibility of changing Indigenous customs by emphasizing evangelical methods. Evaluations of conversion came to the fore in the texts produced by Third Lima Council (1582–83), a meeting spearheaded by the Jesuits who had arrived in Peru by 1568, and in the works composed by its leader, Jesuit José de Acosta. In his famous evangelical tract, *De procuranda Indorum salute* (1588), this clergyman would posit recommendations for relations between friars and Indigenous catechumens as part of his evangelical program. While he engages agrarian rhetoric evocative of Álvarez's own, he reduces the vituperative assertion of impossible transformation into one that emphasizes possible instruction and movement of Indigenous custom toward the Christian ideal. This is not to suggest that he describes a utopian promise of absolute commensurability between Spanish and Indigenous peoples, nor the rapid transformation of the latter's customs into those "perfect" practices of the former. Instead, Indians were, according to Acosta's *De procuranda,* "new plants" (*tyrones teneraque stirpes*) in need of care and "instruction" (*insituerentur*) in customs.[18]

The primary challenge confronted by this evangelical effort was, therefore, a question of *how* to bring about this transformation and how long it would take. While Acosta's neo-Thomist beliefs enabled him to present "bad customs" as a result of practice and not inherent incapacity, his view did implicate a theory of reproduction linked across generations.[19] Sabine

Hyland notes that for neo-Thomists, "customs learned in infancy were considered to have had a profound effect in molding the human soul, and could be eradicated only through generations of education."[20] Thus, it was in the space of education over the long durée that the Third Lima Council would focus its efforts. Friars would have to be "fathers" since their secular counterparts had not transmitted good customs, at least up to the present. Under the heading "Parish priests should educate those of the lowest condition," the Acts told priests to teach social inferiors the rudiments of Christian doctrine as a father would to his children. This shifts the burden of instruction and blame for its failures onto the friar.[21] The Acts note, "Fathers of the family must explain for their children, slaves, and the rest of their family before God." This instruction is critical "so that fathers themselves are not punished by divine law due to the corrupt customs of their children, as happens with frequency and is threatened by the sacred scriptures."[22] Then, noting the affinities between religious and secular paternity, the passage argues that priests must follow the model set by their secular counterparts; friars, like fathers, are held accountable for the customs of "children."[23] This presents a twist for the matter of conversion. While the capacity of Indigenous people comes under scrutiny due to lineage, the responsibility for its transformation rests on the kinship relation they have with the father-friar. While Indigenous peoples' bad customs may be attributed to a material link to an idolatrous past, friars will be accountable before God for these successes or failures in custom.

Religious Examples

To emphasize strategies of evangelization that could change customs, the Third Lima Council focused on instruction as a transformational mechanism that operated outside of lineage. Indeed, as Monique Alaperrine-Bouyer summarizes in her study of elite Indigenous education in colonial Peru, "In reality, there was no clear border between [religious] instruction and education. To convert was to teach."[24] However, if education could modify custom, the failures of earlier evangelical projects suggested that pastoral practices required scrutiny and revision. Friars of the Third Lima Council felt that early evangelists had relative leeway in their strategies and had overlooked too many Indigenous customs in order to facilitate conversion. In part, this flexibility responded to the plurality of Indigenous languages and practices in colonial Peru—no language standard enabled priests to disseminate one version of the doctrine to all peoples and certain elements of Christianity had been privileged above others. However, for the gathered officials of the Third Lima Council, this flexibility was the very object of blame and concern: differences in evangelical presentation enabled the survival of detrimental customs. To ensure the progressive transformation of Indigenous customs, friars had to ensure the stable presentation of their own. To reproduce the customs of an ideal Christian model, there could only be one exemplar.

Control of this example turned toward text. As John Charles notes, "The Church's evangelizing mission drew from the conviction that standards of civility and goodness would find their maximum expression through the Indians' exposure to Spanish and written texts."[25] Yet, friars had been concerned with handwritten texts' mutability since each hand could write something different and introduce new errors. The friars gathered by this Council argued that only copies of a *printed* textual exemplar would overcome the vagrancies of human variability. Only a single textual form, a version approved by the Council, would ensure that "that the doctrine of the natives . . . be *uniform,* without making a difference in even a single syllable for the great damage that has resulted from not having done so in the past."[26] Indeed, print would remove the body from doctrine since the "hand" would no longer be a part of the process. Copies would be produced by a press rather than an amanuensis.

However, while print promised to disseminate precise doctrinal language, the *enunciation* of each syllable returned to an embodied world beyond print. The word takes form in a body, as discussed above, and the embodied exemplar has the power to shape or distort the customs of his pupil. In fact, as Larissa Brewer-García notes, this body was rarely only a European priest. *Mestizo* and Indigenous interpreters were often required to transmit doctrine to converts since friars were limited by their linguistic incapacity, thus creating a distorting chain of relation that meant doctrine and the customs it conveyed could escape the control of friars themselves.[27] In that regard, it is notable that the Acts provide another solution to this linguistic danger: verbal silence and corporeal instruction. As the Acts of the Third Lima Council state, "It is best that clerics called to the divine ministry organize their lives and all their *customs* so that they do not do anything that is not respectful, pious, and full of faith in their habit, their gesture, their movements, discourse, or any other thing. Just as they must also *avoid those small errors* that in them would be grave, so that their *actions* produce the veneration of all."[28] When the instruction of customs becomes the content of education, the priority is not doctrine or text; instead, in this passage, it is the corporeality of an example. Customs take shape in movements, clothes, and behavior—all performative details. Like the warning against differences in syllables, the text cautions against small errors in action. The friar must do more than speak Christian doctrine; he must show it in his daily life. For a friar to model good customs and thus transform Indigenous ones according to his example, it is not only the text that the Council must standardize but the friar's very body.

Given the emphasis on the production and power of standardized text in the Third Lima Council as a means to fight the damage wrought by bodies, this focus on corporeality proves an ironic juxtaposition. Indeed, in one passage, the Acts privilege a friar's ability to make a body "speak" over his ability to convey the doctrine in words. They note, "If no one who knows [the language] appears, the parish, however, shall not be left without a priest, *as long as he does not have bad customs* since it is preferable to send a parish priest who lives correctly over one who speaks well if one had to choose because *life edifies much more than language.*"[29] Customs, in this passage, exist in life and deed over word, and can be observed in the practice of a Christian model and thus reproduced by a catechumen. Therefore, it is critical that the friar behaves according to the standard imposed by the Third Lima Council, even if he cannot engage the text that has been printed. Exemplarity illustrates that the emphasis on doctrinal standardization via print does not have the final say. Rather, the body speaks as its own exemplar.

These articulations of educational exemplarity as a strategy of evangelization undercut the consolidation of Indigenous difference. The Acts invoke biblical precedent in the Old World and create a transatlantic connection that slots the "Indian" into a space of Western similitude. Texts suggest that priests should follow the "example and authority of ancient fathers," thus connecting exemplarity in the New World to that of the Old, insinuating the same efficacious results.[30] In a latter passage, the Acts again assert, "With reason, our elders teach that there is nothing that moves others more toward piety and the cult of God than the *life and example* of those who dedicate themselves to the divine ministry, since, given that these have been elevated from the secular world to a higher vocation, others naturally *turn their eyes* to them like a mirror from which they take that which they should *imitate.*"[31] In this evocation of Church doctrine, the Acts promise that a good life and example encourage the transformation of others via the sight of the ideal. More striking, however, is the fact that this theory creates no distinction between the types of catechumens who imitate: the theory ties the "Indian" to the Old-World model. Imitation is not presented as a sign of

Indigenous incapacity or an instance of parroting misunderstood doctrine (a common accusation lobbed against Indigenous peoples).[32] Rather, it names an evangelical strategy that links New- and Old-World catechumens; it demonstrates the capacity of each to learn from evangelizers. This statement from the Acts resonates with, if not repeats, the language of Acosta in *De procuranda* that again draws from an Old-World and a foundational Christian frame. As above, his text speaks to the power of the example to reshape neophytes based on their observation of the religious model. It states that "Saint Peter . . . advises and asks that pastors become *models* for their flock because their subjects will often look to the example of their betters and naturally conform their customs accordingly."[33] With this emphasis on physical interaction based on act and vision, the standardized text has faded away, even though the terms in this explanatory chain repeat those used to describe the need for print. Instead, the quality of the example that re-*forms* (*conformar*) and reshapes the subject remits to the physical world.

Officially, exemplarity places friars in a position of power since, according to these passages taken from the Acts of the Third Lima Council and *De procuranda,* neophytes "look" to the friar and change their customs accordingly. These works and their logic draw from a longstanding tradition in Church rhetoric where, as Peter Brown summarizes, "the holy man . . . was far more than an exemplar of a previously well-organized and culturally coherent Christianity: very often, he quite simply *was* Christianity"—an important concept when friars were often isolated in far-flung missions.[34] The priest became the embodiment of Christianity and its ultimate authority. As Kenneth Mills posits, engagement with this early Christian logic repeated in colonial Peru. It allowed religious agents to imagine that ideal evangelical results would emerge from their own deeds. As Mills writes, "Obedient and virtuous himself, [the priest] was meant to inspire the same qualities and a situation in which the people under his gaze would 'give themselves over' to his authority."[35] However, Mills notes that just as catechumens would fall under the gaze of the friar, the reverse was true; friars were subject to the scrutinizing gaze of their flock. An exemplar's value as a model was at once his downfall: he would be an exemplar, but a good or bad one. Indeed, as is evident in the entry for "*exemplo*" in the seventeenth-century dictionary by Sebastián de Covarrubias, the good example is undercut by its inverse: the bad one. Covarrubias writes, "One, of course, thinks of the example in terms of its good part, yet we say to give a bad example."[36] "Good" cannot fully encompass the meaning of example, despite the implicit positive attribution to this term. Rather, a bad example lurks behind it.

In colonial Peru, the living example provided a challenge unlike that posed by any classical model or saintly ideal. With figures from the past, pedagogues could extract models to use as guides for contemporary action. Timothy Hampton shows that the historical record could offer suitable models for pupils; elite instructors could reach into the past, extract an exemplar's character, and bring it to a "momentary universality" that would make it relevant for present circumstances.[37] When it came to the "mobilization" of an exemplar in the colonial world, mobility was a liability. Friar-exemplars were not frozen models that could be contemplated at a remove. They inhabited a theater of the present where customs were constantly performed and, most dangerously, open to deviation. It is, therefore, no surprise that religious documents insist upon the regulation of the embodied example since it contains the power to be scrutinized and judged.

Even if the reproduction of the example becomes an evangelical strategy, it is not a one-way discursive site of power. The belief that exemplarity can reform customs enables Indigenous catechumens to blame their own practices on bad Spanish exemplars. As Covarrubias notes, the example is defined by its transfer—not its quality alone. An example is *"given"*; it can be good or bad. Thus, though exemplarity serves as a strategy for friars to confirm their own power to reshape the customs of Indigenous peoples, it also enables witnesses to critique these friars' deviations from the ideal form friars purport to give. A bad copy can be blamed on a bad example. Exemplarity is a form of reproduction that contains its own critique.

Reproducing Bad Customs

One of the most famous Andean[38] engagements with the rhetoric of exemplarity is Guaman Poma de Ayala's *Nueva corónica y buen gobierno* (1615), a text that takes up Christian religious discourse to question imperial biopolitics.[39] Following studies by researchers like Rolena Adorno, scholars have considered exemplarity to offer a meeting between the historiographical and pedagogical sections of Guaman Poma's text: the pre-conquest and colonial history in the "Nueva corónica" and the blunt recommendations that Guaman Poma addresses to King Philip II as a new political platform for the imperial state in the "buen gobierno." As Adorno writes, exemplarity allows Guaman Poma to bring historical events in line with recommendations regarding the treatment of Spanish, African, and Andean peoples as a whole.[40] Each "identity" category—ethnic and political—appears in "the space that exists between history and precept, between the novelistic episode and the maxims that assimilate the biography to the didactic

system."[41] For Adorno, therefore, exemplarity in the *Nueva corónica* operates as a series of case studies that allow Guaman Poma to articulate a vision
for revised colonial praxis. He employs exemplarity to describe the distance
between the ideal and the actual.

That said, scholars have given less attention to Guaman Poma's use of
exemplarity as an articulation of reproduction despite the text's obsessive
focus on procreative sex, illegitimate birth, and *mestizaje*. However, these
acts of sex always intertwine with the question of exemplarity, as shown
in the condemnation of priests' sexual sins framed under a rubric of "bad
examples." For instance, at the conclusion of the summary paragraph that
begins the first chapter dedicated to parish priests ("Capítulo primero de
los P[adres] de las dichas doctrinas deste rreyno del Pirú"), the author questions the double standard of a friar who provides a bad example to his parishioners via his own behavior: "Having some dozen children, how can he
give a good example to the Indians of this kingdom?"[42] In this case, the bad
example seems to proceed from the act of having children and committing
sexual offenses. After seeing that the friar has children and does not respect
the sexual dictates of celibacy, it is impossible to imagine that he could give
a good example to his parishioners. However, the good example is not only
impossible once people have seen the sex act; the bad example also *precedes*
and causes the reproduction of the sex act. Guaman Poma writes of how
friars lead women down a sinful path because women wish to reproduce
the friars' greed and desire: "[Women] don't want to marry because they
go after (*va tras*) the Priest or the Spaniard. And thusly Indians do not
multiply in this Kingdom, but rather *mestizos* and *mestizas* and there is no
remedy."[43] If desire contaminates women, it is because they follow a friar:
they "go after" his example—a verb that indicates sequence, both temporal and spatial, that draws them into the wake of another. While this bad
example leads to sexual reproduction, its first consequence is a violation
in time and space of the customs associated with Christian *policía*. Friars
fail to model the customs they were sent to instruct and, by having women
"follow" their example, allow for the birth of *mestizos y mestizas.*

Guaman Poma makes clear that his vision of "good examples" is an idealized and non-sexual configuration of gendered bodies. Indeed, when Guaman Poma writes that certain Andean groups' customs were less barbarous
than Spaniards had claimed, he employs gender politics and sexuality to
make this point. In a section dedicated to a condemnation of parish priests,
the text describes how Andean religious authorities were far closer to the religious ideals that friars wish to perform, "since the old priests of metals and

idols, daemons and gods, popes of stone . . . acted faithfully and *provided a good example,* as [did] the virgins, *aclla,* and nuns in their temples. And thus, they held everyone else with their justice and law; they were Christians if not for idolatry."[44] Though belief falls short of "true" Christian faith—as they, of course, "have idolatry"—these pre-Christian "priests" *give* a good example. Guaman Poma names the leaders of Andean religiosity according to Christian titles that insert them into a Western religious frame. Because of this faith differential, it is not worship but rather sexual practices of celibacy and enclosure that make these pre-colonial peoples "exemplary" and "Christian-like." Nominatives accrue value via gendered seclusion. Indeed, chaste women are linked in an unbroken sequence of virgin, "aclla," and nun.

Acllas, according to Michael Horswell, were those elite women dedicated to the imperial state as celibate servants (who were potentially offered in marriage to consolidate alliances across the Andes).[45] However, while the role of these women was complex in Andean society, their virginal status was often cause for celebration and a site to project commensurability between Andean and Spanish societies—even in texts besides Guaman Poma's. *Acllas* appeared in Spanish works such as Blas Valera's *Relación de las costumbres antiguas* (1594), which dedicates a chapter to "Acllas, Virgenes Religiosas" and compares them favorably to European nuns and prioresses (though, as a dutiful Christian, Blas Valera posits that the "*acllas* helped spread superstition and 'lies' as agents of a pagan religion").[46] While Guaman Poma does not contest such assertions of earlier idolatry, he does rewrite what it means to "spread" bad practices—and who does so—by leaning on the rhetoric of exemplarity. It is not doctrine but rather bad custom that allows current practices to spread to the Andes' detriment. And, as the papal bull noted, custom is an integral part of evangelization itself. Spaniards' reproduction of customs is cast as a pernicious growth that Europeans brought and disseminated.

Bad customs in the *Nueva corónica,* therefore, do not originate in an Andean lineage and are certainly not "spread" via a reproductive line that begins in an autochthonous religious practice. Rather, as Guaman Poma writes, "The said Christians *brought with them* all of the bad adultery and other mortal sins; under the guise of doctrine, they deflower all of the young girls, and thus beget many *mestizos* in this kingdom."[47] Mortal sins of a sexual kind begin with reproduction occasioned by exemplarity—a birth attributed to pattern *and* subject—even if, as in the passage cited above, Guaman Poma concludes with the birth of mestizos. Practices antithetical to Christianity are not located in an Andean past to be corrected by evangelization; bad customs are shipmates on Spaniards' transatlantic journey.[48] Spaniards cause the transformation of Andean custom through the example of bad behavior, through no fault of Andean peoples' lineage. As Guaman Poma writes via the familiar language of agrarian reproduction, "Now the priests of the eternal God are such and their ministries are such: from the bad father comes the bad son, lost from the things of the true God. From the bad tree comes bad fruit, from the bad seed comes a bad root."[49] As if in response to writers such as Álvarez, who employed agrarian language to condemn Andean soil, Guaman Poma presents a landscape of potential that fails to provide expected yields. This is not, however, the fault of plants that will not grow. On the contrary, in language resonant of Acosta's own vision of paternity, friars are the "fathers," implicated as the model that will determine the shape the "sons" take. By using the evangelical theory of exemplarity, Guaman Poma questions who has good customs and how they transfer. While Guaman Poma does not spare Andean peoples from his condemnations (with a virulent gendered assault against women), his ability to indict Spanish friars places the acquisition of custom outside lineage. Customs are copied from the example, and the example is clear for all to see.

Formal Reproduction

In this regard, Guaman Poma's text is resolutely visual, even beyond the illustrations that have also sustained scholars' attention. It commands the "reader" to look (*mira*) and to think of conversion as a visual practice, where Andean peoples see, evaluate, and reproduce customs. A friar's identity is only as good as it is perceived to be. This need to have others "sign off" on the status of one's customs shows that identity is always, in part, relational, formalized, and witnessed. Customs must be accepted and acknowledged by others. This fact leads me to a final set of texts that share the language of reproduction and exemplarity articulated in the evangelical tracts and Guaman Poma's work discussed above. This is a set of nineteen petitions, now housed in the Archbishopric's Archive of Lima, submitted by potential teachers of first letters in Lima from the seventeenth century who pursue a license to exercise their craft. Like the texts above, each petitioner argues that he can instruct good customs because he can make students reproduce his good example. However, while these texts depend upon the understanding that good customs qualify the instructor, the proof that a teacher has good customs depends upon his performance and certification according to a predetermined exemplar, a form that turns upon textual standardization and documented relations with specific community members.

If customs must be performed according to a predetermined standard to be held true, then the acquisition of a license doubles this regulated "form." While witnesses must know the petitioner in life, they must also correctly register that knowledge on the page. Not only physical contact but also the petition, documentation, and case file determine an instructor's success. Each petitioner's file includes certified testimony from members of the community that details how long they have known the petitioner and where, the witnesses' opinion of the petitioner's customs, life, and example, and a final affirmation that the testimony is accurate and true. Each file in this set closes with a decision from the Vicar General of the Archbishopric of Lima, Don Martín de Velasco y Molina, who gives approval based on the case file in full. But it is not the presence of witnesses alone that confirm the exemplar. Rather, it is the standardized form and the repetition of predetermined language across documents that ensure the successful approval of the file. Form determines what testimony is needed to make the exemplar: it establishes what information matters to the proof of exemplarity, the shape such information will take, and who will be considered a viable interlocutor in the construction of a case. The reproduction of a form thus holds authorial power in its own right; it is a template upon which any potential exemplar must be "related" and confirmed. Thus, the "self-presentation" of a petitioner as a good example depends upon a relation made in form. Good customs and capacity as an exemplar return us to the standardization of the Third Lima Council, where body and text intertwine to make a good example a matter of bureaucratic practice: the ritualized acts of documentation, the practice of witnessing, the language of testimony, and the enactment of text itself. When one claims that he has good customs, he must perform it in the proper channels to make his assertion true.

To that end, community impressions are strikingly uniform. For instance, petitioners such as Baltasar Pérez de Atocha in 1642 presented testimony from witnesses who promise to tell the truth, swearing by God and the cross as required by law.[50] Despite this oath, or perhaps as a consequence of the guiding hand of a notary, each testimonial offers similar details regarding Pérez de Atocha's character and qualifications. Though some witness testimonies do mention the petitioner's experience as a teacher, they all reference the quality of his example or customs. Affirming that he had "seen [Pérez de Atocha] teach Christian doctrine to children as well as to write, read, and count," witness Manuel Pérez's testimony states that Pérez de Atocha is a "virtuous good Christian of good life and example."[51] Another witness, Cristóbal Vásquez, also confirms that the petitioner is "a virtuous man of good life and customs."[52] The last witness, Tomás de Lumbreras, also says that Pérez de Atocha is "a virtuous person of good life and custom."[53] In this gathered testimony, the petitioner's traits take their place in a set of pre-established terms that are repeated by each interlocutor; Pérez de Atocha is always asserted to be a "good example" and a "virtuous person" who leads a "good life."

Despite the frustration that this standardization may provide for the study of these traits, their interlocking arrangement, in fact, determines their meaning. These character traits signify because they align; their definition rests in their syntactical conjunction and reproduction of the standard. That is, an uncontested and unmarked alignment between the good life, good customs, and good example emerges in the conjunction "and." While the ability to use these terms remits to physical exchanges between witnesses and petitioner (Manuel Pérez's testimony states that "[Pérez] has had cordial conversation and interaction" with Pérez de Atocha), these terms gain force in their repetition of boilerplate, textual language.[54] The forms' predetermined standard determines the information needed from a physical encounter, reducing complexity and excising details that such interactions surely entail. The only qualities that matter correspond to the petition's rhetorical and syntactic rules. The repetition of these attributes across testimony does not simply document Christian "customs." It makes them true.

The stakes of these good customs remit, as in the case of the religious tracts discussed above, to the reproductive power of exemplarity. As Velasco y Molina states in his confirmation of Pérez de Atocha's petition, this instructor must teach children Christian doctrine, the catechism, reading, writing, and counting, all while "*giving* them a good example."[55] In turn, a witness who speaks on behalf of Pérez de Atocha, Tomás de Lumbreras, promises that Pérez de Atocha had previously taught children with much care, "without drawing attention to himself or *giving a bad example* of his person for having behaved very well."[56] The witness Pérez concludes his testimony with a pithy, self-evident assertion: "it is very important for this [profession's] exercise . . . virtue and an exemplary life."[57] No explanation is given, nor seems necessary for the concept of exemplarity and its relational terms as the petitions leave no doubt as to its centrality to education. The example is a central method of instruction's reproductive capacity.

This is not to say that Christian lineage and inheritance do not appear in the petitions. The witnesses of Francisco de Sosa's 1658 petition, for instance, attest to the petitioner's "life and customs" as well as to the fact that he is the "child of Old Christian parents."[58] Likewise, in the file submitted by Antonio Jurado Toralba in 1658, witnesses address the petitioner's Old Christian status.[59] Pablo de Noguera states that he knows Jurado Toralba to be the child of Francisco Ruiz Jurado and Francisca Ramos, and knows him to be an "Old Christian clean of the bad race of the Jews, Moors, or the newly converted."[60] Witness Juan Zeberino also notes that Jurado Toralba is an "Old Christian clean of the bad race of the Moors, Jews, and the newly converted" and confirms that Jurado Toralba's parents are known to be the same.[61] And the witness Alonso Pacheco affirms, as well, that he has not "seen, known, heard, or understood anything in contrary" to Jurado Toralba's lineage.[62]

However, what does it mean to "know" this religious lineage? While these boilerplate phrases would serve to confirm Jurado Toralba's status as an Old Christian, they make their case through the performance of customs and the absence—not presence—of proof otherwise.[63] Jurado Toralba's lineage is not a stable fact but rather the accumulation of properly experienced and documented impressions from several community members. Noguera, indeed, writes that Jurado Toralba is "virtuous, humble, of good life and good customs and has always *given* a good example" before noting that he has never *seen* anything to the contrary. While Jurado Toralba's lineage may be "true," the reliance on multiple witnesses illustrates that the truth of Old Christian heritage remains inextricable from presentation and perception by others, as has been well documented by scholars of blood purity interrogations.[64] This performative element of custom—its formal display and relational production—can determine subject status and exemplary capacity.

Even when textual proof of Old Christian status appears, documents cannot be held apart from performance. Testimony for the 1649 petition submitted by the Spanish solicitor Cristóbal de Siles shows as much.[65] The witness Pedro de Carmona affirms that he had always seen Siles "live honestly and discreetly as a good Christian, fearful of God and, in his opinion, giving a very good example in his actions and comportment."[66] However, the witness testimonies provided to confirm Siles's qualifications make no mention of his parentage or lineage. Instead, they note that Siles was a "cha-petón," a recent arrival from Iberia. Given that they may not have known his parentage or past, witnesses place their faith in textual form. Carmona's testimony states that he can confirm Siles's qualifications because he has seen that the standardized form of the body's performance matches the standardized form of text. His document states that Siles has "always *given a very good account of his person and* [the witness] *knows this because of the papers he has seen* as well as by that which had been *said by people who saw and met* [Siles] in said profession."⁶⁷ By citing these papers and "reliable" hearsay, Carmona shows that ascription to a standard at once performed and documented is an important site of encounter between petitioner and witness where customs are seen and known. The relation that gives Siles a viable lineage exists in textual and community relations.

This ability to assert capacity as an exemplar through the repetition of a formal standard in body and text presents an interesting possibil-ity for an elite Indigenous subject who does not meet the requirements of lineage that seemed to precondition the possession and performance of good customs as discussed throughout this chapter. This fact appears in a 1685 document regarding the education of Indigenous peoples in Lima (housed in the Archivo General de la Nación [AGN]), in which an In-digenous solicitor employs this same formal procedure to claim his own status as a subject with good customs capable of giving a good example.⁶⁸ This petition requests payment for Juan Mateo González, a teacher who has already educated poor Indigenous peoples for six months without re-muneration. However, unlike those teachers described above, González is presented as an *indio*.⁶⁹ In a *memorial* (history) included in this file, sev-eral residents of the city—Francisco Velázquez, Mateo de Carvajal, Tomás de Bermudez, Diego Flores, and Felipe Santiago—write in support of González in the name of the community's *"indios vecinos."*⁷⁰ They explain that a license had been issued previously to the friar don Juan Núñez Vela de Rivera to mount a school for the "instruction and education of the poor native Indians of this city."⁷¹ That instructor, however, did not appear for eight months, and in response, these residents recurred to González, *"indio ladino* in the Spanish tongue and of *good customs."*⁷² Like the texts described in the previous sections of the chapter, the Christian friar violated the dic-tates that should have defined him as such. In contrast, the Indigenous man served as the ideal.

The language employed to describe González engages the pre-established form and conventional rhetoric of similar petitions that confirmed the qualifications of Old Christian instructors. Like those documents, González's presents no contradiction between the various characteristics that describe a teacher. It is a text that defines its subject via the relation built in the conjunction "and" both in and across texts. *Indio* and good customs join and make truth through uncontested accrual and juxtaposition, just as the sequential presentation of "custom," "life," and "example" had in the case of the petitions discussed above. The authorizing power of this conjunction in form does not only appear in the testimony of Indigenous community members; it is repeated by Spanish officials who determine González's qualifications as commensurate. After conducting an examination of the Indigenous teacher, the superior of the Church of Desamparados names González "suitable for the instruction of the children for being an *indio of good customs.*"[73]

The text does insinuate that González's status as *indio* will facilitate his instruction of Indigenous pupils, a fact that may seem to diminish his commensurability with other instructors identified as Old Christians. However, it is in the standardized presentation of customs—in body and textual procedure—that the document points to the formal equivalence between González and his Spanish counterparts. In the license issued to González—one that instructs him to teach Spanish letters, doctrine, the Castilian language, and Christian mores to his pupils—González is commanded to instruct children "in the *same form* and manner *as do all other* schoolteachers."[74] While González's pupils will be Indigenous, this emphasis on form is important. It states that he can present customs to students just as would his Old Christian counterparts. In asserting this equivalence in/as form, the approval suggests that González's status as an *indio ladino* does not foreclose his possession of good customs nor his capacity to serve as a good example.[75] Moreover, it suggests that he can reproduce these good customs in others. The reproduction of and in a standard form bridges the distance between Indigenous and Spanish subjects since both groups can be labeled exemplary when they are seen and inscribed according to the choreographed rules of colonial procedure.

A petition such as this one asks scholars to consider fundamental questions that build upon those asked in the previous chapter: what constitutes the resistant "voice," and how can form offer different models of conceiving authorship and the relations that make colonial identities? Unlike the petition that closed this section, Guaman Poma's text has found great success due to the complexity of his work, its size, its illustrations, and, I would venture, its singular voice. When we engage historical documents that contest colonial power, individual voices provide an opportunity to reveal such opposition and epistemological authority. By utilizing methods that incentivize this recovery of difference via a reading "against the grain," we often look for clues of how a writer embeds difference within a work and contests the oppressive force of a colonial apparatus. This method has produced fruitful readings of texts like Guaman Poma's since, while he employs Spanish forms, he engages Indigenous epistemologies in images and writings. The *Nueva corónica* lets us interrogate how Andean communication technologies and knowledges undermine Spanish discursive codes. A newer movement has worked with Ann Laura Stoler's argument to read "along the archival grain," where she poses that readers need not fight against documents to hear the (subaltern) subject.[76] Michelle McKinley, Premo, and van Deusen, among others, have read wills, contracts, and petitions to consider deviations in language as intentioned and indicative of the individual relationships and the textured differences that make colonial life in the Spanish Americas.[77] They have brought a different way of looking at voice within form to colonial studies by considering how form is not limited by the formulaic. These reading methods against and along the grain do share some resonances. Both emphasize experiences, affects, and subjects by highlighting deviations from formal standardization as sites of possibility. They present a rapprochement between the extra-textual subject and the subject on the page.

I have moved in a different direction. I have posed that form's sameness provides an additional means of "reading" colonial relations, racialization, and the constitution of difference. As seen above, by appearing no different *in form* from the exemplary standard, Indigenous peoples interrogate the "content" and consolidation of their difference. They "appear" no different in kind because they take shape via a relational procedure and formal process that is rhetorical, textual, and somatic. This presentation of the self via form might make one highly visible yet, ironically, *too* similar to others. It is no surprise, then, that the occlusions produced by form were problematic for colonial authorities. Viceroy Toledo, according to Charles, "criticized native catechists whose students 'parroted' their lessons without a true grasp of the words that they spoke."[78] In turn, according to Estenssoro Fuchs, extirpation campaigns suggested that Indigenous Christianity was a mere "appearance" and that indigeneity itself had prevented conversion.[79] Likewise, Mills summarizes that friars in pursuit of idolatry finally learned—or uncovered what they believed all along—that "the Indians' attachment to their own religious system had been, as the contemporary rhetoric put it, 'discovered' or 'unmasked'; a secretive and vile 'idolatry' had been revealed beneath the guise of proper Christian acceptance."[80] Indeed, even if a famous extirpator of idolatries, Pablo José de Arriaga in his *Extirpación de la idolatría en el Perú* (1621), could accept the utility of education, where "sons will be better than their fathers, and grandsons better than their fathers and grandfathers," he would still write that Indians were an ontological entity based on their difference from Spaniards. Their true customs remained despite any surface changes.[81]

Ironically, in pursuing and parsing "what is Indigenous" from "what is western" in a text, we might enact the colonial practice that insisted upon Indigenous difference—a practice that refused to accept that form or rhetoric could be "true" in their exercise by non-Spanish subjects. Looking below or beneath form creates a binary in difference—an absolute that makes one type of relation subservient to a kinship of lineage and biology. However, as Jeremy Ravi Mumford wrote of the sixteenth century, "People of all backgrounds struggled to shape their own identities in this chaotic environment. But neither Spaniards nor Andeans knew just what the word 'Indian' was going to mean."[82] Indigenous epistemologies that conflict with Western ones indeed continued throughout this period, as is evident through the manifold and important studies of Guaman Poma's text. Therefore, the stakes in a study of form are not to suggest that Indigenous practice or belief systems disappear into strict Christian values and ideals of custom. On the contrary, friars feared—and realized—that identities presented in a single form could be plural. Form had power because it reproduced and displayed one set of customs, but it might not reveal the survival and scope of Indigenous customs in their true plenitude.

❧ 4

Form and the Future
Use and the Unfinished Work of Evangelization

The friars gathered at the Third Lima Council (1582–83) argued that evangelization could succeed via the standardization of two forms: those of evangelical texts and those of friars' bodies (meaning their behaviors and practices). These forms would serve as templates for the colonial community—namely Indigenous neophytes—to see, learn, and reproduce.[1] To that end, the standardization of Christianity into a textual and embodied form was not a theoretical exercise; it was an evangelical practice that demanded relation. The Archbishop of Lima, Toribio Alfonso de Mogrovejo, articulates this practical fact in a license that opens one of the principal multilingual texts produced by this synod, the *Confessionario para los curas de indios* (1584).[2] As he notes, friars must "take and *use* [this work] in *the form* that the provincial Council *has/is ordered.*"[3] For him, "form" was to be "used" to bring the Andes into a Christian "order" through the repetition of set precepts.

This chapter opens with the archbishop's mandate to show how colonial authorities used form to bring the Andes to order. In turn, it considers the spatial and temporal slippages that inhere in form as method. As this chapter shows through a reading of different multilingual evangelical texts—namely the lexicon, grammar, and guidebook for confessors—form provides a strategy to reshape the ways that Indigenous and Spanish peoples are meant to relate in Christian practice (*policía*). Form could ensure that Spaniards and Indigenous peoples behaved the same way. Nonetheless, a paradox inhered in this evangelical theory, which posed that form could fulfill conversion. As this chapter contends, faith in the "use of form" became less stable as the colonial project radiated outward in space and time. Each successive generation of religious authors posed that older texts exhausted their utility due to linguistic variability, Indigenous practice, and failures in conversion. New forms had to be written to create useful relations and reconstitute order in the Andes. And yet, even these new texts remained ensnared by the same temporal problem of prior works. If older forms could not account for inevitable future change, why should a new form be able to do so?

To answer this question, this chapter explores the logic that subtends "the use of form" in these religious works. Despite these texts' differences as grammars, lexicons, and handbooks for confessors, each work engages the theoretical idea that form can create effective relations that can facilitate evangelization and reshape colonial peoples and their modes of living together. I demonstrate how this theory appears in two texts by the sixteenth-century Dominican Domingo de Santo Tomás, the *Grammatica, o Arte de la lengua general de los Indios de los reynos del Perú* (1560) and the *Lexicon, o Vocabulario de la lengua general del Perú* (1560). Next, I show that later sixteenth- and seventeenth-century texts also ascribe this organizational power to form. However, they decry the shortcomings of earlier authors and their publications, a fact apparent in the seventeenth-century parish priest Juan Pérez Bocanegra's guidebook for confessors, the *Ritual formulario e institucion de curas* (completed 1622, published 1631). Pérez Bocanegra explains that form has not succeeded because prior texts are incomplete, overwrought, or mistranslated. Colonial relations have not been resolved by form because texts were imperfect. Despite this justification for his work, I argue that Pérez Bocanegra also names a temporal trap. While he labors to fix the limitations of texts that precede him, the *Ritual formulario* may also become useless since it, too, addresses an undetermined future that may change.

I conclude by considering a critique levied by Jodi Byrd and Michael Rothberg. As these scholars have posited, readings of Indigenous peoples and colonialism often become a means to talk about the colonizers themselves, even when studies ostensibly focus on indigeneity.[4] In response, I hold that an analysis of form offers one means to recenter Andean peoples in these Spanish and *criollo* texts.[5] Though useful as an organizational strategy, form preserves an opacity that leaves the "content" of indigeneity unspoken by colonial discourses. Form emphasizes surface repetition instead of interior revelation. By emphasizing this opacity produced by form, I suggest that Andean peoples are given a "space" where they are unseen and unorganized by texts that work to subject them to colonial structures of knowledge. These forms certainly create spaces of violence, subjection, and racialization; nonetheless, as each colonial form confronts its limits to capture the plenitude of Indigenous practice, it may also gesture to its own limitations and spaces of possibility.

The Form of Metal, the Form of Gender

As stated throughout this book, the regulatory power of form served as a mainstay in the ideologies of governance and conversion that passed across the Atlantic. Form named the rules of textual standardization, the practices of evangelization, and the behaviors designated as *policía*. Form was a method of colonial organization. These manifestations of form appear in the *Lexicon, o Vocabulario de la lengua general del Perú* (1560) by the influential Dominican Domingo de Santo Tomás. Though printed in Valladolid, this text speaks to the upturned colonial system that had taken root in colonial Peru and the Andes, where conflicts over territory, wealth, and *encomiendas* had obscured evangelical practice. These commercial interests only increased with the discovery of silver at Potosí in 1545,[6] the expansion of a vast mining apparatus, and the development of this region as an economic hub and destination for deracinated subjects—by choice or force.[7] Like other Dominicans such as Las Casas, with whom he was in dialogue, Santo Tomás condemned the consequences of Spaniards' fixation on wealth and the *encomienda* system.[8] He cast the *encomienda* as a pathway to perdition in a letter (1550) to the Council of Indies where he called Potosí a hellmouth into which the Spaniards sacrificed Indigenous bodies to a false god, claiming, "It has been four years . . . since a mouth to hell was discovered where many people enter every year, sacrificed by the greed of Spaniards to their god. It is a silver mine named Potosí."[9] This condemnation presented Christian subjects in the shape of their "pagan" others who were accused of sacrifice and idol worship to *huacas* (objects, bodies, and natural features—including mountains like Potosí, itself—that remained outside of Spanish reasoning). For Santo Tomás, material greed showed Christians to behave as they pretended their catechumens did.[10]

The *Lexicon* emerges from this bellicose context as a work designed to show how textual form can reconstitute evangelical order in the Andes. It does so through the idea of relations as a discourse and practice in form: Christian belief and its concomitant behaviors will take shape in the organization of native languages that can then be used to evangelize and re-form bodily arrangements.[11] Like many other New World lexicons, Santo Tomás works to gather and systematize language as a transformational strategy. He draws from a transatlantic genealogy, organizing his text, he writes, in the "same order" (*mismo orden*) as Antonio de Nebrija, author of the *Vocabulario español-latino* (1494).[12] Bringing something to "order" and putting something in an organized "form" are not dissimilar ideas. Rather, as Sebastián de Covarrubias notes in his 1611 dictionary, the *Tesoro de la lengua castellana o española, orden* is "the placement of things when everything is put in its place. . . . Giving an order so that something is done, is to *give form and order.*"[13] Therefore, when Santo Tomás poses that his text is properly ordered, six times on the second page of his work, he emphasizes that his *Lexicon* gains efficacy through its subjection to a standard form and eventual use alongside his other text, the *Grammatica.* As Santo Tomás writes, the useful tool of the "*Grammar* teaches how to order (*ordenar*) [the Lexicon] and give it harmony and order (*orden*), according to [the *Grammar's*] rules and precepts."[14] The insistence on use/form in this passage is not casual. On the contrary, such a claim is meaningful because it explains that text is ordered for (*para*) something. As Santo Tomás explains in circuitous fashion, order *for* bridges the textual and the physical. It enables the *Lexicon* to support the work of evangelization when friars use the text to facilitate the intertwined organization—ordering—of textual, human, religious, and spiritual bodies.

While this explanation in the *Lexicon* emphasizes how form can make use of New World materials for evangelization, Santo Tomás's text opens with a simile that announces the tension—if not outright opposition—between the use of textual form to create evangelical relations and the current misuse of Indigenous bodies or souls in potentia by Spaniards in their current religious, economic, and corporeal forms of relation in the Andes. He does so by focusing on metal. First, Santo Tomás describes the relationship between his two textual forms—the *Lexicon* (the matter) and its *Grammatica* (the tool)—as one of mutual need. Each text is useless without the other. As he states, "Any type of artisan, faithful reader, however expert he may be and however fine his tools, will be little able to use them or practice [his craft] without matter on which to exercise his art."[15] What good are tools, he asks, without the matter they require? To explain this reciprocity, Santo Tomás turns to the "clear example" of metalwork: "One could use as a clear example any of the professions, but particularly that of the goldsmith or silversmith: He would make little use of his ability to work gold or silver . . . if he did not have the metal that corresponds to his practice."[16] With a quick transition, Santo Tomás uses this allegory to explain how his own texts function at the intersection of art and matter to re-form the Andes: his *Grammatica,* the Arte ("el arte de qualquier lengua"), and the *Lexicon,* as the "matter" at hand ("la materia de que se compone tal oracio[n]"), promise to fulfill the evangelical mission. As he posits, his project organizes this "abundance of vocabulary, which is the matter that the Grammar teaches to order and put into harmony" so that the "grammar is perfect and has matter to be used for the canons and precepts."[17] Ordering terminology into a lexicon gathers the matter that Santo Tomás finds useful for his project, just as the precious raw material of metal can be prepared for a specific use and shaped into a form.

At first glance, this simile appears to have general applicability to the evangelical mission, rather than to function as a specific rejoinder to exploitation taking place in Peru. Santo Tomás not only engages metalworking, but also cites the classical author Protagoras to explain how raw matter can be given a useful form. Yet, though Santo Tomás may cast metal as a "clear example" for his explanation of relations best suited for evangelization, this simile/example is anything but clear or neutral. Metal points to a guiding tension between evangelization and exploitation in the Andes—especially in Santo Tomás's writings. Metal cannot help but point to Potosí, the hell-mouth that Santo Tomás had condemned, and the *encomienda* system. To use metal as a "clear" example is therefore not to illustrate one formation of bodies and practices among many, but rather to evoke differential ways that humans can be made to relate in, what are for Santo Tomás, incompatible fashions. Only a few pages later, the *Lexicon* makes clear how metal names oppositional praxes.[18] When Spaniards orient themselves toward wealth extracted through metal, they turn away from the project of redemption and evangelization. Instead, they show themselves to be "so cruel, so deceitful, so lascivious, and so greedy" (tan crueles, tan mentirosos, tan carnales, y ta[n] cobdiciosos) that the Indians view greed as a guiding tenet of Christianity.[19] The physicality and worldliness ("carnales") of this cardinal sin ("codicia") fosters a relation that cannot be reconciled with evangelization, Christianity, or the organization of language and bodies that undergird the *Lexicon* and its accompanying *Grammatica*.

Notably, these two relations manifested through the simile of metal are cut through with the logics of kinship, gender, and relations. Carnality and greed are not only terms that evoke a desire for metal but also words that conjure the metaphoric alignment between gendered bodies and land—the long tradition posed by Anne McClintock[20] that reaches to early imperial texts. But just as McClintock's reading has been rightfully critiqued for a psychoanalytic generality that flattens the specificity of colonial projects, the European texts that imagine and engage the Andes are not sexualized in the same terms. Like Las Casas's *Brevísima relación,* discussed in chapter 1, Santo Tomás's text engages gender as a means of casting greed and its concomitant desire as incompatible with evangelization. Yet, those who *respond* to his condemnation reformulate gender politics and attraction to metal as a condition of evangelization. An allegory of rape and unreciprocated ravishment becomes a path to marriage. The unsigned "Ánonimo de Yucay frente a Bartolomé de Las Casas" (1571), also known as the "Parecer de Yucay," treats the metals of Potosí as a dowry needed to make the Americas into a bride of Christ. Under this formulation, mineral wealth is the only means by which Christianity could have been "attracted" to the region in order to combat the lack of Indigenous *policía:*

> What else could this mean but that God, with these miserable idolaters and with us, did as does a father with two daughters: one, very fair, modest, and full of grace and elegance, and the other ugly, bleary-eyed, stupid, and bestial. To marry the first, there is little need to give her a dowry. He need only put her in the palace and there, many men will compete to marry her. Regarding the ugly, clumsy, ignorant, and wretched one, this is not enough. She needs a large dowry: many jewels, rich clothes, sumptuous houses, and with this, God and help.... I say this about these Indians, that one of the means of their predestination and salvation was these mines, their treasures, and riches because we clearly see that the Gospel goes flying where these are.... The mines are good among these barbarians; God gave [the mines] to [the barbarians] so that the faith and Christianity be brought and remain here for their salvation.[21]

This passage does not attribute territorial feminization to the Americas alone. Instead, all lands (and their peoples) are feminized and described as in need of marriage to Christianity. However, dowry and beauty become points of differentiation. Europe and Asia[22] required "little" due to their "inherent qualities, great beauty, intelligence, and discretion" (en lo natural, gran hermosura, muchas cieçias, discreçion) and their inborn proximity to Christianity.[23] In contrast, the "miserables"[24] of the Americas found luck in their mines, without which the harbingers of Christ would not have been attracted to this "ugly, hopeless, ignorant, and wretched" bride. These aesthetic qualities are not only gendered but also social labels that describe the Indians' own disorder in terms of the "barbarous" distance from Christian *policía.* In the "Parecer de Yucay," mines are not prohibitive but rather a saving grace, without which salvation would have been impossible.

If we follow Jeremy Ravi Mumford's lead and read this text as the product of Dominican García de Toledo, it presents a strange deviation from the political platform and ethics espoused by other Dominicans such as Las Casas and Santo Tomás.[25] Instead, the "Parecer de Yucay" finds greater resonance with the Jesuit José de Acosta in texts such as *De procuranda Indorum salute* (1588) and *Historia natural y moral de las Indias* (1570), who names an attempted reconciliation of these two forms. As Ivonne del Valle posits through an analysis of the rhetoric of baroque contradiction, Acosta does not celebrate violence or mining but acknowledges that "private business" enabled evangelization.[26] Likewise, with her study of the alignment between religious and financial love (*caritas* and *cupiditas*), Nicole Legnani writes that there can be a rapprochement between economic and evangelical missions.[27] Acosta engages gender to make this reconciliation explicit via a resonant and almost direct gloss of the "Parecer de Yucay."[28] In the *Historia natural y moral de las Indias,* Acosta casts the mines as a gendered handmaiden (if not matchmaker) to conversion, recalling the dictum that "what a father with an ugly daughter does to marry her off is provide her with a large dowry. And this is what God has done with this laborious territory, is give it great riches in the mines."[29] By offering this large dowry to the feminized territory and to the "least *política* people," God encouraged "men to seek out these lands and possess them and, in the process, to speak of their religion and the true God that [the Indians] did not know."[30] Just as did the passage in the "Parecer de Yucay," this statement in Acosta's text casts the mines as a providential presence provided by God, himself, in order to facilitate evangelization. As well, like the "Parecer de Yucay," Acosta's text also presents the peoples of the region as disordered and in need of an organized reformation (they are "gente menos política"—the term pointing to the lack of Christian *policía* via the lack of the *urb* or *polis*—while the "Parecer de Yucay" describes them as "bárbaros"). Unlike in the case of Santo Tomás, where the relational form produced by a sexualized desire for wealth *violates* order, here, economic and evangelical practices *dovetail* because they are gendered and sexualized. For Santo Tomás, the sexualizing procedure of desire is a detrimental violation; for these other writers, it is a providential one that leads to an eventual marriage, making the Andes into the bride of Christ. Thus, what for Santo Tomás was the limit of evangelism becomes recast as the origin and the condition of evangelical possibility. A sexual relation of rape and death is transformed into one of marriage and birth.

While Santo Tomás does condemn this gendered order when it manifests in violence and greed, it would be a mistake to suggest that the text rejects the power and rhetoric of gender as a means to *form* evangelical relations and order outright. On the contrary, we must look to his emphasis on grammar, matter, and the power of form as an evangelical strategy to

understand how gender becomes useful. Gender makes a productive appearance in the *Lexicon* via the evocation of Aristotle's conception of hylomorphism, where there is an inherent and necessary use of form that
imposes shape on matter.[31] As Pietro Li Causi glosses, in hylomorphism
we see a gendered configuration, where "matter" names "raw material" in a
relationship of generation. Here, matter is given shape through its subjection to "*eidos* either as 'form-in-act' or as 'implementation of the principle
of the form.'"[32] With this proposition, Li Causi presents a critical insight to
understand gender's affirmative value in Santo Tomás's text: form and matter exist together as a process and practice that brings matter's immanent
condition into being without passing through a necessarily sexualized logic.
Instead, Santo Tomás emphasizes that matter accrues its particular "use" in
an engendering act of (evangelical) formation that can move away from the
sexual violence of a current expropriative form. Gender "matters" because
it can be formed toward fruitful evangelical ends. As always, this is a matter
(*la materia*) that has purpose in its preordained use ("that is employed" [*se
emplee*]).[33] In the *Lexicon,* the emphasis on hylomorphism emerges in an
evangelical configuration. By revealing Andean matter's inherent Christian
potential, Santo Tomás shows that Christianity can be brought to order
from the peoples and souls of the Americas. Hylomorphism becomes an
organizational cascade. Santo Tomás suggests that his *Lexicon*'s vocabulary
is one type of "matter" to be put in use by his *Grammatica* that will, in turn,
enact/form the Andean landscape and its peoples.

Santo Tomás's engagement with hylomorphism in the transatlantic
Spanish world is not unique. As Ralph Bauer posits, the Second Scholastics
at the University of Salamanca helped solidify the discourse of hylomorphism into an "imperialist ideology" that they "actualized" in America.[34]
Likewise, as scholars such as Orlando Bentancor and Daniel Nemser have
shown, early modern colonialists engaged ideas of hylomorphism to support their economic and evangelical theories of extraction, especially in
the case of Potosí.[35] Through readings of Martin Heidegger, Bentancor
writes that hylomorphism helped explain the creation and management
of a "standing-reserve" of disposable materials (metal and souls) necessary
for the justification and execution of economic and evangelical projects.[36]
Yet, in Santo Tomás's works, the tie between form and matter is cast in
different terms—not least due to his antagonism toward the exhaustion
of bodies toward economic ends.[37] Santo Tomás does not refuse the idea
that Indigenous peoples are matter requiring a Christian form (i.e. organization in *policía*) since this is part of the evangelical project. However, he

excoriates colonial relations that have been instituted around a particular formation of gender—the sexualized *encomienda* and mining apparatus.[38] In the case of Santo Tomás's work, there appears to be a division of forms—economic and evangelical—rather than a synthesis.

While he does not wish these abusive relations to continue, Santo Tomás does not suggest that economic projects have been without use. Economic encounters, he writes, have led to a mutually intelligible form of Quechua among Andean peoples. He writes, "And this language was never so commonly used by all in the past as it is today. Because with the communication, negotiations, and acquisitions that they have with each other at present, and for gatherings in Christian towns and markets, as well as in contracts and in services for Spaniards, peoples from diverse provinces use this general language to understand each other."[39] As a Dominican who censures exploitative relations, it is resonant that Santo Tomás engages the term *servicio,* a word Las Casas used to condemn Spanish abuses of Indigenous peoples.[40] However, he also presents a strange quasi-celebration of the unexpected linguistic outcome of these economic Spanish-Indigenous relations since they can foster communication. If Santo Tomás's project is an organization of intelligible language toward the ends of evangelization, then certain economic practices have enabled a felicitous outcome. They have affected linguistic dissemination and mutual intelligibility.[41] Though Quechua vocabulary and textual forms (namely contracts) have been used to build a colonial system of expropriative and violent relations, Santo Tomás points to the fact that many of these relations can be *converted* to support his own evangelical mission. Santo Tomás can repurpose economic textual forms and use them. Therefore, the *Lexicon* and the *Grammatica* are not only texts. They are also theories that explain how form can produce different types of colonialism. As Santo Tomás poses, form produces social, economic, and/or evangelical relationships; it regulates them, disseminates them, and it can be used to transform them.

Insufficient Pasts, Useful Futures

That said, Santo Tomás includes caveats regarding the power of his text. Without undermining the utility of his work or its method, whereby form can bring evangelical relationships to the Andes and foster *policía* against the devastation imposed by economic exploitation, Santo Tomás points to the limitations caused by a surplus of linguistic "matter" and the inability of the friar to bring it all into his text. Languages and terms which are in use (*usados*) by Indigenous peoples cannot be gathered by one lexicographer alone. Santo Tomás is confronted by regional vocabulary, differential pronunciations, and a plurality of verbs.[42] The author presents these caveats in the "Prologue to the Pious Reader" (Prologo del Auctor al pio Lector) in the *Lexicon* in a series of notes, each of which explains the form, organization, and value of his text as well as its limitations. In his fifth guiding point, Santo Tomás states that there are differences in pronunciation across the Andes regarding Quechua, and while he follows what he posits to be the most common one, his text will contain exclusions and limitations. In turn, his sixth point admits the "lack" (*falta*) of many words, not only those of the natural world,[43] but also of those relating to the religious realm. Plenitude is impossible because of the impossible reach of the researcher, creating what Regina Harrison calls "the lexicographer's plight."[44]

This claim does not, however, undermine the idea that form does work as an evangelical strategy, nor does it belittle Santo Tomás's labor. Rather, it is at once a protestation of false modesty and a temporal proposition. Santo Tomás looks to the future as a site of resolution. As we can see by shifting to the other text by Santo Tomás that accompanies his *Lexicon,* his *Grammatica,* there is a temporal sleight of hand. In the "Prologue by the Author to the Christian Reader" (Prologo del Autor al Christiano Lector) in his *Grammatica,* Santo Tomás goes against typical uses of agrarian metaphors that posit *Indigenous* peoples as "tender plants in the faith." Instead, he casts his own work as "an unripe fruit" (la fructa, no enteramente madura) and a work "born before its time . . . and not fully ripe" (parir este co[n]cepto imperfecto . . . ante de llegar a madurez).[45] If the urgency of publication, of making Quechua known for evangelization, has pushed this work to publication, perfection will arrive in the future via another who "with greater intelligence and skill may finish it" (co[n] mayor erudiction y perfection lo acabe).[46] Form can still organize language (and bodies) into a Christian order. The conclusion simply remains for a future moment. Santo Tomás moves to time as a solution. Form has no failing for the evangelical project, even if Santo Tomás's work is an incomplete iteration of form's logic. Rather it requires future fulfillment—as does evangelization.

Though authors of later evangelical bilingual texts may not address Santo Tomás's works directly,[47] these writers do invoke this call for completion based on past deficiencies. In a compellation of seventeenth-century evangelical Andean texts, Ana Segovia Gordillo has shown how these multilingual works justify their publication through a description of their additions to or improvements upon earlier forms. Alonso de Huerta's *Arte breve de la lengua quechua, general de los yndios de este Reyno del Pirú* (1616), Juan Roxo Mexía y Ocón's *Arte de la lengua general de los indios del Peru* (1648), and Esteban Sancho de Melgar's *Arte de la lengua general del ynga llamada qquechhua* (1691) are part of what she, after Ascensión Hernández de León-Portilla, has called a "cascade of grammars," where a new text is justified as the solution to a previous one's limitations.[48] For instance, Huerta wrote in 1616 that he composed his grammar because two previous works did not satisfy the needs of friars. One was "too long and complex for beginners" (abundoso y amplio, que no es para principiantes) and another "missed many essential topics due to its brevity."[49] In similar fashion, Roxo Mexía y Ocón engaged the language of obligation by positing that he had to supplement the lack of prior texts. "I have been obliged" (me ha obligado), he wrote, to perform this labor because prior works "did not address" certain grammatical matters necessary for instruction. Despite this need to supplement, Roxo Mexia y Ocón did not contest the logic of instruction. In other words, his text would provide the same "*form* of instruction" (*forma de instruirles*), but add content.[50] In each of these texts, we must note that writers do not object to the theory of form—the idea that the organization of language and text could organize Spanish-Indigenous relationships, bodies, towns, and ensure evangelization. Rather, friars needed to revise earlier textual forms and address what each "lacked." They faced a temporal problem rather than a theoretical one.

This temporal dilemma appears in a text that has been well studied for other reasons—namely, its description of Andean cultural practices and acts of colonial subjection. I refer to a handbook for confessors, the *Ritual formulario,* composed by the parish priest Juan Pérez Bocanegra. Though this is a handbook and thus departs from the lexicons and grammars discussed above, it too confronts textual and formal problems: according to Pérez Bocanegra, many of the difficulties he faces are not a problem of Andean character but rather built into the works he has inherited. Pérez Bocanegra posits that gaps must be filled by additions, linguistic errors must be corrected, and documents' organizational difficulties must be sorted out to make evangelical works useful for evangelization in the Andes. He decides that, "Bringing together the different ways [the Sacraments] had been said in Quechua into one [work], and finding so many, so poorly translated, it was better to do away with many of their expressions, [sample] questions, and answers altogether; to add some, supplement others, move conjunctions, verbs, phrases, and imperfections, until the [language] could be reduced (*reducir*) to a useful, pure, unadorned, and intelligible one for friars and Indians alike."[51] As Pérez Bocanegra writes, he has had to work as a reader and editor of previous texts, bringing "many" earlier works into "one" to assemble a text that can standardize and organize evangelization, as well as the bodies and practices that it implicates. He continues to state that he makes one useful text "so that (by the mercy of God) in the celebration of Mass and in the practice of celebrating the canonical hours, we are uniform, as well as in the administration and practice of the holy sacraments, and in the profession of our Christian faith."[52] Like the friars gathered by the Third Lima Council conducted some fifty years prior,[53] Pérez Bocanegra argues that a standard text can standardize evangelical practice, Spanish-Andean "relations," and thus Christianity—how it is lived in body and space—in the Andes. Yet, while he works to revise and reassemble prior works, he does not forswear their intentions or logic. Instead, he takes unintelligible translations and adds to them, fills gaps, and moves parts to "*reduzir*" or reduce—to produce a mutually intelligible and productive Christian organization. With "*reduzir*," Pérez Bocanegra speaks of a restitution of a more perfect Christian form, where language is "brought back to *order*" (buelto a mejor *orden*).

While Pérez Bocanegra is not the only person to speak of this organization of language as an act of *reducir/reducción* (indeed, Santo Tomás does well),[54] his use of the term proves apt to explain how form expresses a link between the ordering of text and that of bodies in the late sixteenth and early seventeenth centuries. While *reducir* and the *reducción* of language describe an attempted return to order after the fragmentation of language begun with the destruction of the Tower of Babel,[55] the *reducción* also names the political and social reorganization of "Indian" subjects. In the 1570s, Viceroy Francisco de Toledo and evangelical agents such as the Jesuits emphasized the need to gather the supposedly "dispersed Indians" and place them into "European-style towns" as a strategy of conversion, thus transforming the *doctrina* into a resettled grid.[56] Though, as Mumford notes, it is critical to remember that the *reducción* was by nature incomplete and selective,[57] an ideology that was put in practice but unfinished, its logic insisted that form was functional. The *reducción* posited that form and repetition could create *policía*.[58] It held that the imposition of spatial, architectonic, intimate, and religious order would bring rhythm and structure to Andean life. That is, the exterior and interior structure of the *polis* (city) would reshape the exterior and interior of the Andean Christian (though a more pessimistic reading, of course, notes that it facilitated the extraction of labor and wealth). As per usual, form was a reproductive practice. Mumford writes how inspectors were told to create *reducciones* that were "identical to one another in every way possible," pointing back to that pre-determined and immutable standard of what it meant to be Christian.[59] Cities were to be laid out with streets extending in a grid shape from a central plaza in the form of an ideal urban environment with a church and *cabildo* marking the town center. As important, if this exterior *polis* was regulated, the "interior" domestic world was also made into a regulated and formalized space through the idea of the *reducción*. Tom Cummins posits that the *reducción* let Church ideology invade the home with the idea of *policía* in mind. Rooms were to have no passageway between each other to ward off the assumed prevalence of sexual sins such as incest.[60] *Policía* could be preserved because the residential interior was visible to the street. The reduction of language into new texts and the reassembly of bodies into new communities meant that form would effect change.[61]

This *future* promise provides a throughline for evangelical methods that undergird Pérez Bocanegra's text. As noted in chapter 3, the Third Lima Council proposed that a standardized form and the production of new relations would solve evangelical failures. Pérez Bocanegra both accepts and repeats this rhetoric. However, since he must "revise" those texts, he speaks to their limitations (a complaint that fills his prologue). Why else would Pérez Bocanegra be obliged to write this *Ritual formulario*? For this reason, we can modify Sara Ahmed's quotation of Henry Petroski, who states that "form follows *failure*," to argue that evangelical form *requires* failure for the composition of new forms.[62] Though failure might overstate the case, the creation of new forms only emerges when previous ones have not completed their mission. Pérez Bocanegra's work to join, supplement, remove, and reorganize text follows on the heels of previous documents that have not finished the promised *reducción* of the words and bodies that populate the Andes.

This need to write a new text shows that the use of form *assumes* future efficacy despite prior failures. The outcome, however, remains a projection. To imagine future possibility, Pérez Bocanegra must obscure a stark reality: his work may also have an infelicitous[63] outcome. Evangelical success is not a present guarantee but rather a future projection that inheres in these colonial forms and the "relations" they *will* (hopefully) produce. This fact is revealed in the rhetoric of "use" and "utility" which saturates the many licenses included in the opening of Pérez Bocanegra's work.[64] It is easy to overlook the future projection that inheres in these licenses, given that they approve publication in its present by confirming the value of the text without insinuating doubt. For instance, in the license provided to the *Ritual formulario,* the leader of the Dominicans in Peru, Luis Cornejo, states that he found the document "very *useful* and necessary for the friars and other priests who labor for the conversion and spiritual good of the Indians [*naturales*]."[65] However, Cornejo has no true knowledge as to the efficacy of this text. It has not been "used." Against this presentism, projection becomes patent in licenses provided by Francisco de Contreras, rector of the Colegio of the Jesuits in Cuzco, and Lorenzo Pérez de Grado, the Bishop of Cuzco. Though they are firm in their certainty, both writers project utility into the future and demonstrate that the usefulness of form is in fact contingent and unproven. Contreras posits that the text is to be celebrated because it "*will* be of utmost utility" ("*será* de grandissima utilidad") "to administer the holy sacraments" (aministrar los santos sacramentos).[66] Likewise, Pérez de Grado promises that the text's "great utility" (*mucha utilidad*) turns upon future possibility. In the license offered to Pérez Bocanegra's text, Pérez de Grado posits that the text *will* bring naturales and friars together and "*will teach* them what they *will/should do*" (*se instruirá* en lo que *deven hazer*).[67] These statements underscore how the future conditions each license and evangelical text as potential, rather than fact. Usefulness remains to be seen. The uncertainty that inheres in the usefulness of form shows that form does not dictate the shape of the colonial future and its configuration. It chases after the future and tries to control it, or as Ivonne del Valle has argued, it imagines a redemptive future with no possible outside.[68] Yet, these futures are constantly confronted with an outside.

This is a problem since reformed customs turn on a future projection. The promise of evangelical change depended on futurity, as del Valle and Andrés I. Prieto have shown. Jesuits like Acosta built their evangelical platform on the belief that *present* difference could be resolved through generational progress.[69] Time and duration, however, remained ambivalent. Even if Acosta emphasized Indigenous capacity for future change, with custom creating a "second nature" that was not fixed,[70] customs were not easily transformed. As del Valle summarizes, friars' "suppression, substitution, and creation of habits"[71] fought against an ossification that had taken place across generations. The variability of form would only make matters worse.

The Question and Not the Answer

This final section returns to a question I broached in chapter 3. It considers how the practice (use) of form undermines the promise that "Indians" can be fully known and transformed into Christian subjects—the purported goal of conversion. To explain this fact, this section focuses on the *Ritual formulario* and shows how standardized repetition often fails to reveal Andean difference. As noted above, the *Ritual formulario* is a handbook for confessors. It emphasizes the need to regulate questions to produce efficacious results; only a uniform document could produce uniform Christians. A problem, however, accompanies uniformity: when evangelism is practiced through the repetition of one set of relations, the outcomes are also uniform. Andean peoples respond as Christians *should* and do not reveal the specificity of their difference. They can never be truly seen if the *Ritual formulario* and the forms dictated by its relations are too formalized.

The obfuscation of difference caused by of the achievement of a goal like religious standardization presents an ironic complication to a colonial text like the *Ritual formulario,* a work that ostensibly divides the confessor from the confessant, the friar from the "Indian"—especially since, as scholars such as Sabine Hyland, Charles, and Kenneth Mills, have shown, friars worked to "discover" supposed Andean intransigence hidden by Christian "forms."[72] However, though a confessional is of course marked by differentiation, it is also deeply procedural and predicated on the constitution of relation. A prompt, and not only a differentiating answer, is central to practice. Though Covarrubias does not define "formulario," the *Diccionario de autoridades* (1726) explains that this term designates a standardizing text that has a regulatory use designed to guide practice. It is "the book or writing that contains the *forms/formulas* that must be observed to *make/do* certain things."[73] This textual "formulario" is a procedural guide, resolutely bureaucratic, and concerned with the execution of practice. Taken to Pérez Bocanegra's text, the *Ritual formulario* shows that the regulatory function is a reciprocal practice where the questioner does not escape scrutiny or standardization. Instead, the practice and the relation it enacts comes to the fore. As a sign of this emphasis on relation, Pérez Bocanegra insinuates that his text is not a resource for the finer points of doctrine. In the "Letter to Friars" (Epistola a los Curas), Pérez Bocanegra emphasizes that his *Ritual formulario* focuses on the execution of repeated questions rather than the explanation of belief—to friars, but perhaps to catechumens as well. He states that "this *Ritual Formulary* does not resolve doubts regarding the matters and forms of the Sacraments. It only deals with what the friar should do in the execution of them."[74] With this summary, Pérez Bocanegra explains that his text does not provide answers to potential questions or doubts, or explanations regarding the meaning of doctrine and ritual. For these, friars can recur to other texts.[75] The *Ritual formulario* does not address form's content or "inside." Instead, his is a text that deals in the composition of repetition, procedure, and relations; it guides the practice, making, and doing of evangelization according to formulaic standards that produce formulaic subjects.

This emphasis on form as a means of standardization provides another entry point into the study of Andean identity in the *Ritual formulario,* distinct from a primary mode of study that has focused on Andean epistemology as the locus of resistance in this text. Scholars have mined the sites where Andeans announce their specificity: in the appearance of Andean communication technologies,[76] the singularity of kinship practices,[77] and ideas of sin that conflict with European ones.[78] For instance, scholars have seen how Andean communication technologies are embedded in the *Ritual formulario*—often evident in Pérez Bocanegra's complaints regarding his difficulties with confession and conversion. Pérez Bocanegra decries the obstacles to confession caused by Andeans' reliance on *khipus*—a communication technology created with a series of knotted cords that could transmit data, history, and memory. He writes that "Indians" bring "certain *khipus,* knots, and memorized [items] to confess" before exchanging the same *khipus* with other parishioners so that they could reuse them in the confessional and repeat the same number of sins.[79] As scholars such as Harrison, Charles, Gary Urton, and others have shown, this condemnation of an Andean communication technology locates Andean specificity *within* a European text. Pérez Bocanegra's condemnations show that Andean epistemology defied Christian rules of remembering and understanding sin[80] and undermined economic allegories of accounting for transgression.[81] Moreover, and ironically, the *khipu* shows how the *Ritual formulario* is disrupted by the standardizing power of an *Andean* relational form. According to the friar's complaint, penitents would share one *khipu* and standardize their answers, repeat each other, and disappear into relations based on this form. As Bruce Mannheim writes, Pérez Bocanegra attempted to prohibit the use of the *khipu* in confession (unlike the Jesuits who encouraged the practice).[82] Yet, Pérez Bocanegra's prohibitions did not solve these problems caused by repetition because, as he writes, many sins required the revelation and verification of "an obscured interior."[83] Andeans "never say . . . the number of sins (more or less) that they have committed, which is necessary for the integrity of confession. Rather, if they said they swore ten times, another ten times they got drunk, had sex, stole, without adding or subtracting from these sins a single number."[84] For Pérez Bocanegra, these Andeans' repetitions suggest that the enumeration of sin[85] has little value since it does not provide a specific "account" of the self. Instead, it is a performance that makes each individual sin and person meaningless to a Christian authority because all have the same, indistinguishable form. When each person looks the same on the outside, the truth value within—belief, understanding, and selfhood—becomes unclear.

Attention to form and the frustration that it produced for colonial authorities thus complicates readings of confession that emphasize the success of evangelical subjection as individualization. If the Third Lima Council and those who took up its mantle worked to inculcate European individualism through an idea of interiority,[86] the insistent "use of form" could ironically undermine these very goals. Repetition got in the way of friars' ability to control the religious message and its "standardized form" since they could not actually see if individual "Indians" understood and believed Christian doctrine as the friars wished. As writes Prieto, the use of the *khipu* suggested an appropriation of authority and belief as something that could be circulated and taught outside of a regulated priestly economy. It suggested that "natives reaffirmed their own agency, critically adopting and rejecting elements of Western culture and morality as they saw fit."[87] Authority, agency, and appropriation is one means of enacting resistance. We might also put an ironic spin on the word "saw." Form as a site of repetition shows how the very inability of colonial agents to "see" what Indigenous peoples adopted and rejected frustrated colonial authorities' very goals. Form produced different relationships than those it was meant to occasion. As this chapter has contended, the successes produced by form as an evangelical strategy inhered in their ability to cast Indigenous peoples in the *shape* of Christianity. Form could produce a recognizable arrangement on the surface, but, friars eventually feared, it could not force the revelation of difference beneath. If form emphasizes the reproduction of a Christian relation among peoples, spaces, objects, and beliefs, only this outside could be seen and verified. While the tenets of Christianity may be performed correctly, the very idea of form—both physical and textual—has inherent complications. As chapter 3 contended, the form itself was an enabling tool of colonial authority and a limitation in its ability to reveal the breadth of cultural practice.[88]

What, then, if we consider the repetition of form as a site of Indigenous presence and absence? As Michel-Rolph Trouillot posited, silence and power enter history at "different angles." Silences, he poses, are plural and must be treated as such since they "enter the process of historical production" in the making of sources, their assembly, retrieval, and attribution of significance.[89] Form is one part of this entry of silence and an ambivalent one. The making of sources such as these evangelical texts is inseparable from the assembly and definition of Indigenous peoples as "Indians." However, form is tied to a silence that is at once a site of opening. Just as form seeks to make the Indigenous person "speak" in the shape of Christianity, form does not always capture or reveal the plenitude of an interior. The imposition of form—at its most successful—reflects form back at colonial authorities. Form speaks in a shape, a performance, a relation, asking that we assume its content rather than "know" it. If this colonial form is used to assemble Indigenous peoples and attribute Christian meaning to behaviors and practices, it also provides a site for difference that is potentially unseen and unspoken.

There is still danger in the celebration of form as a site of opacity. As noted in chapter 3, the logic of an occluded "interior" helped facilitate racialization, violence, and alternate methods of evangelization. Throughout the seventeenth century, evangelical officials compounded their infantilizing view of "Indians" as tender plants with a violent vision of them as weeds holding fast in the New World, most famously in the *campañas de extirpación de idolatrías* in the 1580s led by Cristóbal de Albornoz.[90] Assumptions that Andean intransigence remained "hidden" suggested that form became an obstacle rather than a tool for evangelization and thus justified violence and interrogation. However, we should not treat form as an evangelical strategy relegated to the colonial wastebasket. A friar like Pérez Bocanegra could condemn the use of the *khipu* to suggest that Indigenous peoples had become an undifferentiated mass (i.e., formally opaque) while still arguing for the power of form and its organizational capacity to build new relations, to reduce communities, and to construct identities. Evangelization was a palimpsest of strategies—as were the strategies of resistance that this method of evangelization occasioned.

The daily life of Christianity is, by nature, a ritualistic repetition. In the colonies, much of Christianity and its *policía* was a standardized practice that existed as a formal performance. As writes Jessica Delgado, "the confession-communion sacramental complex" was a procedure "meant to be repeatedly enacted . . . regularly renewed . . . [and] meant to anchor people both individually and communally to God and the church. This anchoring was accomplished socially, somatically, and emotionally through the embodied learning of ritualized repetition and shared physical experiences."[91] Since she points to colonial Christianity writ large, Delgado asks us to consider if Christianity was always a matter of form. With an emphasis on "shared repetitions," Delgado points to the fundamental crux of forms of relation: they are at once an arrangement of bodies into relation and a performance of learned repetition that is formalized and shaped according to a predetermined standard. The texts studied here emphasize this fact. The imposition of the same makes Christianity seem true. Forms of relation are a way of doing life together. Of course, many Andean Christians were earnest in their devotion. Yet the writings of friars reveal a great fear that form might only be practice and not belief. Form was a useful way of organizing Christian life—until it was not.

Coda

"No. But, look here, I'm not inventing this. This is what happened. We have to tell what happened."[1] This plea to history arrives in the middle of the 2010 film *También la lluvia* (directed by Icíar Bollaín), a movie that depicts an international crew in Bolivia as they film a fictitious historical epic restaging the Spanish conquest of the New World.[2] Drawing on a script that charts the destructive encounters of early conquest, the "writers" and "producers" of this film-within-a-film lift much of their material from early colonial texts, especially the Dominican friar Bartolomé de Las Casas's *Brevísima relación de la destrucción de las Indias* (1552). Throughout this recreation, "director" Sebastián (Gael García Bernal) stages multiple pages from that work: he films the dogs of war, presents scenes of massive destruction and enslavement, and rehearses the fruitless pleas of Indigenous peoples. Each scene is captured and depicted on screen to be re-viewed by both the "film crew" and the viewers of *También la lluvia*. However, there is one act ripped from the pages of the *Brevísima relación* that Sebastián fails to represent. Sebastián cries out in vain when Indigenous women "actor/extras" refuse to simulate an act that I discussed at length in chapter 1: infanticide.

In this scene, the women are presented as local mothers selected at random from the crowd who auditioned for a role in the film. When Sebastián explains what they will do, wade in the river and simulate drowning their children, these "mothers" refuse. Despite Sebastián's assurances that no harm will come to the infants since they will be replaced with dolls, the economic incentive of compliance cannot force participation. Shouting over the noise of wailing children, Sebastián requests support from the epic's Andean protagonist Daniel (Juan Carlos Aduviri), who stars as the famous Taíno *cacique* (Caribbean lord) hero/rebel Hatuey. As Daniel argues with the women, one begins to sing a lullaby before she is joined by the others. *También la lluvia* layers their singing over extra-diegetic violins as it cuts to the international "crew" listening intently. Though the "crew" cannot understand the lyrics, the song explains why this scene will never be filmed: infanticide, even simulated, violates the bond that these mothers have with their children. The camera turns to highlight doting mothers and tranquil children, now silent, as the group begins to walk away from the river. Daniel returns and explains to Sebastián that these women will not do the scene. Moreover, "they cannot even imagine the idea of doing it."[3] Here, Sebastián makes his final entreaty to history, exclaiming that "we have to tell what happened," but only receives a shaming critique from Daniel: "There are more important things than your movie."[4] With this final statement, however, Daniel insinuates that *También la lluvia* might want to convey a different message via these women's refusal. The impossible performance of infanticide is transformed from a reflection on the horror of conquest into a critique of Sebastián's myopic focus on his own film at the expense of the neo-colonial conflict that surrounds him.[5]

From its onset, the film makes clear its contemporary stakes: it uses the violent colonial past as an intertext to portray a destructive neo-colonial present. *También la lluvia,* as the film's title indicates, points to a conflict built around water. The movie takes place during the Cochabamba Water War (1999–2000), when attempts to privatize the city's water supply led to protests, civil unrest, and violence between community members and government officials in Bolivia. *También la lluvia* depicts these events as it traces the fictitious filming. The self-centered production team works to insulate itself from local conflicts that keep bleeding over: protestors and armed soldiers block roads, suffering locals appear through the windows of the "crew's" jeeps, delays add to production costs, and actors fail to arrive on set. Strikingly, protagonist Daniel is a leader of the protest movements, making the rebellious historical figure he "plays" have value for the present. He symbolically shouts the film's title, exclaiming that private interests will take "even the rain" from community members who will die without access to water. This present story shows that the past will never be the real object of focus. Each staged scene works to shed light on the present. The Andean setting used to frame the Caribbean conquest shows that Indigenous peoples are still treated as an undifferentiated mass in a Western imaginary;[6] the filming of conquistadors' greed reflects upon the opulence of the film crew that depends on low-wage Indigenous labor; and the extraction of resources like gold points to the avarice of multinational corporations—and, in a reflexive commentary, of the film industry itself.

This constant critique of the neo-colonial present only confirms that staging infanticide was never the point. In fact, with their exit, the women leave a more important object at the center of the frame: water. Their absence shows the river and highlights an object that is, as Daniel says, "more important than your movie."

As a "form of relation," however, this scene does produce a productive conversation with the past. Kinship relations under colonialism depend on forms that shape the arrangements of people, available technologies, and pertinent information. This scene shows how both forms and relations are inflected by conditions of time and space. While the scene points to a "familiar" family configuration, the maternal bond, however "real," is also a networked, relational form structured around the dictates of a film. This scene is not only rhetorical but also procedural. All of the interested parties—both the "filmic" ones and the real ones beyond the screen—are "present" through the practices of scripting, casting,[7] paying,[8] funding, translating, filming, producing, viewing, and distributing. This scene lets us see how kinship is more than a staged maternal tie. It is a network of colonial relations produced in available and relevant forms.

In this book, I have focused on only a few textual forms and the embodied ties they enact such as historical relations, powers of attorney, grammars, and handbooks for confessors. Each form provides a pattern for colonial relations to take shape at a specific moment—a fact no more evident than in this juxtaposition to a film from the twenty-first century. Reading forms of relation with an eye on comparison provides an opportunity to see how colonialism is a "structure rather than an event," as Patrick Wolfe held, while also "both a structure *and* an event," as María Josefina Saldaña-Portillo writes.[9] Or, more precisely, multiple events that resonate because they are relations structured by specific and situated forms that dictate knowledge and organization. Forms and the relations they condition offer a way to see that "structure" is not structuralist, but rather mutable, and not predetermined by transhistorical equivalence. Each event, the anxiety it produces for colonial authorities, and the forms of relation that it occasions make colonialism's structure less immaculate. Forms of relation reveal, as Ann Stoler writes after Foucault, that events are structured by "breach[es] of the self-evident."[10]

Considering how these events take shape in diverse forms can help center the different models of relation that mark colonial worlds. We can expand attention away from certain relations like biology and *mestizaje*,[11] which have, as Shannon Speed (Chickasaw) argues,[12] historically displaced indigeneity. Instead, we can attend to horizontal and gendered forms that do not depend upon the gestation of essentialist identities or nation-states. As writes Bolivian and Aymara scholar Silvia Rivera Cusicanqui, form lets us observe other relations that might have been "realized in spaces that were created by the cultural invader" but are used to produce and reformulate colonial survival.¹³ Forms such as the *relación*, petition, and grammar are such spaces that can and have been opened for other possibilities.

For this reason, I have contended in implicit and explicit ways that relations name how life and its constituent bonds may change. To understand the uncertainty embedded in form requires the suspension of retrospective certainty. Present interlocutors must approach relations as sites of what Anna Brickhouse has called "unsettlement."¹⁴ As Brickhouse proposed, "unsettlement" foregrounds the fallacy of thinking about colonial life as a structure that gains stability with the passage of time. Instead, unsettlement reveals deformations in racialization, starts and stops in attempts at Indigenous removal, and the continual unsettling of colonial mindsets that emerge from the very onset of colonialism. Such insight provides a way to consider how living in and through relation is also a practice of doing and undoing kinship. Possibility emerges in the fact that relation lives in indeterminacy: Indigenous temporality remains, to borrow Rivera Cusicanqui's metaphor, "woven" into the production and reproduction of colonial time, life, and texts as part of the fabric of violence, anxiety, and meaning that defined what it meant to be in relation in the colonial Spanish Americas.¹⁵ Relations—and the forms they take—shift according to the practices, tools, and needs that let subjects live in the colonial Spanish American world. I fight, therefore, to approach the formal conditions of colonialisms while still respecting the contingencies, uncertainties, and differences that make historical events at once *present* and unreachable in their *pastness*. Forms of relation are manifestations of what Valerie Traub calls "cycles of salience," those "recurring moments in which these meta-logics are manifested . . . that is, as *forms of intelligibility* whose meanings recur, intermittently and with a difference, across time."¹⁶ Form provides a site where relations can be constellated in resonance and difference, to find familiarity without collapsing into the same.

This proposition brings me back to the scene of infanticide from *También la lluvia,* where even though it is not shot, it *is* depicted. It is easy to assume that infanticide is fully absent since it is not reenacted. Unlike every other scene of colonial violence staged in *También la lluvia,* only maternal infanticide is not explicitly viewable as part of the film-within-a-film. Instead, this moment focuses on the women "actors"—as have the few readers who attend to this scene. For instance, Andrea Meador Smith condemns this absence, and portrays the scene as a sign of gender and simplification wherein the dismissal of women emphasizes masculine agency at the expense of women's autonomy and complexity. She posits that Daniel's required translation and the lack of subtitles only reinforce a gendered model of women's impotence and "simple-mindedness."[17] When taken to its limit, Smith's argument would hold that even Daniel's translation is superfluous: he merely glosses a maternal impulse that is pre-linguistic and universal since theirs is an act that speaks for itself.

However, this absence of explanation forces *También la lluvia* and its viewers to approach a colonial past that they cannot reach—perhaps against the film's knowledge and intent.[18] In *También la lluvia,* the scene leaves an absence that viewers must "witness" in absentia. It is therefore reaffirmed as impossible and unknowable. As Daniel says, the meaning of infanticide is something that "cannot be imagined," and yet this act and its meaning is something that must be. This is not to be naïve and imagine that these are "real" women/mothers who perform "real" acts of refusal. They are actors. Their refusal to represent infanticide is a scripted representation and the women are instructed to walk off-screen in a stage direction. Yet, if other moments of the film stage the seamless reproduction of the past for presentist purposes, this moment is different. When the film "cannot imagine" or stage infanticide in the same way, it demonstrates the persistence of historical dissonance. There is discomfort, incommensurability, and an unbroachable divide separating the present from the past it strives to use.

These are forms of relation. Though the film depicts kinship as transparent and outside of history, this scene performs the opposite. Transhistorical resonances may feel familiar, but they turn on the contingent possibilities and limitations of formal equivalence. Acts of historical re-creation and narration remake relations with the past since forms are distorted by the constituents who engage them. In studying forms of relation, we reshape their contours and create new ones. Scholarship is part of this re-formation in the present. By entering into relation, a distortion occurs. We—I— reform the way that all interlocutors take shape on the page and become available for the narration of histories and identities. Yet, if colonial subjects created ways to be related to each other, forge new ties, and compose ways of living in concert, I have done my best to also respect those forms of relation that deserve to remain unknown.

NOTES

Introduction

1. Pérez Bocanegra, *Ritual formulario,* 614. The full title of this text is *Ritual formulario e institucion de curas, para administrar a los naturales de este reyno, los santos sacramentos del baptismo, confirmacion, eucaristia, y viatico, penitencia, extremauncion, y matrimonio: con advertencias muy necessarias.* Though published in Lima in 1631, the book was completed in 1622.

2. The Inca "Empire" was an ethnically and politically expansive territory named Tawantinsuyo ("the four parts together") administrated from Cuzco. It incorporated parts of contemporary Colombia to the north; a large swath of the Andean regions of contemporary Bolivia, Ecuador, and Peru; the coastal regions of Chile to the South; and parts of the Amazon to the East. This area was held together through an extensive network of roads, intermarriage, and language. Quechua served as its administrative language and was used to consolidate and maintain cohesion among various ethnic groups. As scholars such as Alan Durston have shown, friars appropriated this strategy and further standardized Quechua to facilitate conversion via practice and publications such as the *Ritual formulario.* Durston, *Pastoral Quechua.*

3. While this image appears in the early pages of Irene Silverblatt's canonical work on gender ideology in the Andes and colonial Peru, *Moon, Sun, and Witches,* in that case, the image serves to illustrate autochthonous Inca practices. Silverblatt, *Moon, Sun, and Witches,* 6. The image also points to one of the friars' central preoccupations during evangelization in the Andes and colonial Peru: "marriage" practice—namely cohabitation and trial marriage. See Harrison, *Sin and Confession;* von Germeten, "Sexuality, Witchcraft, and Honor"; Silverblatt, "Family Values"; and Stavig, "'Living in Offense.'"

4. Pérez Bocanegra, *Ritual formulario,* 613. "Grados de consanguinidad"; "ascendie[n]tes, y descendientes varones, y mugeres." In my citations of original print and manuscript texts, I retain works' original spelling and punctuation, except for a modernization of the u/v and i/j reversal. Further changes are marked with brackets, such as the inclusion of content elided in abbreviations. Unless otherwise noted, all translations are my own. I have engaged the most common Hispanicized spellings of Indigenous-language words and added accents to respect phonetic conventions in modern Spanish. I do not modify or mark scholars' choices in my direct citations of their works.

5. As Tom Cummins notes, this model is not autochthonous or "ethnographic" but rather borrows from biblical and royal genealogical trees. Cummins, "Andean Colonial Towns."

6. Pérez Bocanegra, *Ritual formulario,* 614.

7. Floyd, "Privileging the Local," 379.

8. Emily C. Floyd suggests that these Christian names indicate friars' frequent attempts to overwrite "idolatrous" names that coincided with "Gods" like *Poma* (puma) and *Amaru* (snake). Floyd, "Privileging the Local," 380.

9. Translations in the image insinuate cultural modifications since kinship terms in Quechua are inflected by the gender of the two parties linked by the relation (i.e., the term a man would use for his sister is not the same as that a woman would use). That said, while the translation in the image is not inflected by gender, the text of the *Ritual formulario* does indicate how Quechua kinship terms depend on the gender of the speaker. Michael J. Horswell helps explain the impact of gender-inflected language in conversion practices in the Andes in *Decolonizing the Sodomite.*

10. As Cummins notes, Pérez Bocanegra's visual schema appears in similar woodcuts printed in Peruvian and New Spanish texts in the sixteenth century. Cummins, "Andean Colonial Towns," 222–24.

11. Though Indigenous peoples were technically given dispensation to marry within the third degree by Pope Paul III's Bull of 1537, *Altitudo divini concilii,* friars instructed Indigenous catechumens in matrimonial orthodoxy. For discussions of matrimonial dispensations, see Imolesi, "Doing the Same"; and Rípodas Ardanaz, *El matrimonio en Indias.* Ironically, Kenneth Mills, citing Regina Harrison and Irene Silverblatt, contends that this scrutiny over Inca consanguinity to this degree was unnecessary and that "marriage" within the fourth degree did not exist in Andean traditions. See Mills, "Bad Christians in Colonial Peru," 194.

12. Pérez Bocanegra, *Ritual formulario,* 613. "Se conozcan, y vean mas distintame[n]te."

13. Throughout this book, I use the term "Indigenous"—and acknowledge its inherent problems—when speaking of the first peoples of the Americas to address the movement between transatlantic frames, colonial racializing practices, the complexity of deracination, and my engagement with transnational scholarship. In the context of the Andean region, I reference Jeremy Ravi Mumford's recommendation to engage "Andean" as a specific acknowledgment of groups that share practices due to regional traditions, migrations, intermarriage, and subjection to Inca rule. When possible, I signal groups' specificity and acknowledge how the Spanish empire and scholarship lead to their collapse. I use the category and term "Spanish," while also acknowledging its collapse and imprecision. Mumford, "Litigation as Ethnography," 5.

14. I borrow the term "familiar" from Bianca Premo, who discusses how this word at once implicates and complicates contemporary ideas of kinship in the colonial past. Premo, "Familiar," 298.

15. Butler, "Is Kinship Always Already Heterosexual?," 15. Butler focuses on the US legal context to speak of the polemical dispute over gay marriage.

16. Freeman, "Queer Belongings," 299, emphasis added.

17. Nara Milanich points to this complexity in her interrogation of the methodological and definitional tensions that subtend the study of "family history." Milanich, "Whither Family History?," especially 443–45.

18. Lamana, *Domination without Dominance*, 2.

19. Kazanjian, *Colonizing Trick*, 9. In this case, David Kazanjian speaks to an analysis of "articulation" in the nineteenth-century English Atlantic.

20. Jehlen, "History before the Fact."

21. Adorno, *Polemics of Possession*, 4; and Mignolo, "Cartas, crónicas y relaciones."

22. Covarrubias, *Tesoro de la lengua castellana*, 901.

23. *Diccionario de la lengua castellana* (Madrid, 1737), s.v. "relación," https://apps2 .rae.es/DA.html. "Breve y sucinto informe: que por persona pública se hace en voz o por escrito, al Juez, del hecho de un proceso."

24. *Diccionario de la lengua castellana* (Madrid, 1737), s.v. "relación," https://apps2 .rae.es/DA.html., emphasis added. "Assimismo adherencia ò parentesco à lo largo de una persona con otra: y assi decimos, Pedro *tiene relación* con Juan."

25. Schneider, *Study of Kinship*, 72.

26. Franklin and McKinnon, "Introduction," 2.

27. Lee, *Anxiety of Sameness;* Hering Torres, Martínez, and Nirenberg, *Race and Blood;* and Nirenberg, *Communities of Violence.*

28. Martínez, *Genealogical Fictions*, 104–5. See also Cook, *Forbidden Passages;* Kathryn Burns, "Unfixing Race"; and Martínez, "Black Blood."

29. See, for instance, Mörner, *Race Mixture;* and Padden, *Hummingbird and the Hawk.*

30. Scholars have discussed the consequences of this formation for historiography and cultural studies since it creates a narrative of history where women become biological handmaidens of the future, even in feminist historiography. See Franco, "La Malinche."

31. Tavárez, "Legally Indian"; and Hill, *Hierarchy, Commerce, and Fraud.*

32. Herzog, *Defining Nations.*

33. Rappaport, *Disappearing Mestizo;* Schwartz and Salomon, "New Peoples"; and Twinam, *Public Lives, Private Secrets.*

34. Van Deusen, "Intimacies of Bondage"; Arenal and Martínez-San Miguel, "Refocusing New Spain"; Vieira Powers, *Crucible of Conquest;* Vieira Powers, "Conquering Discourses"; and Wood, "Sexual Violation."

35. Ralph Bauer and Norton, "Introduction"; Dean and Leibsohn, "Hybridity and Its Discontents"; and Cornejo Polar, "Mestizaje e hibridez."

36. Mangan, *Transatlantic Obligations;* Premo, "Familiar"; van Deusen, "Intimacies of Bondage"; van Deusen, "Diasporas, Bondage, and Intimacy"; and Kathryn Burns, "Politics of Mestizaje."

37. Foucault, *History of Sexuality,* 93. For engagements with the grid of intelligibility in studies of colonial racialization, see Nemser, *Infrastructures of Race;* and Stoler, "Tense and Tender Ties."

38. Chakrabarty, *Provincializing Europe.* See also Simpson, *Mohawk Interruptus.*

39. See, among others, Morgan, *Reckoning with Slavery;* Rivera Cusicanqui, *Ch'ixinakax utxiwa;* Pierce, *Argentine Intimacies,* 267–82; TallBear, "Making Love and Relations"; Castellanos, "Introduction"; Heintz, "Crisis of Kinship"; O'Toole, "Bonds of Kinship"; Penyak, "Incestuous Natures"; Pérez, "Family, Spiritual Kinship"; Premo, "Familiar"; Falconí Trávez, Santiago Castellanos, and Viteri, "Resentir lo queer"; Rodríguez, *Sexual Futures, Queer Gestures;* Decena, *Tacit Subjects;* Driskill, Finley, Gilley, and Morgensen, *Queer Indigenous Studies;* Rifkin, *When Did Indians Become Straight?;* Eng, *Feeling of Kinship;* Horswell, *Decolonizing the Sodomite;* Miranda, "Extermination of the *Joyas*"; Justice, "'Go Away, Water!'"; Hartman, *Lose Your Mother;* Povinelli, *Empire of Love;* Ferguson, *Aberrations in Black;* Sigal, *Infamous Desire;* Wolfe, "Land, Labor, and Difference"; Cohen, "Punks"; Lavrin, "Sexuality in Colonial Mexico"; and Spillers, "Mama's Baby, Papa's Maybe."

40. Bourdieu, *Outline of a Theory of Practice,* 35, emphasis in original.

41. Ann Laura Stoler uses this phrase in *Along the Archival Grain* to describe the conditions of documentation that support the felicitous reception of information.

42. Adorno, *Polemics of Possession,* 4. Walter Mignolo turns to "genre" to describe how writing produces a social interface, though he stresses hierarchies of inequality rather than possibility. Mignolo, *Darker Side,* see especially chap. 4, "Genres as Social Practices."

43. Studies of intimacy and colonialism have a genealogy of their own. See, for instance, Lowe, *Intimacies of Four Continents;* Shah, *Stranger Intimacy;* Ballantyne and Burton, *Moving Subjects;* Stoler, *Haunted by Empire;* and Stoler, *Carnal Knowledge.*

44. Stoler, *Along the Archival Grain,* 1.

45. Stoler, "Colonial Archives," 91.

46. Puente Luna, *Andean Cosmopolitans;* Puente Luna and Honores, "Guardianes"; McDonough, *Learned Ones;* Ramos and Yannakakis, *Indigenous Intellectuals;* Charles, *Allies at Odds;* Mills, *Idolatry and Its Enemies;* and Adorno, *Writing and Resistance.*

47. See, for instance, Ruan, "Probanza"; Brewer-García, "Bodies, Texts, and Translators"; Ruan, "Andean Activism"; Dueñas, *"Lettered City";* and Durston, *Pastoral Quechua.*

48. Brewer-García, *Beyond Babel;* Fuentes, *Dispossessed Lives;* Jouve Martín, *Esclavos de la ciudad letrada;* and Bennett, *Africans in Colonial Mexico.*

49. For canonical representations of this position, see Mignolo, *Darker Side;* and Gruzinski, *Mestizo Mind.* In response and building on a long tradition, recent texts by Joanne Rappaport, Tom Cummins, Frank Salomon, Mercedes Niño-Murcia, and John Charles emphasize the inclusion of Indigenous peoples in Western letters. Along these lines, Fernando Bouza Álvarez challenges textual inscription as the early modern period's privileged medium by arguing that European subjects also employed multiple communication technologies. See Rappaport and Cummins, *Beyond the Lettered City;* Salomon and Niño-Murcia, *Lettered Mountain;* Charles, *Allies at Odds;* and Bouza Álvarez, *Communication, Knowledge, and Memory,* 2–3.

50. See Karen Graubart's excellent study on the need for considerations of dialogue across subfields of colonial Andean study to address this collaborative practice of writing. Graubart, "Slaves and Not Vassals."

51. See, for instance, Sigal, "Queer Nahuatl."

52. McKinley, "Till Death Do Us Part."

53. Van Deusen, "Intimacies of Bondage."

54. O'Toole, *Bound Lives.*

55. Delgado, *Laywomen.*

56. Kathryn Burns, *Into the Archive,* 124, 147. Kathryn Burn's excellent study of notarial handbooks, though outside the scope of this book, reveals how manuals help produce formal standardization. See also Stoler, "Colonial Archives."

57. Graubart, "Slaves and Not Vassals"; Puente Luna, *Andean Cosmopolitans;* Premo, *Enlightenment on Trial;* McKinley, *Fractional Freedoms;* Premo, "Before the Law," 261–89; Baber, "Categories"; Mumford, "Litigation as Ethnography"; Honores, "Una sociedad legalista"; Black, "Between Prescription and Practice"; and Kellogg and Restall, *Dead Giveaways.*

58. Stoler, "Colonial Archives," 100.

59. White, *Content of the Form,* xi. Rolena Adorno critiqued the wholesale projection of Hayden White's nineteenth-century European model of historiography onto colonial Spanish American scholarship. Adorno, "Nuevas perspectivas," 16.

60. Van Deusen, *Embodying the Sacred,* 17.

61. Dueñas, *"Lettered City,"* 13.

62. Dean, "Beyond Prescription"; Graubart, "Creolization"; Black, "Between Prescription and Practice"; Kathryn Burns, "Notaries, Truth, and Consequences"; and Luján Muñoz, "Literatura notarial." This is not to say that notarial manuals did not intersect with other conceptions of identity. Rachel O'Toole notes that manuals indicated how testimony should be modified based on the backgrounds of interlocutors. Form is thus inflected by different axes of identity. Personal Correspondence.

63. Glissant, *Poetics of Relation,* 143–44.

64. Van Deusen, *Between the Sacred and the Worldly.*

65. Twinam, *Public Lives, Private Secrets.*
66. Nemser, *Infrastructures of Race.*
67. Cummins, "Andean Colonial Towns."
68. Tortorici, *Sins Against Nature.*
69. Sigal, "Queer Nahuatl."
70. Harrison, *Sin and Confession.*
71. Premo, "Familiar." See also Premo, "Maidens, the Monks, and Their Mothers."
72. Traub, *Thinking Sex,* 10.
73. In this regard, I depart from Roland Greene, who emphasizes keywords he considers *central* to early modern epistemologies. Roland Greene, *Five Words.*
74. This takes inspiration from Lisa Lowe, who writes that her work strives to serve as an investigation and contribution toward "a manner of reading and interpretation." Lowe, *Intimacies of Four Continents,* 21.
75. I borrow this phrase from Bianca Premo. Premo, *Father King.*
76. Muñoz, *Cruising Utopia,* 6, emphasis added.
77. For a study of the promises and difficulties of the rapprochement between queer studies and Indigenous studies articulated via the terms materiality, normativity, and relationality, see Byrd, "What's Normative Got to Do with It?"
78. Tzvetan Todorov made such a claim in *Conquest of America,* posing that writing enabled the conquest.
79. Martínez, "Archives, Bodies, and Imagination." Tortorici also provides an extensive consideration of this challenge in *Sins Against Nature.*
80. Trouillot, *Silencing the Past,* 28–30.

1. Misuse and Maternity

1. In this chapter, I use the general term "Indies" when discussing Bartolomé de Las Casas's text to follow his naming practice and its rhetorical idea of territorial space and evangelical possibility. When I refer to specific geographic sites in his text, I follow Las Casas's naming conventions.
2. Adorno, "Not-So-Brief Story." Adorno helpfully cites French Historian Roger Chartier's lecture at the John Carter Brown Library on February 19, 2015, titled "The Seven Lives of Las Casas's *Brevissima Relacion,* 1552–1822," which divides the text's differential uses into seven periods. The lecture is available at https://www.youtube.com/watch?v=FltEnWApH-8.
3. Verdesio, "Images and War"; Ralph Bauer, "Millennium's Darker Side," 36–37; and Brading, *First America.* See also the essays in Greer, Mignolo, and Quilligan, *Rereading the Black Legend.*
4. The text was composed ten years prior in 1542, the same year that Las Casas wrote the prologue to his more extensive *Historia de las Indias.* For a timeline of Las Casas's textual production, see Edmundo O'Gorman's introduction to the *Apologética historia sumaria* [. . .] (1560–61). Santa Arias discusses Las Casas's

representational practices in the *Historia de las Indias.* Arias, *Retórica, historia y polémica.*

5. Boyer, "Framing the Visual Tableaux," 372–73. As Arias posits, at this juncture of Las Casas's *oeuvre,* the Dominican friar condemned the procedures of Spanish intervention in the Americas and not Spanish intervention itself, though later in life, Las Casas would argue for the full restitution of Indigenous sovereignty. Arias, *Retórica, historia y polémica.* See also Muldoon, "Medieval Canon Law"; Adorno, *Intellectual Life;* Hanke, *All Mankind Is One;* Pennington, Jr. "Bartolomé de las Casas"; Wagner and Parish, *Life and Writings;* and Hanke, *Spanish Struggle for Justice.*

6. Ahmed, *What's the Use?*

7. Though Ivonne del Valle does not highlight "use" as the central axis of her analysis, she engages this term to illustrate how Machiavelli, Bartolomé de Las Casas, and José de Acosta theorize differential relationships between force and political/evangelical ends. Del Valle, "José de Acosta, Violence and Rhetoric."

8. Jáuregui and Solodkow, "Biopolitics," 141.

9. Ginsburg and Rapp, "Politics of Reproduction," 311. This is what Gayle Rubin has termed the sex/gender system, one often manifested in repressive patriarchal systems. See Rubin, "Traffic in Women."

10. In rare cases of child murder by Christians in Iberia, stories take on a different valence: they emphasize martyrdom and heroics. For instance, Numancia, the Peninsular city whose inhabitants resisted Roman soldiers by setting fire to the town and committing suicide, became a legend of bravery. Cervantes's stage version of the story (*El cerco de Numancia* [1581–83]) proves a famous case, as discussed by Bergmann, "Martyrs and Minors."

11. Adorno, *Polemics of Possession,* 6–8; González Echevarría, *Myth and Archive,* 10; and Mignolo, "Cartas, crónicas y relaciones."

12. Las Casas, *Brevísima relación,* 18, 28, 29. "Una vez vide que," "Vídeme," "Otras cosas vide."

13. Rabasa, *Inventing America,* 5.

14. Stone, "Confronting Stereotypes"; Merrim, "Counter-Discourse"; and Avalle-Arce, "Hipérboles del Padre Las Casas."

15. Las Casas, *Brevísima relación,* 5. "No las vido." This is an ironic claim, given that writers such as the *conquistador* of New Spain Bernal Díaz del Castillo condemned Las Casas and his *Brevísima relación* by arguing that the Dominican had not seen the realities of conquest. For a discussion of this conflict as regards the eyewitness, see Adorno, "Discursive Encounter."

16. Las Casas, *Brevísima relación,* 79. "Padres de hijos y mujeres de maridos."

17. Pagden, *Fall of Natural Man,* 71. The question of social organization provided one site of dispute over Spanish dominion as debated by Las Casas and Juan Ginés de Sepúlveda in Valladolid, 1550. For a summary and introduction to these debates, see Adorno, *Polemics of Possession.* See also, Arias, *Retórica,*

historia y polémica; Hanke, *All Mankind Is One;* and Hanke, *Aristotle and the American Indians.*

18. Adorno, *Polemics of Possession,* 107. As Adorno notes, this argument is forcefully made in O'Gorman's study of Las Casas's *Apologética historia sumaria.*

19. Las Casas, *Brevísima relación,* 16, emphasis added. "En la isla Española, que fue la primera, . . . entraron cristianos y comenzaron los grandes estragos y perdiciones destas gentes y que primero destruyeron y despoblaron comenzando los cristianos a tomar las mujeres e hijos a los indios para servirse y *para usar mal dellos.*"

20. Covarrubias, *Tesoro de la lengua castellana,* 988. "El acto y exercicio de usar alguna cosa"; "de costumbre."

21. Las Casas, *Brevísima relación,* 24. "Los hombres a las minas a sacar oro, que es trabajo intolerable, y las mujeres ponían en las estancias, que son granjas, a cavar las labranzas y cultivar la tierra, trabajo para hombres muy fuertes y recios."

22. Las Casas, *Brevísima relación,* 24. "Por estar los maridos apartados, que nunca vían [sic] a las mujeres, cesó entre ellos la generación . . . [y] murieron ellos en las minas de trabajos y hambre, y ellas en las estancias o granjas de lo mesmo."

23. Las Casas, *Brevísima relación,* 28–29. "En tres o cuatro meses, estando yo presente, murieron de hambre por llevalles los padres y las madres a las minas más de siete mil niños."

24. Las Casas, *Brevísima relación,* 24. "Secábasele la leche de las tetas a las mujeres paridas, y así murieron en breve todas las criaturas."

25. Bergmann, "Milking the Poor," 91.

26. Readers might assume that a partial retrospective account of Spanish sexual misuse would discuss children of Spaniards and Indigenous peoples (who would come to be identified as *mestizos* and who had begun to appear in legal documentation as early as the second decade of the sixteenth century). However, throughout the text, there is only one mention of Spanish and Indigenous children, where a Spaniard rapes an Indigenous woman to enslave her children. Berta Ares Queija also notes a similar absence in Las Casas's *Historia de las Indias* (1561, published 1875). Ares Queija, "Relaciones sexuales y afectivas," 253.

27. Muñoz, *Cruising Utopia.* See also scholarship on child separation at the US-Mexico border, such as Yablon-Zug, "Separation, Deportation, Termination."

28. Briggs, *Somebody's Children;* and Stoler, *Carnal Knowledge.*

29. Jacobs, *A Generation Removed;* and Child, *Boarding School Seasons.*

30. Mases, *Estado y cuestión indígena.*

31. Rifkin, *When Did Indians Become Straight?*

32. These historical limitations emerge, in part, from Michel Foucault's periodization in *The Order of Things: An Archaeology of the Human Sciences* (1966) where he emphasized that a European biopolitical state regime emerged in the late eighteenth century and showed its strength through the affirmative management of life. Though Ann Laura Stoler famously critiqued that text's lack of

engagement with empire, she did not question Foucault's periodization. Stoler, *Race and the Education of Desire.*

33. Fray Luis quotes Saint Gregory of Nyssa's "Homily on the Nativity of Christ," a sermon dedicated to the Massacre of the Innocents. Fray Luis de Granada, *Los seis libros de la Retórica eclesiástica.*

34. See Weissberger, "Motherhood and Ritual Murder"; and Dopico Black, "Ghostly Remains." Weissberger dates the trial to 1490, while Dopico Black dates it to 1491.

35. At different times, infants and children of varying ages could receive stays against expulsion. In contrast, older children were condemned to exile due to a belief that they had been indelibly marked by their parents' non-Christian stain. Broggio, "Religious Orders"; and Dopico Black, "Ghostly Remains," 96.

36. García-Arenal, "Baptism and Forced Conversion."

37. Perry, "Between Muslim and Christian Worlds," 180. See also Perry, *Handless Maiden;* and Tueller, "Assimilating Morisco."

38. Martínez Gomis, "Control de los niños moriscos."

39. Dopico Black, "Ghostly Remains," 94.

40. Bianca Premo, *Children of the Father King,* 97.

41. Twinam, "Church, the State, and the Abandoned," 171.

42. Premo, *Children of the Father King,* 99.

43. Mendieta Ocampo, *Hospitales de Lima colonial,* 82; and Premo, *Children of the Father King,* 97.

44. González, "Consuming Interests," 137.

45. Lipsett-Rivera, "Slap in the Face of Honor," 192–93.

46. Las Casas, *Brevísima relación,* 16–17. "Entraban en los pueblos, ni dejaban niños ni viejos, ni mujeres preñadas ni paridas que no desbarrigaban y hacían pedazos, como si dieran en unos corderos metidos en sus apriscos."

47. Las Casas, *Brevísima relación,* 17. "Tomaban las criaturas de las tetas de las madres por las piernas y daban de cabeza con ellas en las peñas."

48. Covarrubias, *Tesoro de la lengua castellana,* 778. "Del nombre latino *mater,* correlativo del hijo . . . en las mugeres es la bulva y lugar do conciben el feto, *latine matrix, genitale arvum.* Virgilio, 3, Geórgica."

49. This reading resonates with works by scholars such as Daniel Nemser, who draw from Sylvia Wynter and Aníbal Quijano to show that "modernity," "race," and a global capitalist system do not originate in a moment posterior to Spanish colonialism's transatlantic foundations. Nemser, *Infrastructures of Race;* Wynter, "Unsettling the Coloniality"; and Quijano, "Coloniality of Power."

50. Jáuregui and Solodkow, "Biopolitics," 134.

51. Las Casas, *Brevísima relación,* 7. "Como la providencia divina tenga ordenado en su mundo que para dirección y común utilidad del linaje humano se constituyesen en los reinos y pueblos reyes como padres y pastores (según los nombra Homero) y, por consiguiente, sean los más nobles y generosos miembros de las repúblicas, ninguna duda de la rectitud de sus ánimos reales se tiene o con recta

razón se debe tener. Que si algunos defectos, nocumentos y males se padecen en ellas, no ser otra la causa sino carecer los reyes de la noticia dellos."

52. As Premo notes, the king's responsibility is cast in patriarchal terms in the *Siete Partidas,* where he is also treated as a loving yet disciplinary father. Premo, *Children of the Father King,* 11. See also Jáuregui and Solodkow, "Biopolitics," 128–34.

53. Richard Graham, *Independence in Latin America: A Comparative Approach* (New York: Knopf, 1972), 6, quoted in Premo, *Children of the Father King,* 6.

54. Las Casas, *Brevísima relación,* 15. "Comúnmente no dejan en las guerras a vida sino los mozos y mujeres."

55. Las Casas, *Brevísima relación,* 63–64. "Como andaban los tristes españoles con perros bravos buscando y aperreando los indios, mujeres y hombres, una india enferma, viendo que no podía huir de los perros que no la hiciesen pedazos como hacían a los otros, tomó una soga y atose al pie un niño que tenían [sic] de un año y ahorcose de una viga. Y no lo hizo tan presto que no llegaron los perros, y despedazaron el niño, aunque antes que acabase de morir lo batizó un fraile."

56. The *Brevísima relación*'s publication coincided with major epidemics in the Americas; in 1545, disease reduced native populations by about one-third in New Spain. Adorno, *Polemics of Possession,* 254.

57. Ruth Hill notes that this practice aligns with a strategy called *sermocinatio,* one included in Luis de Granada's rhetorical recommendations for swaying interlocutors. Hill, "Hearing Las Casas Write," 62.

58. Las Casas, *Brevísima relación,* 80. "Sin fe y sin sacramentos." In most of Las Casas's work, Indigenous salvation will not depend on baptism. For an understanding of his different interpretations of theology, baptism, and condemnation, see Orique, "To Heaven or Hell," 1495–526.

59. The conclusion of this scene is notable due to its explicit reworking of an alleged source text, the "Carta que escribieron varios padres de la órden de Santo Domingo, residentes en la isla Española á Mr. de Xeveres." In an almost identical scene, the Spaniards are said to take a child from an Indigenous mother and feed it to a hungry dog before her eyes. There is no religious redemption to conclude that scene. "Carta que escribieron varios padres," 402. Juan Durán Luzio discusses this scene and the letter as a source for the *Brevísima relación.* Durán Luzio, *Bartolomé de Las Casas,* 114–40.

60. Jensen, *Baptismal Imagery in Early Christianity,* 54.

61. McClintock, *Imperial Leather,* 29. In her reading of Las Casas's *De unico vocationis modo,* No calls this a "maternalist metaphor of non-violence." Between 1537 and 1557, Las Casas put this method into practice in the region of Alta Verapaz (contemporary Guatemala).

62. For the Spanish context, see Bergmann, "Milking the Poor"; Nadeau, "Authorizing the Wife/Mother"; and Nadeau, "Blood Mother/Milk Mother." For

the Spanish Americas, see Rappaport, *Disappearing Mestizo;* Brewer-García, "Bodies, Texts, and Translators"; and Earle, *Body of the Conquistador.*

63. Tortorici, "Reading the (Dead) Body"; Robert Burns, *Underworlds,* 1446; and Rodríguez and Calvo, "Sobre la práctica del aborto," 32. Nora Jaffary notes that the *Siete Partidas* "cautioned punishment" for acts committed against infants under three days old. Jaffary, "Reconceiving Motherhood," 5.

64. For instance, as María de los Angeles Rodríguez and Thomas Calvo note, Jesuit missionaries in Sinaloa described abortion as a sign of diabolism and women's authority against Jesuit religious inroads. Rodríguez and Calvo, "Sobre la práctica del aborto," 33. See also texts by religious authorities in Mesoamerica, such as Diego de Landa, *Relación de las cosas de Yucatán* (1566) and Bernardino de Sahagún, *Historia general de las cosas de la Nueva España* (1580s) and, in Peru, such as Pablo José de Arriaga, *Extirpación de la idolatria en el Perú* (1621). For a treatment of religious extirpation and child sacrifice, see Redden, "Angelic Death and Sacrifice"; and Haskett, "Dying for Conversion," 186.

65. Castro, *Another Face of Empire,* 109–10; and Durán Luzio, *Bartolomé de Las Casas,* 114–40.

66. "Carta que escribieron varios padres," 418. "Como las madres viesen que no podian engendrar ni criar hijos, sin que por ello padesciesen intolerables trabajos y crueldades, eran compelidas, ó á no se empreñar, ó si estaban preñadas á mover, ó si parian, á matar el hijo por no dejarlo en tan áspero sacrificio é cativerio como ellas estaban, é finalmente, porque al no podian hacer. Y por esta causa les han levantado que la culpa del no multiplicar era en las indias, que como bestias mataban á sus hijos, lo cual es imposible que de ninguna gente se diga, lo que no se puede decir de ninguna bestia fiera, aunque fuese tigre ó serpiente, mas antes todo animal quiere criar su hijo; pero ellas, como dicho es, no pudiendo sufrir las crueldades de los castellanos, querian estar libres para poder servir á los cristianos segun sus apetitos."

67. Covarrubias, *Tesoro de la lengua castellana,* 369–70. "Se toma muchas vezes por engendrar, como dezir: Esta tierra cría hombres valientes y robustos. En Cilicia se cría mucho açafrán, en Córdova se crían buenos cavallos, etc. Este mantenimiento cría cólera, y estotro melancholía. Criar aves, cevarlas. Criar conejos, tenerlos caseros. El contento cría buena sangre."

68. Las Casas, *Brevísima relación,* 113. "Un pedazo de una carta y relación"; "que escribió cierto hombre." This letter appears in a 1552 edition of the *Brevísima relación,* held by the John Carter Brown Library and a 1553 edition held by the University of Pennsylvania. Many other language editions of the text that I have consulted also contain the letter. For instance, it is included in full in the 1583 English translation, *The Spanish Colonie,* and in excerpts in the 1689 translation, *Popery truly display'd in its bloody colours.* The 1701 French translation, *La découverte des Indes Occidentales par Les Espagnols,* includes the letter in full.

69. Las Casas, *Brevísima relación,* 115, emphasis added. "Y al tiempo que el dicho capitán salió del Quito sacando tanta cantidad de naturales, descasándolos, ... salió una mujer con un niño chiquito en los brazos tras él, dando voces, diciéndole que no le llevase a su marido, porque tenía tres niños chiquitos y que ella no los podría criar y que se le morirían de hambre, y visto que la primera vez le respondió mal, tornó a segundar con mayores voces, diciendo que sus hijos *se le habían de morir* de hambre, y visto que la mandaba echar por ahí y que no le quiso dar a su marido, dio con el niño en unas piedras y lo mató."

70. Las Casas, *Brevísima relación,* 17. "Daban de cabeza con ellas en las peñas."

71. The language of infanticide and "*querer*" is repeated in a letter from the *Visita* (1550?) where the *oidor* Lorenzo Lebrón de Quiñones describes women who also committed infanticide because they "did not want to see their children in the captivity and servitude that they were in." L. Lebrón de Quiñones, *Carta del licenciado . . .* (1554). Qtd. in Rodríguez and Calvo, "Sobre la práctica del aborto," 33.

72. Las Casas, *Brevísima relación,* 46. "Acaeció mujer matar su hijo para comello, de hambre."

73. For an extensive treatment of the trajectory of cannibalism as a foundation of colonial structures, see Jáuregui, *Canibalia;* and Sylvia Wynter, "Unsettling the Coloniality."

74. Las Casas, *Brevísima relación,* 6.

75. Lira, "Bartolomé de Las Casas and the Passions of Language," 95–96.

76. See the conclusion where I discuss the ethics of repeating violence, a question that has been engaged by Fred Moten and Saidiya Hartman and is acknowledged there.

77. Hortense J. Spillers, "Notes on an Alternative Model: Neither/Nor," in *The Year Left 2: An American Socialist Yearbook,* ed. Mike Davis et. al. (London: Verso, 1987), 176–77. Qtd. in Avery Gordon, *Ghostly Matters,* 163.

78. Kimberly Brown, *Repeating Body,* 8.

79. I only touch upon the possibilities and demands for comparison to enslaved women's experiences around maternity. In a US academic context, discussions of enslaved women's maternity and infanticide have been powerfully affected by Toni Morrison's novel *Beloved* (1987), a touchstone for many of the texts I engage here.

80. Adorno, *Polemics of Possession,* 41.

81. As Rabasa notes, Durán claimed to see idolatry "in sowing, in reaping, in storing grain, even in plowing the earth." Rabasa, "Writing and Evangelization," 72. For a discussion of this disenchantment with early evangelical endeavors, see the classic text Clendinnen, *Ambivalent Conquests;* for a reading of the Indigenous response in the period, see Tedlock, "Torture in the Archives."

2. Recomposing Legitimacy

1. The original manuscript has not been located. A transcribed copy from 1574 is housed in El Escorial and does not include original signatures. Julien, "Introduction," xxviii. See Nicole Legnani's introduction for an extensive review of later editions of the *Instrucción*. I cite Catherine Julien's transcribed version and respect her unmodernized orthography. While I have consulted Julien's translations, translations are my own.

2. Titu Cusi, *Instrucción*, 160. "Lo rrelato y ordeno."

3. Titu Cusi, *Instrucción*, 162. "No se el ffrase y la manera que los españoles thienen en semejantes avisos."

4. As Julien notes, the association between these forms in the *Instrucción* text is ambiguous. Since no original exists, we only have the *relación* and the *poder* copied and bound together. These texts provide both continuities and discontinuities in their productions; the *relación* and the *poder* feature the same scribe and are notarized on the same day. Each is witnessed by the same two Augustinian friars. However, while each document has three Inca witnesses, these men are not the same for the *relación* and the *poder*. Julien, "Introduction," xvi-xvii.

5. Lamana, *Domination without Dominance*, 8. MacCormack also describes the different compositional practices that mark early histories of Peru in "History, Historical Record."

6. In her focus on the sixteenth century, Jane Mangan has shown that a traditional, essentialist opposition between legitimacy and illegitimacy limits scholars' understanding of the ways that these terms designated practice and perception. See Mangan, *Transatlantic Obligations*, 4.

7. As Ann Twinam's meticulous research demonstrates, individuals and groups negotiated, asserted, and manipulated the ways that legitimate or illegitimate status defined their identities. Twinam, *Public Lives, Private Secrets*. For discussions of the attribution of legitimacy or illegitimacy to various populations in the colonial Spanish Americas, see, among others, Rappaport, *Disappearing Mestizo;* Mangan, "Moving Mestizos"; Bennett, *Colonial Blackness;* Martínez, *Genealogical Fictions;* Vieira Powers, *Crucible of Conquest;* Hill, "*Casta* as Culture"; Kathryn Burns, "Politics of Mestizaje"; Dueñas-Vargas, *Hijos del pecado;* Mannarelli, *Pecados públicos;* and Seed, *Love, Honor, and Obey.*

8. For a discussion of differing nomenclatures of community membership in the early modern Spanish Atlantic, see Herzog, *Defining Nations.*

9. See Lamana, *Domination without Dominance;* Adorno, *Polemics of Possession;* Julien, "Toledo and His Campaign"; Julien, *Reading Inca History;* Hyland, "Conversion, Custom, and 'Culture'"; Pagden, *Fall of Natural Man;* Hanke, *All Mankind Is One;* Wagner and Parish, *Bartolomé de Las Casas;* and Hanke, *Spanish Struggle for Justice.*

10. Lamana, *Domination without Dominance,* 161.

11. This frame is compounded by readings of Túpac Amaru, Titu Cusi's younger brother and the final Inca of Vilcabamba. After his capture by Martín García Óñez de Loyola, Túpac Amaru was condemned to death in the town square of Cuzco. Brian Bauer, Halac-Higashimori and Cantarutti, *Voices from Vilcabamba,* 16; and Kubler, "Neo-Inca State."

12. Upon Manco Inca's move to Vilcabamba, Spaniards shifted their support to Manco Inca's half-brother Paullu Topa Inca and other Inca allies who remained in Cuzco. Paullu Topa's troops supported Spanish incursions into Vilcabamba, including one that enabled a brief capture of Titu Cusi. Brian Bauer, "Vilcabamba," 4.

13. Lamana, *Domination without Dominance,* 125.

14. Brian Bauer, "Vilcabamba," 3.

15. Millones Figueroa, "Colonial Andean Texts," 188.

16. Julien dates the negotiation of this text to 1565. Julien, "Toledo and His Campaign," 244.

17. For a suspicious reading of Titu Cusi's motivations, see Cattan, "En los umbrales."

18. Scholars do not agree on Titu Cusi's facility in Spanish or the amount of time he spent in Cuzco—a representation of the indecision regarding the text's authorial control. Though Titu Cusi was raised in Vilcabamba, he was captured in a raid by the forces of Diego de Almagro, after which he was placed in the home and under the care of Pedro de Oñate, a Spanish resident of Cuzco. Scholars differ, however, on the year of his capture, the amount of time that Titu Cusi remained in Cuzco—ranging from two to seven years—and the impact that this stay had on his linguistic and cultural skills. See Vincent Lee, "Vilcabamba," 748; Brian Bauer, Halac-Higashimori and Cantarutti, *Voices from Vilcabamba,* 97n9; Julien, "Introduction," x; and Ralph Bauer, "Introduction," 12–13.

19. Titu Cusi, *History,* 160. "Yo, Martin de Pando, escrivano de comission por el muy yllustre señor liçençiado Lope Garçia de Castro, governador que ffue destos rreynos, doy ffee que todo lo arriba escripto lo rrelato y ordeno el dicho padre a ynsistion del dicho don Diego de Castro."

20. Ralph Bauer also considers the text to have a third form, an "introduction" or *instrucción* that presents the text to King Philip, while Julien combines this "introduction" with the *relación* form. Julien, "Introduction," xv; and Ralph Bauer, "Introduction," 22.

21. Titu Cusi, *History,* 164, emphasis added. "De la misma manera *sy yo lo dixiese y declarase.*"

22. Titu Cusi, *History,* 2. "Rreçivido muchas merçedes y favor."

23. Titu Cusi, *History,* 4. "Debaxo de cuyo anparo yo me he puesto."

24. For instance, scholars attend to the simultaneous use of Quechua and Christian terminology in the *Instrucción* to consider if Titu Cusi or his translator

provided the critique of Spanish violence. Cattan, "Palabras que no se tradujeron"; Roy, "El discurso neo-inca"; Gose, *Invaders as Ancestors,* 68; and Zevallos, "Reflexiones."

25. Cattan, "En los umbrales," 38–39.

26. Lienhard, *La voz y su huella,* 157. See also Mazzotti, *Coros mestizos*; Jakfalvi-Leiva, "De la voz a la escritura"; and Chang-Rodríguez, "Forgotten Indian Chronicle," 87–95.

27. Julien, "Introduction," xix.

28. Mazzotti, *Coros mestizos,* 96–97. Frank Salomon argues that while Christian *relaciones* partake in a strict chronology of cause and effect, Andeans presented historical events as parts of repeating patterns. See Salomon, "Chronicles of the Impossible"; see also Covey, "Chronology, Succession, and Sovereignty," 174; No, "La heterogeneidad suturada"; Verdesio, "Traducción y contrato"; and Chang-Rodríguez, *Apropiación del signo.*

29. For a description of how Indigenous peoples used this concept in colonial Mexico to recuperate status, see Villella, *Indigenous Elites and Creole Identity.*

30. Titu Cusi, *History,* 2, emphasis added. "Yo, don Diego de Castro Titu Cussi Yupangui, nieto de Guaina Capac e hijo de Mango Ynga Yupangui, *señores naturales* que fueron de los rreinos y provinçias del Piru." The *poder* opens with an identical formation, though it directly names Titu Cusi the "Sapay Inca" or ruler: "I, the Sapay Inca Don Diego de Castro Titu Cusi Yupanqui, son and first-born heir to Manco Inca Yupanqui and grandson of Huayna Capac, who were natural lords of these kingdoms and provinces of Peru" (Yo, el sapai ynga don Diego de Castro Tito Cusi Yupangui, hijo mayorazgo que soy de Mango Ynga Yupangui y nieto de Guaina Capac, señores naturales que ffueron destos rreynos e provinçias del Piru). Titu Cusi, *History,* 164. Nowack posits that Titu Cusi had betrayed his own illegitimacy in earlier negotiations and thus needed to correct these admissions. Nowack, *"Las mercedes que pedía,"* 68–69.

31. Titu Cusi, *History,* 4, emphasis added. "Bien creo que por nuebas de muchas personas se abra publicado quien fueron los *señores naturales* antiguos desta tierra y de donde y como proçedieron, y por esso no me quiero detener açerca desto."

32. Chamberlain, *"Señor Natural,"* 130. See also Millones Figueroa, "De señores naturales a tiranos," 96.

33. Las Casas, *Doce dudas,* 194–95. "El Rey católico de Castilla, nuestro Señor, es obligado, de necesidad de salvarse, a restituir en el reyno o reynos del Perú al susodicho Rey Tito y a los demás Señores Yngas lo que fuere suyo." See also Roy, "El discurso neo-inca," 92.

34. Adorno, *Polemics of Possession,* 41.

35. Garrett, "Inca Ancestry and Colonial Privilege," 760.

36. Through a reading of correspondence between Philip II and Toledo, Catherine Julien illustrates how Las Casas's anti-colonial rhetoric had seeped into colonial Peru. Julien, "Toledo and His Campaign," 256. This conflict is also discussed by Adorno, *Polemics of Possession,* 52.

37. Earlier histories had been shaped by the continuing cultural dominance of the Incas and relied on songs and ballads highly mediated by the Incas themselves. See Julien, *Reading Inca History;* MacCormack, *On the Wings of Time;* and Murra, "'*Nos hazen mucha ventaja.*'"

38. See Hanke, "Viceroy Francisco de Toledo."

39. As MacCormack notes, Sarmiento's dedication to Philip II includes a disputation of Las Casas's arguments and an attack on the tyranny of the Incas. MacCormack, *On the Wings of Time,* 19n47. Karen Graubart's study of Spanish historiography on the Inca shows how arguments both for and against Inca tyranny turned on representations of gender and kin relationships. Graubart, "Indecent Living."

40. Jeremy Ravi Mumford provides an extensive and useful review of scholarship on marriage regulations and practice in sixteenth-century colonial Peru, with both Spanish and Inca antecedents. Mumford, "Child Marriage in Early Colonial Cuzco."

41. Covarrubias, *Tesoro de la lengua castellana,* 757. Covarrubias concludes his point via an epigraph taken from Latin poet Marcus Valerius Martialis that describes the forced marriage of two cohabitants as an act which, again, draws marriage and law to the fore. "Vulgarmente entendemos el nacido de legítimo matrimonio; en rigor, legítimo es todo aquello que se haze conforme a la ley, *latine leigitimus, quod est iustum, aequum; conueniens, lege, more, atque instituto maiorum factum.*"

42. Premo, "Custom Today," 359. As Premo notes, custom played a large role in legal disputes over Indigenous authority.

43. Sarmiento, *Historia de los Incas,* 279. "Es averiguado que es cosa falsa y sin razón ni derecho decir que agora hay en estos reinos ninguna persona del linaje de los ingas que puedan pretender derecho a la sucesión del ingazgo deste reino del Pirú, ni por ser señores naturales ni legítimos, porque no lo eran, ni por haber quedado alguno que aun conforme a sus leyes." He then notes that Manco Inca is a "bastardo," knowledge which is public among them ("que entre éstos es público"). Luis Millones Figueroa discusses these passages in "Colonial Andean Texts," 187.

44. Zuidema, "Guaman Poma on Inca Hierarchy," 442.

45. Herzog, "Colonial Law and 'Native Customs,'" 310.

46. Titu Cusi, *History,* 4, emphasis added. "Avisar a su Magestad de como yo soy el hijo *ligitimo.*"

47. Titu Cusi, *History,* 4. "El primero y mayorazgo, que my padre Mango Ynga Yupangui dexo entre otros muchos." Scholars have reaffirmed that this is not

true given that Sayri Túpac had preceded Titu Cusi, already negotiated with Spaniards, and abandoned the territory.

48. As María Elena Martínez writes, Viceroy Toledo encouraged Indigenous artists to produce portraits of the "Sapa Incas" or rulers and their Coyas/queens to suggest a genealogical line. Martínez, "Indigenous Genealogies," 176.

49. Titu Cusi, *History,* 6, emphasis added. "Hijo que ffue de Guaina Capac e nieto de Tupa Ynga Yupangui, y ansy por sus abolengos deçendiendo *por linea rrecta* ffue el señor prençipal de todos los rreynos del Piru señalado para ello por su padre Guaina Capac y tenido y obedeçido por tal."

50. Titu Cusi, *History,* 8, emphasis added. "Todo su poderio y mando como su padre Guaina Capac se lo avia dexado"; "un hermano suyo *mayor* aunque *bastardo.*"

51. Titu Cusi, *History,* 12, emphasis added. "Aunque hijos de Guaina Capac, de parte de las madres de sangre suez [soez] e baxa, e my padre ffue *hijo ligitimo* de sangre rreal como lo ffue Pachacuti Ynga, aguelo de Guayna Capac." While "low and common blood" is clunky, I choose this direct translation due to its resonance with Spanish blood purity and its juxtaposition with the invocation of "royal blood" that immediately follows.

52. Rostworowski de Diez Canseco and Murra, "Succession," 417.

53. See Jenkins, "Inka Conical Clan." Each social unit could assert family divisions, distributions of wealth, and access to territory. See also Sherbondy, "Panaca Lands," 179; Jakfalvi-Leiva, "De la voz a la escritura"; and Rostworowski de Diez Canseco and Murra, "Succession," 417, 420.

54. Rostworowski de Diez Canseco and Murra, "Succession," 420.

55. Julien, *Reading Inca History,* 32.

56. Zuidema, "Guaman Poma on Inca Hierarchy," 445.

57. Sarmiento de Gamboa, *Historia de los Incas,* 201. "Porque, aunque la costumbre destos tiranos era quel primero y mayor hijo legítimo heredase el estado, pocas veces lo guardaban, antes señalaban al que más amor tenían o a cuya madre más amaban o el que de los hermanos más podía y se quedaba con todo." Also qtd. in Millones Figueroa, "Señores Naturales," 98n13. Millones Figueroa offers a discussion of Sarmiento de Gamboa's general construction of the Incas as tyrants in "De señores naturales a tiranos."

58. Legnani, "Introduction," 35.

59. Ralph Bauer, "Introduction," 37. Ralph Bauer quotes Julien, *Reading Inca History,* 43.

60. Ralph Bauer, "Introduction," 40.

61. Titu Cusi, *History,* 38, 40. "Aunque le solteis vosotros y de mas oro e plata que cabe en quatro bohios, no se soltara de mi parte si no me da primero a la señora coya, su hermana, llamada Cura Ocllo, por mi muger."

62. According to Raquel Chang-Rodríguez, this scene in the *Instrucción* foregrounds the Spanish violation of two epistemological orders: Christian ethics and Andean reciprocity. By expounding Spanish impropriety according to

multiple codes, the text justifies Manco Inca's response to an array of possible interlocutors. Chang-Rodríguez, "Rebelión y religión," 178.

63. Titu Cusi, *History,* 76. "Una yndia muy hermosa, peinada y muy bien adereçada, para darsela en lugar de la *coya* que ellos pedian."

64. Titu Cusi, *History,* 76, emphasis added. "Dixeron que no les *paresçia* a ellos."

65. Titu Cusi, *History,* 78. "Por tentarlos hizo sacar otras mas de beynte, casy de aquella suerte, unas buenas y otras mejores."

66. Titu Cusi, *History,* 78. "Ya que le paresçio a my padre que hera tienpo, mando que saliese una, la mas prençipal muger que en su casa tenia, conpañera de su hermana la coya, la qual le paresçia casy en todo, en espeçial sy se bestia como ella, la qual se llamava Ynguill (que quiere dezir 'fflor'), y que aquella les diesen, la qual salio alli en presençia de todos, vestida y adereçada ni mas ni menos que coya (que quiere dezir 'rreyna')."

67. Julien has noted that Ynguill is later identified as married to Juan Pizarro and not Gonzalo Pizarro. She attributes this misidentification to the greater fame of Gonzalo in Titu Cusi's eyes. Titu Cusi, *History,* 79n74. See also Julien, "Francisca Pizarro."

68. Titu Cusi, *History,* 40, emphasis added. "*La avia visto* y enamoradose della, porque hera muy hermosa."

69. Titu Cusi, *History,* 76, emphasis added. "*Desconoçiendo* la coya, dixieron que no les *paresçia* a ellos."

70. Rostworowski de Diez Canseco and Murra, "Succession, Coöption to Kingship, and Royal Incest," 422.

71. Titu Cusi, *History,* 77n71.

72. Titu Cusi, *History,* 78, emphasis added. "Como sy fuera su muger *ligitima.*"

73. Titu Cusi, *History,* 80. "Amistad avia de durar mucho entre los dos por causa del quñadazgo."

74. Kathryn Burns, "Politics of Mestizaje," 14. See also Berta Ares Queija, "Mancebas de españoles."

75. Titu Cusi, *History,* 134. "¿En una muger bengais vuestros enojos? ¿que mas hiziera otra muger como yo?; dados priesa a acabarme porque se cunpla vuestro apetito en todo." I follow Catherine Julien's translation of "se cunpla vuestro apetito en todo," though this phrase proves ambiguous in meaning given its pseudo-sexual connotations.

76. Mangan, *Transatlantic Obligations,* 29.

77. Ralph Bauer, "Introduction," 41.

78. Titu Cusi, *History,* 78. "Mucho de norabuena, haze lo que quisierdes"; "rrio mucho."

79. Chang-Rodríguez, "Forgotten Indian Chronicle," 92.

80. Titu Cusi, *History,* 78. "Dava gritos como una loca"; "espanto y pabor"; "no queria arrostrar a semejante gente."

81. Titu Cusi, *History,* 78. "En aquella estava el ser el suelto o no."

82. This meeting led to the production of a treaty, which included an abridged version of Manco Inca's biography. Nowack, "Provisiones de Titu Cusi Yupangui," 145. For tables denoting the documents and dates of communiqués that traveled among parties during these negotiations, see Nowack, "Provisiones de Titu Cusi," 151–56. For an additional discussion of textual traffic and terms of negotiation, see Nowack, "Mercedes que pedía," 57–91. See also Guillén Guillén, "Documentos inéditos."

83. This was the bridge that separated the territory of Vilcabamba from the region that Spaniards more comfortably inhabited, including Cuzco. Brian Bauer, Halac-Higashimori and Cantarutti, *Voices from Vilcabamba,* document 3, "Diego Rodríguez de Figueroa's Journey into Vilcabamba."

84. Titu Cusi, *History,* 152. "Despues desto torno otra bez a venir el tesorero Garça de Melo con despachos de vuestra Señoria, el qual me aconsejo, por lo que yo le adverti, que casasemos a mi hijo don Phelipe Quispe Tito con su prima doña Beatriz; y ansy lo conçertamos, como se hiziesen las pazes que despues hezimos en Acobanba por mandado de vuestra Señoria, el e yo traiendo para ello los testigos que vuestra Señoria señalo, a lo qual se hallo pressente Diego Rodriguez como corregidor y Martin de Pando como secretario."

85. Catherine Julien observes that "Titu Cusi gives the wrong name. He means Juan de Matienzo, the *oidor* or judge who had come from the high court (*audiencia*) of Charcas." Titu Cusi, *History,* 153n167. Given that Matienzo was instrumental to the Andean resettlement projects sponsored by Toledo (called the *reducción*), this statement shows that the lines of "antagonism" and "collaboration" are confused—a constitutive element of this elite negotiation of a colonial project-in-process.

86. Julien, "Toledo and His Campaign," 250.

87. See, among others, Mangan, *Transatlantic Obligations,* 26; Horswell, "Negotiating Apostasy in Vilcabamba," 102–3; Julien, "Toledo and His Campaign," 248–50; and Legnani, "Introduction," 33–37.

88. This process of linear inheritance followed a Spanish legal system where the estate was given to one descendent, rather than the "corporate" Inca system that entitled other relatives to financial wealth gained from the territory. Covey and Elson, "Ethnicity, Demography, and Estate Management," 311.

89. Levillier, *Gobernantes del Perú,* 264–65. "Envió a nuestra magestad el testimonio de como se bautizo el hijo del ynga y porque en uno de los capítulos que con el ynga se hizieron se contiene que este niño se case con hija que quedo de sayretopa por manera que son primos y primos dos vezes porque aca estos en su ynfidilidad se casavan hermanos con hermanos."

90. Levillier, *Gobernantes del Perú,* 265. "Es menester que vuestra magestad mande que se trayga dispensación de Roma pues la causa es tan vastante para que su santidad la de que es bolberse estos xpos y la paz y el sosiego deste Reyno."

91. Perhaps this was because while Quispe Titu lived in Vilcabamba, Beatriz had been raised in Cuzco in the convent of Santa Clara where she was placed in 1563 to "learn good [Christian] customs" (*buenas costumbres*). Burns, *Colonial Habits,* 27.

92. Mangan, *Transatlantic Obligations,* 26.

93. As Mumford writes, it is unclear if this was done at the bequest of Beatriz's mother, Kusi Warkay. Mumford, "Child Marriage in Early Colonial Cuzco," 431.

94. See Lamana, "Testamento y el codicilo," 48; Kathryn Burns, "Politics of Mestizaje," 22–24; Chang-Rodríguez, "Princesa incaica Beatriz Clara"; and Rostworowski de Diez Canseco, "Repartimiento de doña Beatriz," 153–58.

95. Guengerich, "Mining the Colonial Archive," 66–67. Guengerich posits that Vilcabamba should not be seen as a territory held by one leader but as a contested space. Kusi Warkay would, thus, be one of these leaders despite her distance from Vilcabamba. See Guengerich, "Capac Women."

96. Quispe-Agnoli, "Taking Possession," 266. Though Quispe-Agnoli does not focus on Kusi Warkay, I extend her argument to destabilize masculine autonomy around Cristóbal Maldonado's actions.

97. Mumford, "Child Marriage in Early Colonial Cuzco," 431–32.

98. Guengerich, "Mining the Colonial Archive," 66.

99. According to correspondence between Viceroy Toledo and the Crown, Beatriz was "given the choice" to remain in the convent or marry and selected the latter. Rostworowski de Diez Canseco, "Repartimiento de Beatriz," 156.

100. As Marie Timberlake shows in her study of the seventeenth-century *Matrimonio de García de Loyola con Ñusta Beatriz,* a painting hung in the Jesuit Church of Cuzco, this marriage between the "last legitimate heir to the Inka throne" and the "grand nephew of San Ignacio de Loyola" provided the Jesuits with a means of narrating their order's importance to Andean politics. Timberlake, "Painted Colonial Image."

101. Her convent entry is held in the Archivo Regional de Cuzco. Protocolo Notorial: Juan de Pineda, 1656, fol. 648. This text is also published in Angulo, "Libro original," 158. While I have consulted the archival document, I reproduce Angulo's transcription for its standardized orthography: "Doña Beatriz Yupangui. Hija de Sayre Topa Ynga, entró en la casa Doñá en doze de Agosto del año de mil y quinientos y sesenta y tres años; trájola a la casa el Padre fray Melchor de los Reyes, de la Orden de Señor Santo Domingo, para que criase y deprendiese buenas costumbres en la dicha casa; no se concertó lo que ha de dar para sus alimentos.—Casóse con Martín de Loyola, Comendador del avito de Calatrava, Capitán de la Guardia del Señor Virrey don Francisco de Toledo."

102. Horswell, "Negotiating Apostasy," 100.

103. Horswell, "Negotiating Apostasy," 100.

3. Good Examples

1. "Ad instruendum incolas & habitatores praefatos in fide Catholica, & bonis moribus imbuendum destinare debeatis." Cocquelines, *Bullarum Privilegiorum*, 234. Alaperrine-Bouyer translates "moribus" as "custom" in her citation of this section of the papal bull: "Adoctrinar a los indígenas y habitantes dichos en la fe católica e imponerlos en las buenas *costumbres.*" Alaperrine-Bouyer, *Educación de las elites,* 13. The language of "good customs" was reiterated in Charles V's edicts of 1540 and 1563. Dueñas, *"Lettered City,"* 27n48.

2. Kelley, "'Second Nature,'" 132.

3. Martínez, *Genealogical Fictions,* 103.

4. Along these lines, Carolyn Dean notes that the Jesuits José de Acosta and Bernabé Cobo in sixteenth-century Peru employed infantilizing rhetoric to describe Indigenous peoples. She also points to similar language used by the seventeenth-century extirpator of idolatries, Pablo José de Arriaga. Dean, "Familiarizando el catolicismo," 170.

5. The term *indio ladino* designated Indigenous peoples with varying degrees of ability in spoken and written Spanish. Their status as translators, religious intermediaries, and litigants made them polemical figures in the colonial landscape. I build upon the work of scholars who have attended to Indigenous peoples' and *indio ladinos'* use of bureaucratic procedure to contest their marginalization from colonial authority and the codification of their difference. See, for instance, Charles, "En los foros," 203–22; Charles, *Allies at Odds;* Charles, "More *Ladino* than Necessary"; Mills, "Bad Christians in Colonial Peru"; Mills, "Limits of Religious Coercion"; and Adorno, "Images of *Indios Ladinos.*"

6. This familiarity with the historiographic and evangelical codes of imperial administration remits to Guaman Poma's autobiography: he served as a former interpreter in Indigenous lawsuits and as an assistant of the Mercedarian friar Martín de Murúa, author of the *Historia general del Piru* (1580–1616). See Cummins and Anderson, *Getty Murúa;* and Adorno, *Guaman Poma and His Illustrated Chronicles,* 30–31.

7. Kelley, "Second Nature," 135.

8. As R. Jovita Baber and Tamar Herzog note, performance and visible perception of behavior could determine the viability of one's membership in a community. For instance, Herzog notes that "acting" as a member of the community could create the "public image that they were citizens or natives." Herzog, *Defining Nations,* 24; and Baber, "Categories." See also Rappaport, *Disappearing Mestizo.*

9. Nancy van Deusen speaks to the fact that Indigenous enslavement continued despite these regulations. van Deusen, *Global Indios.*

10. Rabasa, *Without History,* 104. The importance of "costumbres" in legal discussions and disputes is too extensive to account for here. For an introduction to

this topic, see Premo, "Custom Today"; Herzog, "Colonial Law and 'Native Customs'"; Martínez, *Genealogical Fictions,* 156; and Tedlock, "Torture in the Archives." For applications of 'customary law' in Andean communities today, see Hernández, *Racial Subordination in Latin America,* 12; and Salomon and Niño-Murcia, *Lettered Mountain.*

11. Martínez, *Genealogical Fictions,* 103.

12. See, among others, Tortorici, *Sins Against Nature;* Carlos A. Jáuregui, *Canibalia;* and Horswell, *Decolonizing the Sodomite.*

13. Torres de Mendoza, *Colección de documentos inéditos,* 183. "Para que no se maten ni coman, ni sacrifiquen, como en algunas partes se hacia"; "el uso de pan y vino y aceite y otros muchos mantenimientos; paño, seda, lienzo, caballos, ganados, herramientas y armas, y todo lo demas que Despaña ha habido . . . con que viven ricamente; y que de todos estos bienes, gozarán los que vinieren á conocimiento de nuestra Sancta Fée catolica y Nuestra obidiencia."

14. Alaperrine-Bouyer, *Educación de las elites,* 182–83; and Hyland, "Conversation, Custom and 'Culture,'" 281. Though the foundation of these schools had been called for in the 1570s under the mandate of the recently arrived Viceroy Francisco de Toledo, the first was not founded until 1618 in El Cercado, Lima, and the latter in 1621 in Cuzco. Dueñas, *"Lettered City,"* 16.

15. The classic study of this historical timeline is Ricard, *Spiritual Conquest of Mexico.* Inga Clendinnen also provides a foundational touchstone for this affective shift, emphasizing Franciscans in the Yucatan peninsula. See Clendinnen, *Ambivalent Conquests.* For the Peruvian context, see Estenssoro Fuchs, *Del paganismo a la santidad.*

16. See Rappaport and Cummins, *Beyond the Lettered City* as well as Charles, *Allies at Odds.*

17. Álvarez, *De las costumbres,* 318. "De las costumbres de los indios se puede entender cuán imperitos y torpes están para todas las cosas que se pretenden plantar en ellos. Y porque para lo que importa—ser cristianos—aún es necesario ser adornados de buenas y políticas costumbres, humanas y de honra, y en ellos no hay alguna, ¿cómo vendrán a ser cristianos?"

18. Luciano Pereña translates this phrase to "plantas nuevas y tiernas" in his Latin-Spanish edition of the text. Acosta, *De procuranda,* 1:461. See also Ditchfield, "What Did Natural History Have to Do with Salvation?" 162–63.

19. For the Spanish American context, jurists of the School of Salamanca, such as Francisco de Vitoria, followed Thomas Aquinas in arguing that custom ("consuetudo") created habits ("mores") that ossified as "second nature." Pagden, *Fall of Natural Man,* 100.

20. Hyland, "Conversion, Custom and 'Culture,'" 289.

21. Lisi, *Tercer Concilio Limense,* 127. For accessibility, I cite Lisi's Spanish translations of the original Latin. English translations are my own. "Los párrocos deben educar a los de condición más baja."

22. Lisi, *Tercer Concilio Limense,* 127. "Los padres de familia . . . han de dar razón a Dios de sus hijos, esclavos y del resto de la familia. . . . Para que los padres mismos no sean castigados por mandato divino a causa de las costumbres corruptas de los hijos, como sucede a menudo y amenazan las sagradas escrituras."

23. This passage remits to the Spanish legal tradition in which patriarchy was not synonymous with paternity. Bianca Premo discusses these distinctions in "Maidens, the Monks, and Their Mothers."

24. Alaperrine-Bouyer, *Educación de las elites,* 14. "En realidad, no existía entonces una frontera nítida entre instrucción y educación. Convertir era instruir."

25. Charles, *Allies at Odds,* 15.

26. Toribio Medina, *La imprenta en Lima,* 28 (original title and imprint *Tercero Cathecismo y exposicion de la Doctrina Christiana, por Sermones. Para que los Curas y otros ministros prediquen y enseñen a los Yndios y a las demas personas conforme a lo que en el Sancto Concilio Provincial de Lima se proveyó* [Ciudad de los Reyes: Antonio Ricardo, 1585]). Alan Durston highlights the same passage in his quotation of the 1584 first publication of this text which was reissued the following year with copy edits and, ironically, changes. See Durston, *Pastoral Quechua,* 102, 331n59. "[U]na de las cosas de mayor substancia que se trató en el Concilio Provincial . . . fué dar orden en que la doctrina de los naturales . . . fuesse *uniforme,* sin hacer diferencia ni aún en sólo una sílaba por el gran daño que ha resultado de no haberse hecho así en lo pasado."

27. See Brewer-García, *Beyond Babel;* and Toribio Medina, *La imprenta en Lima,* 28.

28. Lisi, *Tercer Concilio Limense,* 175, 177, emphasis added. "Por ello, conviene que los clérigos convocados al dominio del señor compongan su vida y todas sus *costumbres* de tal modo que ni en su hábito, ni en su gesto, ni en el modo de andar, el discurso o cualquier otra cosa hagan nada que no sea grave, moderado y lleno de religión, así como también que *eviten los delitos leves* que en ellos serían gravísimos, para que sus *acciones* produzcan veneración a todos."

29. Lisi, *Tercer Concilio Limense,* 155, emphasis added. "Si no apareciere ninguno que la sepa, no ha de dejar de proveerse sin embargo la parroquia con un sacerdote cualquiera, *mientras no sea de malas costumbres,* pues es preferible enviar un párroco que viva correctamente a uno que hable bien, si hubiera que elegir uno, porque la *vida edifica mucho más que la lengua.*"

30. Lisi, *Tercer Concilio Limense,* 111. "El ejemplo y la autoridad de los antiguos padres."

31. Lisi, *Tercer Concilio Limense,* 175, emphasis added. "Pues con razón nuestros mayores enseñan que no hay nada que mueva más a la piedad y al culto de Dios al resto que *la vida y ejemplo* de aquellos que se dedicaron al divino ministerio, pues, como se ve que han sido elevados del siglo a un puesto superior, naturalmente los otros *vuelven sus ojos* a ellos como a un espejo de donde toman lo que *imitar.*"

32. See Harrison, *Sin and Confession*. The idea of imitation does not only appear in religious texts that codify Indigenous difference. One of the petitions held in the Papeles Importantes collection at the Archbishopric Archive of Lima (hereafter AAL), the collection studied in this chapter, explicitly describes *criollo* education as imitation. In Francisco de Sosa's 1658 petition to be a teacher, the witness Joseph Santos testifies to Sosa's Christianity by stating that he saw Sosa's parents "raise and nourish" their son and, in turn, saw their son "*imitate* his Christian parents." AAL, Papeles Importantes, leg. 5, exp. 19 (1658), 2v-3r, emphasis added. Santos is identified as a vecino of the city and is 44 years old. "Los vido criar y alimentar"; "hijo de tales y tan cristianos padres *imitándoles.*"

33. Acosta, *De Procuranda*, 131. "San Pedro . . . aconseja y pide a los pastores que se conviertan en *modelos* del rebaño, porque los súbditos miran de ordinario los ejemplos de los superiores y de acuerdo con ellos conforman de una manera connatural sus costumbres."

34. Brown, "Saint as Exemplar," 9. For a discussion of the use of exemplarity and the rhetoric of the example in the constitution of religious education, see Newman, *Permeable Self,* especially chap. 1, "Teacher and Student: Shaping Boys."

35. Mills, "Bad Christians in Colonial Peru," 184, emphasis added.

36. Covarrubias, *Tesoro de la lengua castellana,* 575. "Absolutamente exemplo se toma en buena parte, pero dezimos dar mal exemplo."

37. Hampton, *Writing from History,* 21.

38. Though situated in a wider Andean context, Guaman Poma identifies with his father's Yarovilca lineage, claiming that this group predates the Incas in authority and prestige. Adorno, *Writing and Resistance,* 5.

39. Despite the "failure" of this text in the period of its composition (as it remains unclear if the document was ever read by its intended recipient Philip II), Guaman Poma's *Nueva corónica* has become dramatically successful in studies of Andean resistance to imperialism. The text and its author often serve as near metonyms for *indio ladino* or the lettered Indigenous person who could contest the mechanisms of empire by engaging its language and discursive forms. The full text of the *Nueva corónica* is available online: http://www.kb.dk/permalink /2006/poma/info/en/frontpage.htm. For a summary of recent scholarship, see Adorno, *Guaman Poma and His Illustrated Chronicles.*

40. Though I focus on exemplarity and its European resonances in Guaman Poma's text, scholars' extensive and striking research demonstrates the simultaneous articulation of Andean codes in the *Nueva corónica*—be they spatial representations of order, cultural practices of sexuality and religiosity, or communication technologies. See, among many others, Rasmussen, *Queequeg's Coffin;* Brokaw, *History of the Khipu;* Quispe-Agnoli, *La fe andina;* Horswell, *Decolonizing the Sodomite;* and Adorno, *Writing and Resistance.*

41. Adorno, *Writing and Resistance,* 52.

42. Guaman Poma, *Nueva corónica,* 576. "Teniendo una dozena de hijos, ¿cómo puede dar buen egenplo a los yndios deste rreyno?"

43. Guaman Poma, *Nueva corónica,* 579, emphasis added. "No se quieren casar porque *va tras* del padre o del español. Y ací no multiplica yndios en este rreyno, cino mestizos y mestizas y no ay rremedio."

44. Guaman Poma, *Nueva corónica,* 582–83, emphasis added. "Cómo antigos saserdotes de metales y de ýdolos y demonios, dioses, pontífises de piedra . . . uzavan fielmente y *dava buen egenplo* como las vírgenes, aclla, y monjas en sus tenplos. Y ací los demás tenían a su justicia y ley; eran cristianos ci no tubiera ydúlatra."

45. While outside the scope of this reading, Horswell shows that Guaman Poma erases non-normative Andean gender politics to create a sex-gender system more commensurate with Christian logic. Horswell, *Decolonizing the Sodomite,* 86, 109–10.

46. Blas Valera, *Las costumbres antiguas del Perú,* 38–47; and Hyland, *Jesuit and the Incas,* 166.

47. Guaman Poma, *Nueva corónica,* 226, emphasis added. "Todo lo malo adulterio y otros pecados mortales *trajo concigo los dichos cristianos;* con color de la dotrina desvirga a todas las donzellas y aní [sic] paren muchos mestisos en este rreyno."

48. In his account of history prior to the Spanish conquest, Guaman Poma directs his ire toward the Incas against his own identification with the Yarovilca people.

49. Guaman Poma, *Nueva corónica,* 583. "Agora los saserdotes del eterno Dios bibo son tales y sus ministros son tales; del mal padre sale mal hijo, perdido de las cosas de Dios verdadero. Del mal árbol sale mala fruta, de la mala cimiente sale mala rraýs."

50. AAL, Papeles Importantes, leg. 5, exp. 9 (1642), 3f. Pérez de Atocha is documented as a "natural de Lima." Solicitors' ages are not always listed in the petitions. Paula Martínez Sagredo has published an article on the historiography of Indigenous education in the Andes that transcribes parts of this petition. Since it was published after the completion of this book, I did not have the opportunity to consult it. Paulina Martínez Sagredo, "Sobre la castellanización y educación de los indígenas en los andes coloniales: materiales, escuelas y maestros." *Diálogo Andino* no. 61 (2020): 41–54.

51. AAL, Papeles Importantes, leg. 5, exp. 9 (1642), fol. 2r. "Persona buen christiano virtuoso de buena vida y exemplo por lo qual le [h]a visto exercitarse en enseñar la doctrina christiana a los niños y a leer escrevir y contar." The notary records Manuel Pérez to be a resident of the city, more or less fifty years old, and family of the inquisitor don Antonio de Castro.

52. AAL, Papeles Importantes, leg. 5, exp. 9 (1642), fol. 2v. "Hombre virtuoso y de buena vida y costumbres." According to the text, Vásquez is the "ayudante de las compañías de los pardos" or a ranking officer in the company of the *pardo* militia and forty years old.

53. AAL, Papeles Importantes, leg. 5, exp. 9 (1642), fol. 3r. "Persona virtuosa de buena vida y costumbres." The notary lists Lumbreras as a "natural" (native) and "morador" (inhabitant) of the city.

54. AAL, Papeles Importantes, leg. 5, exp. 9 (1642), fol. 2r. "Le [h]a tratado y comunicado familiarmente."

55. AAL, Papeles Importantes, leg. 5, exp. 9, (1642), fol. 3v, emphasis added. *"Dandoles* buen *exemplo."*

56. AAL, Papeles Importantes, leg. 5, exp. 9, (1642), fol. 3r, emphasis added. "Sin *dar nota ni mal exemplo* de su persona por aver procedido muy bien."

57. AAL, Papeles Importantes, leg. 5, exp. 9, (1642), fol. 2r. "Es muy importante para el dicho exercisio . . . virtud y vida exemplar."

58. AAL, Papeles Importantes, leg. 5, exp. 19 (1658), 4f. Fol. 1r. "Vida y costumbres, y de como es hijo de padres christianos viejos." Francisco de Sosa is said to have arrived from Panama.

59. AAL, Papeles Importantes, leg. 5, exp. 18 (1658), 5f. Jurado Toralba is listed as a "natural de Lima."

60. AAL, Papeles Importantes, leg. 5, exp. 18 (1658), fol. 2r. "Cristiano viejo y limpio de toda mala raza de judios ni moros ni de los nuevamente convertidos." Pablo de Noguera is listed as "español" (Spaniard), a "vecino" (citizen) of the city, and seventy years old.

61. AAL, Papeles Importantes, leg. 5, exp. 18 (1658), fol. 3r. "Christiano biejo limpio de toda mala raça de moros y judios y de los nuebamente conbertidos." Zeberino is identified as a "natural" (native) of the city, a master carpenter, and forty-four years old.

62. AAL, Papeles Importantes, leg. 5, exp. 18 (1658), fol. 4r. "Visto sabido oydo ni entendido cossa en contrario." Pacheco is identified as a "vecino" (citizen) of the city and 54 years old.

63. See, among many, Martínez for an account of how witness testimonies were required to prove *limpieza* in Iberia as well. Martínez, *Genealogical Fictions,* especially Part 1, "Iberian Precedents," 1–91.

64. See Kamen, *Spanish Inquisition,* particularly chap. 7, "Structure and Politics," 137–73.

65. AAL, Papeles Importantes, leg. 5, exp. 13 (1649), 6f. Siles is noted to have been a school teacher in Seville and Cadiz, Spain.

66. AAL, Papeles Importantes, leg. 5, exp. 13 (1649), fol. 3r. "Proceder mui honesta y rrecoxidamente como buen xptiano (cristiano) temeroso de Dios y de su conciencia dando mui buen exemplo en sus acciones y proceder." Carmona is listed as a "maestro de escuela" (schoolteacher) and sixty years old.

67. AAL, Papeles Importantes, leg. 5, exp. 13 (1649), fol. 3v. "Siempre [h]a dado mui buena quenta de su persona savelo assi por los papeles que [h]a visto como por averselo dicho personas que le vieron y conocieron en el d[ic]ho ministerio."

68. Archivo General de la Nación (hereafter AGN), Gobierno 2, caja 868, leg. 92 (1685), 5f. The following texts refer to this document: Charles, *Allies at Odds;* Alaperrine-Bouyer, *Educación de las elites,* 146–47; and Vargas Ugarte, "La instrucción primaria." While each mentions the petition as evidence of *indio ladinos'* capacity for litigation, those works do not conduct a close analysis of the petition or its formal structures. According to Alaperrine-Bouyer, González may have been a student at the Jesuit Colegio del Príncipe since a Juan González appears in the student list in 1657. Fittingly, as John Charles notes, the Jesuits complained that graduates of this school became troublesome litigants in the colonial legal system. Charles, "Trained by Jesuits," 62.

69. There is no specification of Juan Mateo González's background or birthplace in the document. Should this man be the same as the González listed in the student list of the Colegio del Príncipe, his place of origin is only slightly clarified. Alaperrine-Bouyer notes that of the ninety-five entries in the ledger book of the Jesuit Colegio del Príncipe from 1648–58, only seventeen are identified by place of origin. These include Cajamarca, Cajatambo, Canta, Chancay, Huamalies, Huamanga, Huarochirí, Huaylas, Jauja, Lima, Tarma, and Yauyos. Alaperrine-Bouyer, *Educación de las elites,* 137.

70. Though unspecified, this may be the community of El Cercado, the Indigenous town located on the limits of Cuzco. As Alcira Dueñas writes, Lima and its Indigenous neighborhoods like El Cercado housed "uprooted Indian immigrants (*mitayos,* artisans, *yanaconas* [native retainers subject to a colonial overlord]) of different ethnicities from the highlands, the coast and perhaps the Amazon ... [as well as a] significant portion of Afro Peruvians." Notably, El Cercado was the location of the Colegio del Príncipe where "Juan González" had been educated. Dueñas, *"Lettered City,"* 195–96.

71. AGN, Gobierno 2, Caja 868, leg. 92 (1685), fol. 2. "Enseñanza y educación de los yndios pobres naturales de esta ciudad."

72. AGN, Gobierno 2, Caja 868, leg. 92 (1685), fol. 2v, emphasis added. "Indio ladino en lengua española y de *buenas costumbres.*"

73. AGN, Gobierno 2, Caja 868, leg. 92 (1685), fol. 3r, emphasis added. "A proposito para la enseñanza de los muchachos por ser *yndio de buenas costumbres.*"

74. AGN, Gobierno 2, Caja 868, leg. 92 (1685), fol. 4r, emphasis added. "De la *misma forma* y manera que lo hacen *los demas* m[aest]ros de escuela."

75. Charles notes that the seventeenth-century Viceroys Martín Enríquez de Almanza and Pedro de Toledo y Leiva established provisions allowing priests to use the most "ladino" or lettered Indigenous persons to teach children up to fourteen the Castilian language and literacy. Charles, *Allies at Odds,* 20.

76. Stoler, *Along the Archival Grain.*

77. McKinley, "Till Death Do Us Part"; Premo, "Familiar"; and van Deusen, "Diasporas, Bondage, and Intimacy."

78. Charles, *Allies at Odds,* 24.

79. Estenssoro Fuchs, *Del paganismo a la santidad,* 311–12.
80. Mills, "Limits of Religious Coercion," 88.
81. Arriaga, *Extirpación de la idolatría en el Perú,* 24. "Los hijos serán mejores que sus padres, y los nietos mejores que padres y abuelos." Though the masculine plural could include men and women, I have used male terminology as a sign of the period's gendered logic and the ambivalence around women's role in the reproduction of custom.
82. Mumford, "Aristocracy on the Auction Block," 39.

4. Form and the Future

1. The Provisión Real to the first *Doctrina Christiana y catecismo para la instruccion de los Indios* notes that the monolithic "reformation of friars" ("reformación de los sacerdotes") and the establishment of "uniform" ("uniforme") catechisms would allow priests to reproduce the standard example of Christian practice—faith and behavior—in Indigenous catechumens. Toribio Medina, ed., *La imprenta en Lima,* 5.
2. *Confessionario para los curas de indios.*
3. *Confessionario para los curas de indios,* A recto. Also qtd. in Toribio Medina, *La imprenta en Lima,* 23, emphasis added. "Saqueys y *useys* en *la forma* que por el dicho Concilio Provincial *está ordenado.*"
4. Byrd and Rothberg, "Between Subalternity and Indigeneity."
5. The idea of single authorship can occlude the frequent participation of Indigenous, *mestizo,* and peoples of African origin and descent in the making of colonial texts. While not the focus of this chapter, production history provides a means of seeing the different methods of "writing" and agency in colonial documents. Within this body of scholarship, see Brewer-García, *Beyond Babel;* Bigelow, "Imperial Translations"; and Yannakakis, "Making Law Intelligible." See also note 11.
6. For a summary of this "discovery" by the Andean Diego Gualpa and an exploration of the epistemological transformation of the Andean Potoc'chi into the colonial Potosí, see Lane, *Potosí.*
7. Bigelow, *Mining Language;* and Lane, *Potosí.* As Jane Mangan has shown, the deracination occasioned by Potosí created unique opportunities for women to participate in colonial markets. See Mangan, *Trading Roles.*
8. Santo Tomás casts a long shadow over the religious history of Peru despite his brief ten-year stay in the region. After serving as the Dominican provincial and the bishop of Charcas, as well as the first examiner of Quechua in the Viceroyalty of Peru, he worked in Spain to advocate on behalf of Indigenous Andeans. Most famously, he collaborated with Las Casas to outbid Spanish *encomenderos* who attempted to buy rights to the *encomienda* system in perpetuity. For discussions of Santo Tomás and these conflicts, see Legnani, *Business*

of Conquest; Harrison, *Sin and Confession;* and Wagner with Parish, *Bartolomé de las Casas,* among others.

9. Santo Tomás, "Carta al Consejo de Indias," 15. "Habrá cuatro años . . . se descubrió una boca del infierno por la que entran cada año gran cantidad de gente, que la codicia de los españoles sacrifica a su dios, y es una mina de plata que llaman Potosí." This is perhaps the most famous statement made by Santo Tomás and it has been used to support interpretations of colonial systems and the role of Potosí within them, notably by Enrique Dussel. Dussel, *El encubrimiento del otro,* 65–66.

10. Kris Lane and others position Santo Tomás as the Peruvian counterpart to Las Casas. Works by both writers were offered as evidence of Spain's unique violence (in the Americas and Europe) to underpin the so-called "Black Legend." Not incidentally, Theodor de Bry's engravings that portrayed Spanish violence against Indigenous peoples in his six-volume *America* (1590–1618) represent scenes taken from Las Casas's *Brevísima relación* and Santo Tomás's works, according to Lane, *Potosí,* 31–32.

11. There is a long and rich tradition of study regarding the consideration of Indigenous, *mestizo,* and peoples of African descent in the composition of multilanguage grammars and evangelical texts that cannot be summarized here. For recent appraisals of this tradition, see Brewer-García, "Agency of Translation." For consideration of missionary standardization and translation, see, among others, Durston, *Pastoral Quechua.* For an early work on *indios ladinos* (lettered Indigenous peoples) as participants in the tradition of translation and composition, see Adorno, *Writing and Resistance.*

12. As Regina Harrison notes, Antonio Nebrija's studies of Latin—the *Introductiones latinae* (1481) and the *Introductiones in latinam grammaticem* (1540)—provided the base for Indigenous language grammars. Harrison, "Language and Rhetoric," 6.

13. Covarrubias, *Tesoro de la lengua castellana,* 838, emphasis added. "La colocación de las cosas, quando cada una está puesta en su lugar. . . . Dar orden para que se haga una cosa, *es dar la forma, y orden.*"

14. Santo Tomás, *Lexicon,* ii verso, emphasis added. "El Arte [de la grammatica] enseña *ordenar* y disponer por concierto, y *orden,* conforme a sus reglas y preceptos."

15. Santo Tomás, *Lexicon,* ii recto. "El artifice de qualquier arte (pio Lector,) Por muy experto q[ue] sea en el, y por muy acabados instrumentos que para exercitarlo te[n]ga, muy poco le aprovecha[n] para el exercicio del, si no tiene materia en que exercitarlos."

16. Santo Tomás, *Lexicon,* ii recto. "Como se podria poner claro exemplo en todos los officios, y particularmente en el aurifice, o platero: Al qual poco aprovecharia ser muy sabio en la lavor de oro, o plata . . . si no tuviesse metal en que los exercitar."

17. Santo Tomás, *Lexicon,* ii verso—iii recto. "Abundancia de vocablos, q[ue] es la materia que el Arte enseña ordenar y disponer por concierto . . . el arte sea perfecto, y tenga materia en que sus canones y preceptos se emplee[n]."

18. John D. Blanco and Ivonne del Valle, among others, have considered how biopolitics reconcile spiritual and economic colonial projects, a question I consider below. See the special edition of *Política común* edited by Blanco and del Valle and their essay "Reorienting Schmitt's Nomos."

19. Santo Tomás, *Lexicon,* iv verso.

20. McClintock, *Imperial Leather.* For an important engagement with McClintock's conception of desire and material culture in colonial Spanish America, see O'Toole, "Devotion."

21. Pérez Fernández, *El anónimo de Yucay,* 159–60. "¿Qué significa esto sino que se hubo Dios, con estos gentiles miserables y con nosotros, como sea un padre que tiene dos hijas: la una muy blanca, muy discreta y llena de graçias y donaires, la otra muy fea, lagañosa, tonta y bestial? Si ha de casar la primera, no ha menester dote sino ponerla en palaçio, que allí andarán en competencia los señores sobre quién se casará con ella. A la fea, torpe, neçia, desgraçiada, no basta esto sino darle gran dote: muchas joyas, ropas ricas, sumptuosas casas, y con todo eso Dios y ayuda. . . . Así, digo destos indios que uno de los medios de su predestinaçión y salvación fueron estas minas, tesoros y riquezas, porque vemos claramente que donde las hay va el Evangelio volando. . . . Buenas son las minas entre estos bárbaros, pues Dios se las dio para que les llevasen la fee y cristiandad y conservaçión en ella y para su salvación."

22. Note that Asia does not include the Pacific Island region populated by those defined as the "indios del oriente." For instance, Ricardo Padrón notes that a 1720 letter written by the missionary Gaspar de San Agustín called peoples of the Spanish Pacific "indios asiáticos," different from the "indios naturales de América" in capacity, though "they are all commonly referred to as 'indios.'" Padrón, *Indies of the Setting Sun,* 279–80. See also van Deusen, *Global Indios,* 224.

23. Pérez Fernández, *El anónimo de Yucay,* 159.

24. "Miserable" was not a category attributed to Indigenous persons alone. This term first applied to women, children, and other persons considered bereft of paternal authority. It afforded one legal privileges under the aegis of the Crown. For a discussion of the miserable and its extension to Indigenous peoples, see Goldmark, "Pity and Empire"; Sempat Assadourian, "Fray Bartolomé de Las Casas"; Castañeda Delgado, "La condición miserable." I thank Kristine Steenbergh, Katherine Ibbett, and the editors at Cambridge University Press for the opportunity to think through these questions.

25. Perhaps this divergence can be attributed to a sympathy between the author and the Viceroy, given that the two were cousins. See Mumford, "Francisco de Toledo," 50. In general, like those texts described above, this work supported

Viceroy Francisco de Toledo's position regarding Inca illegitimacy and rejected the political platform posed by Las Casas (and thus implicitly, Santo Tomás) by arguing that the Incas did not have sovereignty over the Andes.

26. Del Valle, "José de Acosta, Violence and Rhetoric," 60.

27. See Legnani, *Business of Conquest.*

28. Tom Cummins points to the repetition of the "Parecer de Yucay" in Acosta's text, as does Sabine MacCormack. Cummins, "Andean Colonial Towns," 232n25; and MacCormack, *Religion in the Andes,* 264.

29. Acosta, *Historia natural y moral,* 220. "Que hace un padre con una hija fea para casarla, que es darle mucha dote, eso había hecho Dios con aquella tierra tan trabajosa, de dalle mucha riqueza de minas."

30. Acosta, *Historia natural y moral,* 212. "Gente menos política. . . . los hombres a buscar aquellas tierras y tenellas, y de camino comunicar su religión y culto del verdadero Dios a los que no le conocían."

31. Skrzypek, "Editor's Introduction"; Bentancor, *Matter of Empire,* 8–15.

32. Li Causi, "Hybridization as Speciation?," 7. See also Laqueur, *Making Sex,* especially chap. 2, "Destiny is Anatomy." I thank Larissa Brewer-García for pointing me toward these texts.

33. Santo Tomás, *Lexicon,* iii recto.

34. Worthy of note, Ralph Bauer emphasizes that the use of hylomorphism was not an evangelical universal. He shows how Franciscans did not describe inert matter in potentia that was given form but instead employed the language of medicine to diagnose "corrupted" matter that required "re-formation." Ralph Bauer, *Alchemy of Conquest,* 218.

35. It is for this reason that scholars such as Daniel Nemser and Orlando Bentancor work to consider how there is sympathy between evangelization and economic exploitation, which Nemser has called "primitive spiritual accumulation." Both engage hylomorphism to articulate this coincidence between the two forms of colonialism, but approach gender differently. Bentancor argues against a binary gendered model via a reading of self-generating metal in Alvaro Alonso Barba's *Arte de los metales* (1640), while Nemser does not focus on gender. Nemser, "Primitive Spiritual Accumulation"; and Bentancor, "Matter."

36. Bentancor, "Matter."

37. Li Causi, "Hybridization as Speciation?"; and Summers, "Form and Gender," 261.

38. Nicole Legnani points to ideological tension between Las Casas and Acosta in the *Business of Conquest,* chap. 4, "The Specter of Las Casas in the Political Theology of José de Acosta." For a distinct approach to the intersections of capitalism, evangelism, and Acosta's thought, see del Valle, "Jesuit Baroque," 155.

39. Santo Tomás, *Lexicon,* iii verso–iiii recto. "Y nunca esta le[n]gua en los tiempos antiguos fue tan generalmente usada quasi de todos como el dia de oy. Porque

co[n] la communicacion, tracto, y grangerias que al presente tiene[n] unos con otros, y concurso en los pueblos de los christianos, y mercados dellos, assi para sus contractaciones, como para servicio de los españoles, para ente[n]derse entre si los de diversas provincias, usan desta general."

40. See my discussion of this term in chapter 1.

41. While the contracts mentioned above are likely textual, Andean *khipus* also served as forms used in "accounting" for historical and economic exchanges. See, among many works, Pillsbury, "Writing Inca History"; Urton, *Inka History in Knots;* Curatola Petrocchi and Puente Luna, *El quipu colonial;* Brokaw, *History of the Khipu;* Urton, "Sin, Confession"; and Salomon, *Cord Keepers.*

42. As both Regina Harrison and Bruce Mannheim note, Santo Tomás likely worked with a dialect of the central and peripheral Andes. Harrison, "Language and Rhetoric," 7; and Mannheim, *Language of the Inka,* 140.

43. Santo Tomás, *Lexicon,* vi verso. Among his list, Santo Tomás includes "trees, seeds, fruits, birds, fish, animals, professions, and the tools used for them" (De arboles, de semillas, de fructas, de aves, de pexes, de animales, de officios, de instrumentos dellos).

44. Harrison, "Language and Rhetoric," 7.

45. Santo Tomás, *Grammatica,* viii recto.

46. Santo Tomás, *Grammatica,* viii verso. This passage is also quoted in Segovia Gordillo, "Gramáticas misioneras," 469–70.

47. Segovia Gordillo, "Gramáticas misioneras," 471. Ana Segovia Gordillo posits that later texts do not make direct mention of Santo Tomás's *Arte, y vocabulario.* However, as I note, these works use the same logic of form as a strategy of evangelization.

48. Segovia Gordillo, "Gramáticas misioneras," 485; and Hernández de León-Portilla, "Primeras gramáticas mesoamericanas," 6.

49. Huerta, *Arte breve de la lengua quechua,* 18. "El uno es tan corto, que le faltan muchas cosas."

50. Roxo Mexía y Ocón, *Arte de la lengua general de los indios del Peru,* 13v.

51. Pérez Bocanegra, *Ritual formulario,* [27–28]. "Juntando pues en uno, las maneras de dezir en la lengua Quechua, e hallado tantas, y tan mal traduzidas, que estuvo bien quitar totalmente, muchas locuciones, interrogaciones, responsiones; añadir, y suplir otras, mudar las copulas, y verbos, frasis, è impertinencias, en todos ellos hasta las reduzir a un lenguaje usado, casto, inafectado, è inteligible, assi a todos los Curas, como a los Indios."

52. Pérez Bocanegra, *Ritual formulario,* [27]. "Para que como (por la misericordia de Dios) en la celebracion de la Missa, y reglas de rezar el Oficio divino, somos conformes, tambien lo seamos, en la administracion, y practica de los Sacramentos santos, y en la profession de nuestra Christiana Religion."

53. As noted in chapter 3, Jesuits spearheaded the Third Lima Council. Pérez Bocanegra struggled with the Jesuits since they were afforded control over the

parish of Andahuaylillas in 1628 after seven years of dispute. Ironically, one of the licenses approving the publication of his text is from a Jesuit head of the Colegio of Cuzco, as discussed below. See Charles, *Allies at Odds,* 97–99; Charles, "Unreliable Confessions," 30; and Harrison, "Pérez Bocanegra's *Ritual formulario,*" 270.

54. In the prologue to his grammar, Santo Tomás writes, "I began to work to *reduce* that language to the Arte." ("Comence a tractar de *reduzir* aquella lengua a Arte"). Santo Tomás, *Grammatica,* ii verso–iii recto, emphasis added.

55. Cummins, "Andean Colonial Towns," 203.

56. While Simon Ditchfield aligns the creation of this *reducción* with the Jesuits, Ralph Bauer notes that the Commissary General of the Franciscan Order, Fray Martín de Valencia, told the twelve "apostles" of Mexico to "reduce" Indigenous peoples to the Church as early as 1523. See Ditchfield, "What Did Natural History Have to Do with Salvation?," 144–68; Ralph Bauer, *Alchemy of Conquest,* 236.

57. Mumford, *Vertical Empire,* 87. The canon of studies on the *reducción* is too large to discuss here. For recent appraisals of the *reducción* that connect this practice to extraction economies, see Bigelow, *Mining Language;* and Nemser, *Infrastructures of Race.* For a consideration of the *reducción*'s afterlives, see Van-Valkenburgh, "Unsettling Time."

58. Irene Silverblatt, *Modern Inquisitions,* 111.

59. Mumford, *Vertical Empire,* 87.

60. Cummins, "Andean Colonial Towns," 217–18; and Durston, "Un régimen urbanístico," 101.

61. Rappaport and Cummins, *Beyond the Lettered City,* 233–38; and Durston, "Un regimen urbanístico," 61.

62. Henry Petroski, *The Evolution of Useful Things* (New York: Vintage, 1994), 20, quoted in Ahmed, *What's the Use?,* 25.

63. With "infelicitous," I evoke J. L. Austin's concept of the performative that points to the unintentional misrecognition of the discursive act. Austin, *How to Do Things with Words.* I thank Emma Stapely for this insight.

64. See also, for instance, the licenses to Franciscan friar Luis Jerónimo de Oré's compendious history and multilingual confessional handbook replete with hymnal, the *Symbolo catholico indiano* (1598). These licenses also engage the rhetoric of "use" to describe the value of the text. A committee commissioned by the Archbishop of Lima confirms that the text "can be and must be *used*" for evangelical endeavors (se pueda *usar* y *use* de el) because it is of "benefit for the Indians" (beneficio destos naturales). Likewise, from the very opening of the text, García Hurtado de Mendoza—the Viceroy of Peru and Marquez de Cañete—describes how Oré "has written some books in the general language that are *very useful and beneficial*" (ha compuesto algunos libros en la lengua general muy *utiles* y *provechosos*) for evangelization. Oré, *Symbolo*

catholico indiano 4r, emphasis added. For an extensive study of Oré's textual production and his role in the creation of Peruvian identity, see Andrango-Walker, *Saberes coloniales.*

65. Pérez Bocanegra, *Ritual formulario,* b2r–v, emphasis added. "Muy *util,* y necessario para los Curas, y demas Sacerdotes, que tratan de la conversion, y bien espiritual de los Naturales."

66. Pérez Bocanegra, *Ritual formulario,* n.p., emphasis added.

67. Pérez Bocanegra, *Ritual formulario,* b1r–v, emphasis added.

68. Del Valle, "José de Acosta," 7.

69. See chapter 3 for an extended discussion of custom.

70. Prieto, "Confessing to be an Indian," 530.

71. Del Valle, "Colonial Regimes," 13–17.

72. Mills, *Idolatry and Its Enemies;* Hyland, "Conversion, Custom, and Culture." We need to remember that there are different spaces in which self-identifying as "Indian" is a productive and opportune choice. It can be strategic, not only a negative imposition.

73. *Diccionario de autoridades,* s.v. "formulario," emphasis added. "El libro, o escríto en que se contienen las *fórmulas* que se han de observer para *la execución* de algunas cosas."

74. Pérez Bocanegra, *Ritual formulario,* n.p. This description of form and matter evokes the sacrament and the invocation of the Word, where bread and wine become the body and blood of Christ, a form of hylomorphism associated with St. Thomas Aquinas. "Que no se resuelven en este Ritual, y Formulario, dudas, acerca de las materias, y formas, &c. de los Sacramentos; sino solamente lo que [h]à de hazer el Cura, en la solene celebracion dellos."

75. Regina Harrison notes that different texts present specifications and a range of explanations according to their perception of Andean "capacity," taking, for example, the difference between the *Catecismo breve* versus the *mayor* (1584) produced by the Third Lima Council as a case in point. Harrison, "Literatura de la evangelización," 278–79.

76. See among others Prieto, "Confessing to be an Indian"; Brokaw, *History of the Khipu;* Charles, *Allies at Odds;* Charles, "Unreliable Confessions"; and Harrison, "Pérez Bocanegra's *Ritual formulario.*"

77. Von Germeten, "Sexuality, Witchcraft, and Honor"; Stavig, "Living in Offense"; and Silverblatt, *Moon, Sun, and Witches.*

78. Harrison, *Sin and Confession,* 120–27. See also Urton, "Sin, Confession"; and Horswell, *Decolonizing the Sodomite,* among others.

79. Pérez Bocanegra, *Ritual formulario,* 111. "Ciertos quipos, ñudos, y memorias, que traen para coufessarse [sic]."

80. While the *khipu* functioned as a method of "counting," a practice that could dovetail with the metaphoric spiritual "account" of one's sins in the West,

Harrison posits that Andeans would not conduct a Christological, numeric tracking of sin. Harrison, "Pérez Bocanegra's *Ritual formulario*," 276–78.

81. The economic use of the *khipu* might have supported the European rhetoric of the market that infused the language of sin: a sin was a "debt" that required "repayment." However, Urton has contended that the economic rhetoric inscribed in the *khipu* did not adjust to European epistemology but rather remained tied to "native reality." Urton, "Sin, Confession," 825. See also Harrison, *Sin and Confession*, 23–25; and Harrison, "Teaching Restitution."

82. Mannheim, "Nation Surrounded," 390–92.

83. Prieto, "Confessing to Be an Indian"; and Gruzinski, "Individualization and Acculturation."

84. Pérez Bocanegra, *Ritual formulario*, 117, corrected from erroneous numbering of page 137. "Ni tampoco declara el numero de los pecados (poco mas, ò menos) que [h]a cometido, que es necessario para la integridad de la confession. Antes si dize jurò diez vezes, otras diez, se emborrachò, fornicò, hurtò: sin añidir, ni quitar en quantos pecados confiessan este numero."

85. Harrison, "Pérez Bocanegra's *Ritual formulario*," 276.

86. Prieto, "Confessing to Be an Indian," 531.

87. Prieto, "Confessing to Be an Indian," 539, emphasis added.

88. This reading thus contravenes canonical works that posit the role of confession in the constitution of Indigenous individuation. See, for example, Klor de Alva, "Birth of Modern Ethnography"; Foucault, *History of Sexuality*.

89. Trouillot, *Silencing the Past*, 26, 28.

90. Movements such as the Taki Onqoy proposed the revolt of Andean *huacas* (deities) against Spaniards and their Gods. The violent attempts to extirpate the Taki Onqoy produced relations throughout the Andes that determined how friars and Andeans understood each other. The understanding of such movements might have been severely distorted by the anxieties of Spanish friars themselves. See Cristóbal de Molina, *Relación de las fábulas y ritos;* and Cristóbal de Albornoz, *Instrucción*.

91. Delgado, *Laywomen*, 39.

Coda

1. Bollaín, *También la lluvia*. "No. Pero, a ver, no me lo estoy inventando. Esto es lo que sucedió. Tenemos que contar lo que pasó."

2. While I do not address this extra layer, a third, intermittent "film" appears throughout *También la lluvia*. María (Cassandra Ciangherotti)—a film assistant—shoots documentary footage of the process, interviews members of the film-within-a-film crew and tracks the local conflict.

3. Bollaín, "Ni siquiera se pueden imaginar la idea de hacerlo."

4. Bollaín, "Hay cosas más importantes que tu película."

5. Elisabeth L. Austin provides a summary of theoretical approaches scholars have taken to this film in "Consuming Empathy in *También la lluvia* (2010)," 314n2.

6. The "film crew" does discuss this collapse as a problem for the "authenticity" of the historical epic, though this concern disappears as the film progresses. The potential collapse and performance of identity did mark the real casting process. As Andrea Meador Smith and Isabel Santaolalla have noted, Aduviri is not a *cochabambino* but an *alteño,* making his casting a potential collapse in indigeneity. In an interview with the Bolivian newspaper *Los Tiempos* on January 19, 2011, Aduviri commented on the difference between *cochabambinos, paceños,* and *alteños* and the research he conducted to represent the Cochabamba community. See Smith, "Savages and Saviours," 320–21; Santaolalla, *Cinema of Iciar Bollaín,* 206; and "Juan Carlos Aduviri."

7. Paul Joseph Lennon and Caroline Egan comment on the similarities and differences between Aduviri and Daniel's casting. While they note that a "Making of *También la lluvia*" featurette included on the DVD presents Aduviri stating that this opportunity "fell out of the sky . . . as a story that we needed to tell," they also show that Aduviri is a professional actor. Aduviri's quotation appears in a highly mediated section of the DVD and fits neatly into the rhetorical narrative of the film, with a play on the title itself ("falling from the sky" evoking rain). Lennon and Egan, "Conversion and Colonial History," 946–47.

8. Critics Roger Ebert and Stephen Holden questioned if Bollaín and Laverty underpaid Bolivian extras. Lennon and Eagan, "Conversion and Colonial History," 937. While the film-within-a-film "pays" extras 2 dollars per day, Bollaín paid extras 20 dollars per day. The salary for extras in Hollywood and New York at the time was 139 dollars per day. Smith, "Savages and Saviours," 327n6.

9. Wolfe, "Settler Colonialism and the Elimination of the Native," 388, 390; and Saldaña-Portillo, "Indians Have Always Been Modern," 226.

10. Stoler, *Along the Archival Grain,* 37.

11. Despite the refutation of this model by generations of scholars, emphasis on procreation has retained purchase in scholarship in subtle ways—in the elision of metaphors of culture with ideas of biology; in brief treatments of biology *as* gender; and in general, discursive practice. See for instance Gruzinski, *Mestizo Mind;* and Sidbury and Cañizares-Esguerra, "Mapping Ethnogenesis." For a critique of the persistence of this model, see Graubart. "Toward Connectedness and Place."

12. Speed, "Structures of Settler Capitalism in Abya Yala," 786–87.

13. Silvia Rivera Cusicanqui, *"Ch'ixinakax utxiwa,"* 107.

14. Brickhouse, *Unsettlement of America.*

15. Rivera Cusicanqui speaks of the possibility of viewing the intercultural in "weaving." Silvia Rivera Cusicanqui, *"Ch'ixinakax utxiwa,"* 106–7; Also qtd. in Saldaña 227. As scholars have well-considered, Andean peoples, friars, and colonial authorities focused on the temporalities of religion, marriage,

and death and interrogated how these conditioned colonial life. This is particularly apparent in the case of an Andean text that has been read in terms of its epistemological and temporal density, *The Huarochirí Manuscript: A Testament of Ancient and Colonial Andean Religion,* eds. and trans. Frank Salomon and George L. Urioste (Austin: University of Texas Press, 1991). For discussions of colonial temporality and its impacts on daily life see, among others, Ramos, *Death and Conversion;* and Gose, *Invaders as Ancestors,* among others. For a theoretical consideration of the intersection of Indigenous and settler colonial temporalities, see Rifkin, *Beyond Settler Time.*

16. Traub, "Present Future of Lesbian Historiography," 126. The interrogation of transhistorical family forms and sexuality has been a polemic in US queer studies, where debates have focused on identification and difference across time. Scholars can be put into roughly two schools, those who claim the value of ahistoricism, such as Carla Freccero, Jonathan Goldberg, and Madhavi Menon, and those focused on periodization and genealogy, such as Valerie Traub and David Halperin. However, the extensive focus on European literature and epistemology in both camps reveals the potential displacement of colonial relations and temporality. This is despite the emphasis on the colonial world as an important touchstone for those working in the ahistorical camp. See Traub, *Thinking Sex;* Freccero, "Figural Historiography"; Menon, *Unhistorical Shakespeare;* Halperin, *How to Do the History of Homosexuality;* Traub, *Renaissance of Lesbianism;* and Goldberg, *Sodometries.* For a general, if partial, overview of this debate, see Traub, "New Unhistoricism," 21–39.

17. Smith, "Savages and Saviours," 324–25.

18. This reading builds on Fred Moten and Saidiya Hartman's conversation on the paradox of ethical representations of gendered violence under the conditions of enslavement. Hartman refuses to represent an oft-described scene of violence regarding Aunt Hester from the *Narrative of the Life of Frederick Douglass* (1845) to call attention to viewers' frequent inurement to such moments. Moten, however, contends that "swerve[ing] away from [the scene] . . . runs right back to [it]." Even the refusal to describe is a description in evocation and absentia. Hartman, *Scenes of Subjection,* 3–4; and Moten, *In the Break,* 5.

Bibliography

Acosta, José de. *De procuranda Indorum salute.* 1588. Edited and translated by Luciano Pereña. Madrid: Consejo Superior de Investigaciones Científicas, 1984.

———. *Historia natural y moral de las Indias.* 1590. Edited by José Alcina Franch. Madrid: Historia 16, 1987.

Adorno, Rolena. "The Discursive Encounter of Spain and America: The Authority of Eyewitness Testimony in the Writing of History." *William and Mary Quarterly* 49, no. 2 (1992): 210–28.

———. *Guaman Poma and His Illustrated Chronicles from Colonial Peru: From a Century of Scholarship to a New Era of Reading.* Copenhagen: Museum Tusculanum Press, 2001.

———. *Guaman Poma: Writing and Resistance in Colonial Peru.* Austin: University of Texas Press, 1986.

———. "Images of *Indios Ladinos* in Early Colonial Peru." In Andrien and Adorno, *Transatlantic Encounters,* 232–70.

———. The *Intellectual life of Bartolomé de Las Casas.* New Orleans: Graduate School of Tulane University, 1992.

———. "The Not-So-Brief Story of the *Brevísima relación de la destrucción de las Indias.*" In Orique and Roldán-Figueroa, *Bartolomé de las Casas, O.P.,* 29–57.

———. "Nuevas perspectivas en los estudios literarios coloniales hispanoamericanos." *Revista de crítica literaria latinoamericana* 14, no. 28 (1988): 11–28.

———. *The Polemics of Possession in Spanish American Narrative.* New Haven: Yale University Press, 2007.

Ahmed, Sara. *What's the Use? On the Uses of Use.* Durham, NC: Duke University Press, 2019.

Alaperrine-Bouyer, Monique. *La educación de las elites indígenas en el Perú colonial.* Lima: Institut français d'études andines, 2007.

Albornoz, Cristóbal de. *Instrucción para descubrir todas las guacas del Pirú y sus camayos y haziendas.* 1584. In Urbano and Duviols, *Fábulas y mitos,* 161–98.

Alconini, Sonia and R. Alan Covey, eds. *The Oxford Handbook of the Incas.* Oxford: Oxford University Press, 2018.

Álvarez, Bartolomé. *De las costumbres y conversion de los indios del Perú: Memorial a Felipe II.* 1588. Edited by Maria del Carmen Martín Rubio, Juan J.R. Villarías Robles, and Fermín del Pino Díaz. Madrid: Ediciones Polifemo, 1998.

Andrango-Walker, Catalina. El *Símbolo católico indiano* (1598) *de Luis Jerónimo de Oré: Saberes coloniales y los problemas de la evangelización en la región andina.* Madrid: Iberoamericana, 2018.

Andrien, Kenneth J., and Rolena Adorno, eds. *Transatlantic Encounters: Europeans and Andeans in the Sixteenth Century.* Berkeley: University of California Press, 1991.

Angulo, Domingo, ed. "Libro original que contiene la fundacion del monesterio de monxas de señora Sta Clara desta cibdad del Cuzco [. . .]" *Revista del Archivo Nacional del Perú* 11, nos. 1–2 (1939): 55–95 and 157–84.

Arenal, Electa, and Yolanda Martínez-San Miguel. "Refocusing New Spain and Spanish Colonization: Malinche, Guadalupe, and Sor Juana." In *A Companion to the Literatures of Colonial America,* edited by Susan Castillo and Ivy Schweitzer, 174–94. Hoboken, NJ: Blackwell Publishing Ltd., 2005.

Ares Queija, Berta. "Mancebas de españoles, madres de mestizos. Imágenes de la mujer indígena en el Perú colonial temprano." In *Las mujeres en la construcción de las sociedades iberoamericanas,* edited by Pilar Gonzalbo Aizpuru and Berta Ares Queija, 15–39. Sevilla: Consejo Superior de Investigaciones Científicas, 2004.

———. "Relaciones sexuales y afectivas en tiempos de conquista. La Española (1492–1516)." In *Congreso Internacional Cristóbal Colón 1506–2006,* edited by Consuelo Varela, 237–56. Palos de la Frontera, Spain: Ayuntamiento de Palos de la Frontera, 2006.

Arias, Santa. *Retórica, historia y polémica: Bartolomé de Las Casas y la tradición intelectual renacentista.* Lanham, MD: University Press of America, 2001.

Arias, Santa, and Eyda M. Merediz, eds. *Approaches to Teaching the Writing of Bartolomé de Las Casas.* New York: Modern Language Association of America, 2008.

Arriaga, Pablo Joseph de. *La extirpación de la idolatría en el Perú.* 1621. Edited with preliminary study and notes by Henrique Urbano. Cuzco, Peru: Centro de Estudios Regionales Andinos "Bartolomé de Las Casas," 1999.

Austin, Elisabeth L. "Consuming Empathy in *También la lluvia* (2010)." *Chasqui* 46, no. 2 (2017): 313–29.

Austin, J. L. *How to Do Things with Words.* Oxford: Clarendon Press, 1962.

Avalle-Arce, Juan Bautista. "Las hipérboles del Padre Las Casas." In *Dintorno de una época dorada,* 73–100. Madrid: Ediciones José Porrúa Turanzas, S.A., 1978.

Baber, R. Jovita. "Categories, Self-Representation and the Construction of the *Indios.*" *Journal of Spanish Cultural Studies* 10, no. 1 (2009): 27–41.

Ballantyne, Tony, and Antoinette Burton. *Moving Subjects: Gender, Mobility, and Intimacy in an Age of Global Empire.* Urbana Champaign, IL: University of Illinois Press, 2009.

Bauer, Brian, Madeleine Halac-Higashimori and Gabriel E. Cantarutti, eds. *Voices from Vilcabamba: Accounts Chronicling the Fall of the Inca Empire.* Boulder: University Press of Colorado, 2016.

Bauer, Ralph. *The Alchemy of Conquest: Science, Religion, and the Secrets of the New World.* Charlottesville: University of Virginia Press, 2019.

———. Introduction to *An Inca Account of the Conquest of Peru,* by Titu Cusi Yupanqui, 1–56. Translated and annotated by Ralph Bauer. Boulder: University Press of Colorado, 2005.

———. "Millennium's Darker Side: The Missionary Utopias of Franciscan New Spain and Puritan New England." In *Finding Colonial Americas: Essays Honoring J. A. Leo Lemay,* edited by Carla Mulford and David S. Shields, 33–49. Newark: University of Delaware Press, 2001.

Bauer, Ralph, and Marcy Norton. "Introduction: Entangled Trajectories: Indigenous and European Histories." *Colonial Latin American Review* 26, no. 1 (2017): 1–17.

Bennett, Herman L. *Africans in Colonial Mexico: Absolutism, Christianity, and Afro-Creole Consciousness, 1570–1640.* Bloomington: Indiana University Press, 2003.

———. *Colonial Blackness: A History of Afro-Mexico.* Bloomington: Indiana University Press, 2010.

Bentancor, Orlando. "Matter, Form, and the Generation of Metals in Alvaro Alonso Barba's *Arte de los metales.*" *Journal of Spanish Cultural Studies* 8, no. 2 (2007): 117–33.

———. *The Matter of Empire: Metaphysics and Mining in Colonial Peru.* Pittsburgh, PA: University of Pittsburgh Press, 2017.

Bergmann, Emilie L. "Martyrs and Minors: Allegories of Childhood in Cervantes." In *Gender and Early Modern Constructions of Childhood,* edited by Naomi J. Miller and Naomi Yavneh, 193–208. Farnham, England: Ashgate, 2011.

———. "Milking the Poor: Wet-nursing and the Sexual Economy of Early Modern Spain." In *Marriage and Sexuality in Medieval and Early Modern Iberia,* edited by Eukene Lacarra Lanz, 90–114. London: Routledge, 2002.

Bigelow, Allison Margaret. "Imperial Translations: New World Missionary Linguistics, Indigenous Interpreters, and Universal Languages in the Early Modern Era." In *American Literature and the New Puritan Studies,* edited by Bryce Traister, 93–110. Cambridge: Cambridge University Press, 2017.

———. *Mining Language: Racial Thinking, Indigenous Knowledge, and Colonial Metallurgy in the Early Modern Iberian World.* Williamsburg, VA: Omohundro Institute of Early American History and Culture, 2020.

Black, Chad Thomas. "Between Prescription and Practice: Licensure and Women's Legal Identity in Bourbon Quito, 1765–1810." *Colonial Latin American Review* 16, no. 2 (2007): 273–98.

Blanco, John D., and Ivonne del Valle, "Reorienting Schmitt's *Nomos:* Political Theology, and Colonial (and Other) Exceptions in the Creation of Modern and Global Worlds," *Política común* 5 (2014): n.p. https://doi.org/10.3998/pc.12322227.0005.001.

Bollaín, Icíar, dir. *También la lluvia.* 2010; Chatsworth, CA: Image Entertainment, 2012.

Boone, Elizabeth Hill, and Tom Cummins, eds. *Native Traditions in the Postconquest World: A Symposium at Dumbarton Oaks.* Washington, D.C.: Dumbarton Oaks Research Library and Collection, 1998.

Bourdieu, Pierre. *Outline of a Theory of Practice.* Translated by Richard Nice. Cambridge: Cambridge University Press, 1977.

Bouza Alvarez, Fernando J. *Communication, Knowledge, and Memory in Early Modern Spain*. Translated by Sonia López and Michael Agnew. Philadelphia: University of Pennsylvania Press, 2004.

Boyer, Patricio. "Framing the Visual Tableaux in the *Brevísima relación de la destrucción de las Indias.*" *Colonial Latin American Review* 18, no. 3 (2009): 365–82.

Brading, D. A. *The First America: The Spanish Monarchy, Creole Patriots, and the Liberal State 1492–1867*. Cambridge: Cambridge University Press, 1991.

Brewer-García, Larissa. "The Agency of Translation in Colonial Latin America: Rethinking the Roles of non-European Linguistic Intermediaries." In *Routledge Hispanic Studies Companion to Colonial Latin America and the Caribbean (1492–1898)*, edited by Yolanda Martínez-San Miguel and Santa Arias, 379–92. London: Routledge, 2021.

———. *Beyond Babel: Translations of Blackness in Colonial Peru and New Granada*. Cambridge: Cambridge University Press, 2020.

———. "Bodies, Texts, and Translators: Indigenous Breast Milk and the Jesuit Exclusion of Mestizos in Late Sixteenth-Century Peru." *Colonial Latin American Review* 21, no. 3 (2012): 365–90.

Brickhouse, Anna. *The Unsettlement of America: Translation, Interpretation, and the Story of Don Luis de Velasco, 1560–1945*. Oxford: Oxford University Press, 2014.

Briggs, Laura. *Somebody's Children: The Politics of Transracial and Transnational Adoption*. Durham, NC: Duke University Press, 2012.

Broggio, Paolo. "The Religious Orders and the Expulsion of the Moriscos: Doctrinal Controversies and Hispano-Papal Relations." In *The Expulsion of the Moriscos from Spain: A Mediterranean Diaspora*, edited by Mercedes Garcia-Arenal and Gerard A. Wiegers, 156–78. Leiden: Brill, 2014.

Brokaw, Galen. *A History of the Khipu*. Cambridge: Cambridge University Press, 2010.

Brown, Kimberly Juanita. *The Repeating Body: Slavery's Visual Resonance in the Contemporary*. Durham: Duke University Press, 2015.

Brown, Peter. "The Saint as Exemplar in Late Antiquity." *Representations* 1, no. 2 (1983): 1–25.

Burns, Kathryn. *Colonial Habits: Convents and the Spiritual Economy of Cuzco, Peru*. Durham, NC: Duke University Press, 1999.

———. "Gender and the Politics of Mestizaje: The Convent of Santa Clara in Cuzco, Peru." *Hispanic American Historical Review* 78, no. 1 (1998): 5–44.

———. *Into the Archive: Writing and Power in Colonial Peru*. Durham, NC: Duke University Press, 2010.

———. "Notaries, Truth, and Consequences." *American Historical Review* 110, no. 2 (2005): 350–79.

———. "Unfixing Race." In Greer, Mignolo, and Quilligan, *Rereading the Black Legend*, 188–204.

Burns, Robert I., S.J., ed. *Underworlds: The Dead, the Criminal, and the Marginalized.* Vol. 5 of *Las Siete Partidas,* translated by Samuel Parsons Scott. Philadelphia: University of Pennsylvania Press, 2000.

Butler, Judith. "Is Kinship Always Already Heterosexual?" *Differences: A Journal of Feminist Cultural Studies* 13, no. 1 (2002): 14–44.

Byrd, Jodi A. "What's Normative Got to Do with It?: Towards Indigenous Queer Relationality." *Social Text* 38, no. 4 (2020): 105–23.

Byrd, Jodi A., and Michael Rothberg. "Between Subalternity and Indigeneity: Critical Categories for Postcolonial Studies." *Interventions* 13, no. 1 (2011): 1–12.

"Carta que escribieron varios padres de la órden de Santo Domingo, residentes en la isla Española á Mr. de Xevres." In *Colección de documentos inéditos relativos al descubrimiento, conquista y organización de las antiguas posesiones españolas de América y Oceanía, sacados de los Archivos del Reino, y muy especialmente del de Indias.* Vol. 7, edited by D. Luis Torres de Mendoza, 397–430. Madrid: Frias y Compañia, 1867.

Castañeda Delgado, Paulino. "La condición miserable del indio y sus privilegios." *Anuario de Estudios Americanos* 28 (1971): 245–335.

Castellanos, M. Bianet. "Introduction: Settler Colonialism in Latin America." *American Quarterly* 69, no. 4 (2017): 777–81.

Castro, Daniel. *Another Face of Empire: Bartolomé de Las Casas, Indigenous Rights, and Ecclesiastical Imperialism.* Durham, NC: Duke University Press, 2007.

Cattan, Marguerite. "En los umbrales de la *Instrucción* de Titu Cusi Yupanqui." *Histórica* 35, no. 2 (2011): 7–44.

———. "Las palabras que no se tradujeron en la *Instrucción* de Titu Cusi Yupanqui." *Hipogrifo: Revista de literatura y cultura de Siglo de Oro* 4, no. 2 (2016): 169–95.

Chakrabarty, Dipesh. *Provincializing Europe: Postcolonial Thought and Historical Difference.* Princeton, NJ: Princeton University Press, 2000.

Chamberlain, Robert S. "The Concept of the *Señor Natural* as Revealed by Castilian Law and Administrative Documents." *Hispanic American Historical Review* 19, no. 2 (1939): 130–37.

Chang-Rodríguez, Raquel. *La apropiación del signo: Tres cronistas indígenas del Perú.* Tempe, AZ: Arizona State University, 1988.

———. "A Forgotten Indian Chronicle: Titu Cusi Yupanqui's *Relación de la conquista del Perú.*" *Latin American Indian Literatures Journal: A Review of American Indian Texts and Studies* 4, no. 2 (1980): 87–95.

———. "La princesa incaica Beatriz Clara y el dramaturgo ilustrado Francisco del Castillo." In *Mujer y cultura en la colonia hispanoamericana,* edited by Mabel Moraña, 51–66. Pittsburgh: Instituto Internacional de Literatura Iberoamericana, 1996.

———. "Rebelión y religión en dos crónicas indígenas del Perú de ayer." *Revista de crítica literaria latinoamericana* 14, no. 28 (1988): 175–93.

Charles, John. *Allies at Odds: The Andean Church and Its Indigenous Agents, 1583–1671.* Albuquerque: University of New Mexico Press, 2010.

———. "Felipe Guaman Poma de Ayala en los foros de la justicia eclesiástica." In *Los indios, el Derecho Canónico y la justicia eclesiástica en la América virreinal*, edited by Ana de Zaballa Beascoechea, 203–22. Madrid: Iberoamericana, 2011.

———. "'More *Ladino* than Necessary': Indigenous Litigants and the Language Policy Debate in Mid-Colonial Peru." *Colonial Latin American Review* 16, no. 1 (2007): 23–47.

———. "Trained by Jesuits: Indigenous *Letrados* in Seventeenth-Century Peru." In Ramos and Yannakakis, *Indigenous Intellectuals*, 60–78.

———. "Unreliable Confessions: Khipus in the Colonial Parish." *The Americas* 64, no. 1 (2007): 11–33.

Child, Brenda J. *Boarding School Seasons: American Indian Families, 1900–1940*. Lincoln: University of Nebraska Press, 1998.

Clendinnen, Inga. *Ambivalent Conquests: Maya and Spaniard in Yucatan, 1517–1570*. Cambridge: Cambridge University Press, 1987.

Cocquelines, Charles, ed. *Bullarum privilegiorum ac diplomatum Romanorum Pontificum: Amplissima collectio cui accessere Pontificum omnium vitae, notae, & indeces opportuni*. Vol. 3, pt. 3. Roma, 1743.

Cohen, Cathy J. "Punks, Bulldaggers, and Welfare Queens: The Radical Potential of Queer Politics?" *GLQ: A Journal of Lesbian and Gay Studies* 3, no. 4 (1997): 437–65.

Confessionario para los curas de indios: Con la instrucion contra sus ritos: y Exhortacion para ayudar a bien morir: y summa de sus privilegios: y forma de Impedimentos del Matrimonio. Compuesto y traduzido en las lenguas quichua, y aymara. Por autoridad del Concilio Provincial de Lima, del año de 1583. Ciudad de los Reyes: Antonio Ricardo, 1585.

Cook, Karoline P. *Forbidden Passages: Muslims and Moriscos in Colonial Spanish America*. Philadelphia: University of Pennsylvania Press, 2016.

Cornejo Polar, Antonio. "Mestizaje e hibridez: Los riesgos de las metáforas. Apuntes." *Revista Iberoamericana* 63, no. 180 (1997): 341–44.

Covarrubias, Sebastián de. *Tesoro de la lengua castellana o española según la impresión de 1611, con las adiciones de Benito Remingo Noydens publicadas en la de 1674*. Edited by Martín de Riquer. Barcelona: S.A. Horta, 1943.

Covey, R. Alan. "Chronology, Succession, and Sovereignty: The Politics of Inka Historiography and Its Modern Interpretation." *Comparative Studies in Society and History* 48, no. 1 (2006): 169–99.

Covey, R. Alan, and Christina M. Elson. "Ethnicity, Demography, and Estate Management in Sixteenth-Century Yucay." *Ethnohistory* 54, no. 2 (2007): 303–35.

Cummins, Thomas B. F. "Forms of Andean Colonial Towns, Free Will, and Marriage." In *The Archaeology of Colonialism*, edited by Claire L. Lyons and John K. Papadopoulos, 199–240. Los Angeles: Getty Research Institute, 2002.

Cummins, Thomas B. F., and Barbara Anderson, eds. *The Getty Murúa: Essays on the Making of Martín de Murúa's* Historia General del Piru, *J. Paul Getty Museum Ms. Ludwig XIII 16*. Los Angeles: Getty Research Institute, 2008.

Curatola Petrocchi, Marco, and José Carlos de la Puente Luna, eds. *El quipu colonial: Estudios y materiales.* Lima: Pontificia Universidad Católica del Perú, 2013.

Dean, Carolyn. "Beyond Prescription: Notarial Doodles and Other Marks." *Word & Image: A Journal of Verbal/Visual Enquiry* 25, no. 3 (2009): 293–316.

———. "Familiarizando el catolicismo en el Cuzco colonial." In *Incas e indios cristianos: Elites indígenas e identidades cristianas en los Andes coloniales,* edited by Jean-Jacques Decoster, 169–94. Lima: Institut français d'études andines, 2002.

Dean, Carolyn, and Dana Leibsohn. "Hybridity and Its Discontents: Considering Visual Culture in Colonial Spanish America." *Colonial Latin American Review* 12, no. 1 (2003): 5–35.

Decena, Carlos Ulises. *Tacit Subjects: Belonging and Same-Sex Desire among Dominican Immigrant Men.* Durham, NC: Duke University Press, 2011.

Delgado, Jessica L. *Laywomen and the Making of Colonial Catholicism in New Spain, 1630–1790.* Cambridge: Cambridge University Press, 2018.

Del Valle, Ivonne. "Jesuit Baroque." *Journal of Spanish Cultural Studies* 3, no. 2 (2002): 141–63.

———. "José de Acosta: Colonial Regimes for a Globalized Christian World." In *Coloniality, Religion, and the Law in the Early Iberian World,* edited by Santa Arias and Raúl Marrero-Fente, 3–26. Nashville, TN: Vanderbilt University Press, 2014.

———. "José de Acosta, Violence and Rhetoric: The Emergence of Colonial Baroque." *Calíope: Journal of the Society for Renaissance and Baroque Hispanic Poetry* 18, no. 2 (2013): 46–72.

Ditchfield, Simon. "What Did Natural History Have to Do with Salvation? José de Acosta SJ (1540–1600) in the Americas." In *God's Bounty? The Churches and the Natural World,* edited by Peter Clarke and Tony Claydon, 144–68. Woodbridge, UK: Boydell Press, 2010.

Dopico Black, Georgina. "Ghostly Remains: Valencia, 1609." *Arizona Journal of Hispanic Cultural Studies* 7 (2003): 91–100.

Driskill, Qwo-Li, Chris Finley, Brian Joseph Gilley, and Scott Lauria Morgensen, eds. *Queer Indigenous Studies: Critical Interventions in Theory, Politics, and Literature.* Tucson: University of Arizona Press, 2011.

Dueñas, Alcira. *Indians and Mestizos in the "Lettered City": Reshaping Justice, Social Hierarchy, and Political Culture in Colonial Peru.* Boulder: University Press of Colorado, 2010.

Dueñas-Vargas, Guiomar. *Los hijos del pecado: Ilegitimidad y vida familiar en la Santafé de Bogotá colonial.* Bogotá: Editorial Universidad Nacional, 1997.

Durán Luzio, Juan. *Bartolomé de las Casas ante la conquista de América: Las voces del historiador.* Heredia, Costa Rica: Editorial de la Universidad Nacional, 1992.

Durston, Alan. *Pastoral Quechua: The History of Christian Translation in Colonial Peru, 1550–1650.* Notre Dame, IN: University of Notre Dame Press, 2007.

———. "Un régimen urbanístico en la América Hispana colonial: El trazado en damero durante los siglos xvi y xvii." *Historia* 28 (1994): 59–115.

Dussel, Enrique. *El encubrimiento del otro: Hacia el origen del mito de la modernidad.* Quito: Ediciones ABYA-ALA, 1994.

Earle, Rebecca. *The Body of the Conquistador: Food, Race, and the Colonial Experience in Spanish America, 1492–1700.* Cambridge: Cambridge University Press, 2012.

Edelman, Lee. *No Future: Queer Theory and the Death Drive.* Durham, NC: Duke University Press, 2004.

Eng, David L. *The Feeling of Kinship: Queer Liberalism and the Racialization of Intimacy.* Durham, NC: Duke University Press, 2010.

Estenssoro Fuchs, Juan Carlos. *Del paganismo a la santidad: La incorporación de los indios del Perú al catolicismo, 1532–1750.* Translated by Gabriela Ramos. Lima: Institut français d'études andines, 2003.

Falconí Trávez, Diego, Santiago Castellanos, and María Amelia Viteri. "Resentir lo queer en América Latina: diálogos desde/con el Sur." In *Resentir lo queer en América Latina: diálogos desde/con el Sur,* edited by Diego Falconí Trávez, Santiago Castellanos, and María Amelia Viteri, 9–18. Barcelona: Egales Editorial, 2014.

Ferguson, Roderick A. *Aberrations in Black: Toward a Queer of Color Critique.* Minneapolis: University of Minnesota Press, 2004.

Fisher, Andrew B., and Matthew D. O'Hara, eds. *Imperial Subjects: Race and Identity in Colonial Latin America.* Durham, NC: Duke University Press, 2009.

Floyd, Emily C. "Privileging the Local: Prints and the New World in Early Modern Lima." In *A Companion to Early Modern Lima,* edited by Emily A. Engel, 360–84. Leiden: Brill, 2019.

Foucault, Michel. *The History of Sexuality.* Vol. 1. *An Introduction,* translated by Robert Hurley. New York: Vintage, 1990.

Franco, Jean. "La Malinche: From Gift to Sexual Contract." In *Critical Passions: Selected Essays,* edited by Mary Louise Pratt and Kathleen Newman, 71–88. Durham, NC: Duke University Press, 1999.

Franklin, Sarah, and Susan McKinnon. Introduction to *Relative Values: Reconfiguring Kinship Studies,* edited by Sarah Franklin and Susan McKinnon, 1–25. Durham, NC: Duke University Press, 2001.

Freccero, Carla. "Figural Historiography: Dogs, Humans, and Cynanthropic Becomings." In *Comparatively Queer: Interrogating Identities Across Time and Cultures,* edited by Jarrod Hayes, Margaret R. Higonnet, and William J. Spurlin, 45–68. New York: Palgrave, 2010.

Freeman, Elizabeth. "Queer Belongings: Kinship Theory and Queer Theory." In Haggerty and McGarry, *Companion,* 295–314.

Fuentes, Marisa J. *Dispossessed Lives: Enslaved Women, Violence, and the Archive.* Philadelphia: University of Pennsylvania Press, 2016.

García-Arenal, Mercedes. "Theologies of Baptism and Forced Conversion: The Case of the Muslims of Valencia and Their Children." In *Forced Conversion in*

Christianity, Judaism and Islam, edited by Mercedes García-Arenal and Yonatan Glazer-Eytan, 354–85. Leiden: Brill, 2020.

Garrett, David T. "Inca Ancestry and Colonial Privilege." In Alconini and Covey, *Oxford Handbook of the Incas,* 759–76.

Ginsburg, Faye, and Rayna Rapp. "The Politics of Reproduction." *Annual Review of Anthropology* 20 (1991): 311–43.

Glissant, Édouard. *Poetics of Relation.* Translated by Betsy Wing. Ann Arbor: University of Michigan Press, 1997.

Goldberg, Jonathan. *Sodometries: Renaissance Texts, Modern Sexualities.* Stanford: Stanford University Press, 1992.

Goldmark, Matthew. "Pity and Empire in the *Brevísima relación de la destrucción de las Indias* (1552)." In *Compassion in Early Modern Literature and Culture: Feeling and Practice,* edited by Kristine Steenbergh and Katherine Ibbett, 257–72. Cambridge: Cambridge University Press, 2021.

González Echevarría, Roberto. *Myth and Archive: A Theory of Latin American Narrative.* Cambridge: Cambridge University Press, 1990.

González, Ondina E. "Consuming Interests: The Response to Abandoned Children in Colonial Havana." In González and Premo, *Raising an Empire,* 137–62.

González, Ondina E., and Bianca Premo, eds. *Raising an Empire: Children in Early Modern Iberia and Colonial Latin America.* Albuquerque: University of New Mexico Press, 2007.

Gordon, Avery F. *Ghostly Matters: Haunting and the Sociological Imagination.* Minneapolis: University of Minnesota Press, 2008.

Gose, Peter. *Invaders as Ancestors: On the Intercultural Making and Unmaking of Spanish Colonialism in the Andes.* Toronto: University of Toronto Press, 2008.

Granada, Fray Luis de. *Los seis libros de la Retórica Eclesiástica, o Método de predicar,* edited by Manuel López-Muñoz. Logroño: Instituto de Estudios Riojanos, 2010.

Graubart, Karen B. "As Slaves and Not Vassals: Interethnic Claims of Freedom and Unfreedom in Colonial Peru." *Población y sociedad: revista de estudios sociales* 27, no. 2 (2020): 30–53.

———. "The Creolization of the New World: Local Forms of Identification in Urban Colonial Peru, 1560–1640." *Hispanic American Historical Review* 89, no. 3 (2009): 471–99.

———. "Indecent Living: Indigenous Women and the Politics of Representation in Early Colonial Peru." *Colonial Latin American Review* 9, no. 2 (2000): 213–35.

———. "Toward Connectedness and Place." *William and Mary Quarterly* 68, no. 2 (2011): 233–35.

Greene, Roland. *Five Words: Critical Semantics in the Age of Shakespeare and Cervantes.* Chicago: University of Chicago Press, 2013.

Greer, Margaret R., Walter D. Mignolo, and Maureen Quilligan, eds. *Rereading the Black Legend: The Discourses of Religious and Racial Difference in the Renaissance Empires.* Chicago: University of Chicago Press, 2007.

Gruzinski, Serge. "Individualization and Acculturation: Confession among the Nahuas of Mexico from the Sixteenth to the Eighteenth Century." Lavrin, *Sexuality and Marriage,* 96–117.

———. *The Mestizo Mind: The Intellectual Dynamics of Colonization and Globalization.* Translated by Deke Dusinberre. New York: Routledge, 2002.

Guaman Poma de Ayala, Felipe. *Nueva corónica y buen gobierno.* 1615. Edited by John V. Murra, Rolena Adorno, and Jorge L. Urioste. 3 vols. Mexico, D.F.: Historia 16, 1980.

Guengerich, Sara Vicuña. "Capac Women and the Politics of Marriage in Early Colonial Peru." *Colonial Latin American Review* 24, no. 2 (2015): 147–67.

———. "Mining the Colonial Archive: The Global Microhistory of a Peruvian Coya." *Modern Philology* 119, no. 1 (2021): 61–76.

Guillén Guillén, Edmundo. "Documentos inéditos para la historia de los incas de Vilcabamba: La capitulación del gobierno español con Titu Cusi Yupanqui." *Historia y Cultura* 10 (1977) 47–93.

Haggerty, George E., and Molly McGarry, eds. *A Companion to Lesbian, Gay, Bisexual, Transgender, and Queer Studies.* Malden, MA: Blackwell Publishing, 2007.

Halperin, David M. *How to Do the History of Homosexuality.* Chicago: University of Chicago Press, 2002.

Hampton, Timothy. *Writing from History: The Rhetoric of Exemplarity in Renaissance Literature.* Ithaca: Cornell University Press, 1990.

Hanke, Lewis. *All Mankind Is One: A Study of the Disputation Between Bartolomé de Las Casas and Juan Ginés de Sepúlveda in 1550 on the Intellectual and Religious Capacity of the American Indian.* DeKalb: Northern Illinois University Press, 1974.

———. *Aristotle and the American Indians: A Study in Race Prejudice in the Modern World.* Chicago: Henry Regnery Company, 1959.

———. *The Spanish Struggle for Justice in the Conquest of America.* Philadelphia: University of Pennsylvania Press, 1949.

———. "Viceroy Francisco de Toledo and the Just Titles of Spain to the Inca Empire." *The Americas* 3, no. 1 (1946): 3–19.

Harrison, Regina. "The Language and Rhetoric of Conversion in the Viceroyalty of Peru." *Poetics Today* 16, no. 1 (1995): 1–27.

———. "Literatura de la evangelización: Catecismos, confesionarios y sermones." In *Literaturas orales y primeros textos coloniales,* edited by Juan C. Godenzzi and Carlos Garatea, 275–308. Vol. 1 of *Historia de las literaturas en el Perú,* edited by Raquel Chang Rodríguez and Marcel Velásquez Castro. Lima: Pontificia Universidad Católica del Perú, 2017.

———. "Pérez Bocanegra's *Ritual formulario:* Khipu Knots and Confession." In *Narrative Threads: Accounting and Recounting in Andean Khipu,* edited by Jeffrey Quilter and Gary Urton, 266–90. Austin: University of Texas Press, 2002.

———. *Sin and Confession in Colonial Peru: Spanish-Quechua Penitential Texts, 1560–1650.* Austin: University of Texas Press, 2014.

———. "Teaching Restitution: Las Casas, the *Rules for Confessors,* and the Politics of Repayment." In Arias and Merediz, *Teaching the Writings of Bartolomé de Las Casas,* 132–40.

———. "The Theology of Concupiscence: Spanish-Quechua Confessional Manuals in the Andes." In *Coded Encounters: Writing, Gender, and Ethnicity in Colonial Latin America,* edited by Francisco Javier Cevallos-Candau, Jeffrey A. Cole, Nina M. Scott, and Nicomedes Suárez Aráuz, 135–50. Amherst: University of Massachusetts Press, 1994.

Hartman, Saidiya V. *Lose Your Mother: A Journey Along the Atlantic Slave Route.* New York: Farrar, Straus and Giroux, 2007.

———. *Scenes of Subjection: Terror, Slavery, and Self-Making in Nineteenth-Century America.* New York: Oxford University Press, 1997.

Haskett, Robert. "Dying for Conversion: Faith, Obedience, and the Tlaxcalan Boy Martyrs in New Spain." *Colonial Latin American Review* 17, no. 2 (2008): 185–212.

Heintz, Lauren. "The Crisis of Kinship: Queer Affiliations in the Sexual Economy of Slavery." *GLQ: A Journal of Lesbian and Gay Studies* 23, no. 2 (2017): 221–46.

Hering Torres, Max S., María Elena Martínez, and David Nirenberg, eds. *Race and Blood in the Iberian World.* Zurich: Lit Verlag, 2012.

Hernández, Tanya Katerí. *Racial Subordination in Latin America: The Role of the State, Customary Law, and the New Civil Rights Response.* Cambridge: Cambridge University Press, 2013.

Hernández de León-Portilla, Ascensión. "Las primeras gramáticas mesoamericanas: Algunos rasgos lingüísticos." *Historiographía Linguistica* 30, no. 1/2 (2003): 1–44.

Herzog, Tamar. "Colonial Law and 'Native Customs': Indigenous Land Rights in Colonial Spanish America." *The Americas* 69, no. 3 (2013): 303–21.

———. *Defining Nations: Immigrants and Citizens in Early Modern Spain and Spanish America.* New Haven: Yale University Press, 2003.

Hill, Ruth. "*Casta* as Culture and the *Sociedad de Castas* as Literature." In *Interpreting Colonialism,* edited by Byron R. Wells and Philip Stewart, 231–59. Oxford: Voltaire Foundation, 2004.

———. "Hearing Las Casas Write: Rhetoric and the Façade of Orality in the *Brevísima relación,*" Arias and Merediz, *Teaching the Writings of Bartolomé de Las Casas,* 57–65.

———. *Hierarchy, Commerce, and Fraud in Bourbon Spanish America: A Postal Inspector's Exposé.* Nashville: Vanderbilt University Press, 2005.

Honores, Renzo. "Una sociedad legalista: Abogados, procuradores de causas y la creación de una cultura legal colonial en Lima y Potosí, 1540–1670." PhD diss., Florida International University, 2007.

Horswell, Michael J. *Decolonizing the Sodomite: Queer Tropes of Sexuality in Colonial Andean Culture.* Austin: University of Texas Press, 2005.

———. "Negotiating Apostasy in Vilcabamba: Titu Cusi Yupanqui Writes from the *Chaupi*." *Romanic Review* 103, nos. 1–2 (2012): 81–110.

Huerta, Alonso de. *Arte breve de la lengua quechua.* 1616. Introduction by Ruth Moya and transcription by Eduardo Villacís. Quito: Proyecto Educación Bilingüe Intercultural, 1993.

Hyland, Sabine. "Conversion, Custom, and 'Culture': Jesuit Racial Policy in Sixteenth-Century Peru." PhD diss., Yale University, 1994.

———. *The Jesuit and the Incas: The Extraordinary Life of Padre Blas Valera, S.J.* Ann Arbor: The University of Michigan Press, 2003.

Imolesi, María Elena. "Doing the Same but With Different Arguments: Matrimonial Dispensations in the Indigenous and Spanish Population of Colonial Charcas." *Journal of the Max Planck Institute for European Legal History* 27 (2019): 131–42.

Jacobs, Margaret D. *A Generation Removed: The Fostering and Adoption of Indigenous Children in the Postwar World.* Lincoln: University of Nebraska Press, 2014.

Jaffary, Nora E. "Reconceiving Motherhood: Infanticide and Abortion in Colonial Mexico." *Journal of Family History* 37, no. 1 (2012): 3–22.

Jákfalvi-Leiva, Susana. "De la voz a la escritura: La 'Relación' de Titu Cusi (1570)." *Revista de crítica literaria latinoamericana* 19, no. 37 (1993): 259–77.

Jáuregui, Carlos A. *Canibalia: Canibalismo, calibanismo, antropofagia cultural y consumo en América Latina.* Madrid: Iberoamericana, 2008.

Jáuregui, Carlos A. and David Solodkow. "Biopolitics and the Farming (of) Life in Bartolomé de las Casas." In Orique and Roldán-Figueroa, *Bartolomé de las Casas, O.P.,* 127–66.

Jehlen, Myra. "History before the Fact: Or, Captain John Smith's Unfinished Symphony." *Critical Inquiry* 19, no. 4 (1993): 677–92.

Jenkins, David. "The Inka Conical Clan." *Journal of Anthropological Research* 57, no. 2 (2001): 167–95.

Jensen, Robin M. *Baptismal Imagery in Early Christianity: Ritual, Visual, and Theological Dimensions.* Grand Rapids, MI: Baker Academic, 2012.

Jouve Martín, José Ramón. *Esclavos de la ciudad letrada: Esclavitud, escritura y colonialismo en Lima, 1650–1700.* Lima: Instituto de Estudios Peruanos, 2005.

"Juan Carlos Aduviri, de personaje anónimo a un paso del Goya." *Los Tiempos,* January 1, 2011. https://www.lostiempos.com/actualidad/cultura/20110119/juan-carlos-aduviri-personaje-anonimo-paso-del-goya.

Julien, Catherine. "Francisca Pizarro, la cuzqueña, y su madre, la coya Ynguill." *Revista del Archivo Regional del Cusco* 15 (2000): 53–74.

———. "Francisco de Toledo and His Campaign against the Incas." *Colonial Latin American Review* 16, no. 2 (2007): 243–72.

———. Introduction to *History of How the Spaniards Arrived in Peru: Dual-Language Edition* by Titu Cusi Yupanqui, vii–xxix. Translated by Catherine Julien. Indianapolis, IN: Hackett Publishing Company, 2006.

———. *Reading Inca History.* Iowa City: University of Iowa Press, 2000.

Justice, Daniel Heath. "'Go Away, Water!': Kinship Criticism and the Decolonization Imperative." In *Reasoning Together: The Native Critics Collection,* edited by Craig S. Womack, Daniel Heath Justice, and Christopher B. Teuton, 147–68. Norman: University of Oklahoma Press, 2008.

Kamen, Henry. *The Spanish Inquisition: A Historical Revision.* New Haven, CT: Yale University Press, 1997.

Kazanjian, David. *The Colonizing Trick: National Culture and Imperial Citizenship in Early America.* Minneapolis: University of Minnesota Press, 2003.

Kelley, Donald R. "'Second Nature': The Idea of Custom in European Law, Society, and Culture." In *The Transmission of Culture in Early Modern Europe,* edited by Anthony Grafton and Ann Blair, 131–72. Philadelphia: University of Pennsylvania Press, 1990.

Kellogg, Susan, and Matthew Restall, eds. *Dead Giveaways: Indigenous Testaments of Colonial Mesoamerica and the Andes.* Salt Lake City: University of Utah Press, 1998.

Klor de Alva, José Jorge. "Sahagún and the Birth of Modern Ethnography: Representing, Confessing, and Inscribing the Native Other." In *The Work of Bernardino de Sahagún: Pioneer Ethnographer of Sixteenth-Century Aztec Mexico,* edited by José Jorge Klor de Alva, H. B. Nicholson, and Eloise Quiñones Keber, 31–52. Albany: University at Albany, State University at New York, 1988.

Kubler, George. "The Neo-Inca State (1537–1572)." *Hispanic American Historical Review* 27, no. 2 (1947): 189–203.

Lamana, Gonzalo. *Domination without Dominance: Inca-Spanish Encounters in Early Colonial Peru.* Durham, NC: Duke University Press, 2008.

———. "El testamento y el codicilo de doña Beatriz Clara Coya de Loyola, hija de don Diego Sayri Túpac Ynga Yupangui y de la Coya doña María Cusi Huarcay." *Revista del Archivo Departamental del Cusco* 14 (1999): 45–60.

Lane, Kris. *Potosí: The Silver City That Changed the World.* Oakland: University of California Press, 2021.

Laqueur, Thomas. *Making Sex: Body and Gender from the Greeks to Freud.* Cambridge, MA: Harvard University Press, 1992.

Las Casas, Bartolomé de. *Brevísima relación de la destrucción de las Indias.* 1552. Edited by José Miguel Martínez Torrejón. Madrid: Real Academia Española, 2013.

———. *Doce dudas.* 1564. Edited by Paulino Castañeda Delgado. Vol. 11, no. 2 of *Obras completas.* Madrid: Alianza Editorial, 1992.

Lavrin, Asunción, ed. *Sexuality and Marriage in Colonial Latin America.* Lincoln: University of Nebraska Press, 1989.

———. "Sexuality in Colonial Mexico: A Church Dilemma." In Lavrin, *Sexuality and Marriage,* 47–95.

Lee, Christina. *The Anxiety of Sameness in Early Modern Spain.* Manchester: Manchester University Press, 2016.

Lee, Vincent R. "Vilcabamba: Last Stronghold of the Inca." In Alconini and Covey, *Oxford Handbook of the Incas,* 741–58.

Legnani, Nicole. *The Business of Conquest: Empire, Love, and Law in the Atlantic World.* Notre Dame, IN: University of Notre Dame Press, 2020.

———. Introduction to *Titu Cusi: A 16th Century Account of the Conquest,* by Diego de Castro Titu Cusi Yupanqui, 1–72. Adapted by Nicole Legnani. Cambridge: Harvard University Press, 2005.

Lennon, Paul Joseph, and Caroline Egan. "Conversion and Colonial History in Icíar Bollaín's *También la lluvia* (2010)." *Bulletin of Hispanic Studies* 96, no. 9 (2019): 935–52.

Levillier, Roberto, ed. *Gobernantes del Perú. Cartas y papeles, siglo XVI; Documentos del Archivo de Indias.* Vol. 3. Madrid: Sucesores de Rivadeneyra, 1921.

Li Causi, Pietro. "Hybridization as Speciation? The Viewpoint of Greek Folk Biology (and Aristotle) on the Mutation of Species." Paper presented at the 7th Europaeum Classics Colloquium, Ravenna, November 21, 2008. https://papers.ssrn.com/sol3/papers.cfm?abstract_id=1323052.

Lienhard, Martín. *La voz y su huella: Escritura y conflicto étnico-social en América Latina (1492–1988).* La Habana: Casa de las Américas, 1990.

Lipsett-Rivera, Sonya. "A Slap in the Face of Honor." In *The Faces of Honor: Sex, Shame, and Violence in Colonial Latin America,* edited by Lyman L. Johnson and Sonya Lipsett-Rivera, 179–200. Albuquerque: University of New Mexico Press, 1998.

Lira, Obed Omar. "Bartolomé de Las Casas and the Passions of Language." PhD diss., Harvard University, 2017.

Lisi, Francesco Leonardo, ed. *El Tercer Concilio Limense y la aculturación de los indígenas sudamericanos: Estudio crítico con edición, traducción y comentario de las actas del concilio provincial celebrado en Lima entre 1582–1583.* Salamanca, Spain: Ediciones Universidad de Salamanca, 1990.

Lowe, Lisa. *The Intimacies of Four Continents.* Durham, NC: Duke University Press, 2015.

Luján Muñoz, Jorge. "La literatura notarial en España e Hispanoamerica, 1500–1820." *Anuario de estudios americanos* 38 (1981): 101–16.

MacCormack, Sabine. "History, Historical Record, and Ceremonial Action: Incas and Spaniards in Cusco." *Comparative Studies in Society and History* 43, no. 2 (2001): 329–63.

———. *On the Wings of Time: Rome, the Incas, Spain, and Peru.* Princeton, NJ: Princeton University Press, 2007.

———. *Religion in the Andes: Vision and Imagination in Early Colonial Peru.* Princeton, NJ: Princeton University Press, 1991.

Mangan, Jane E. "Moving Mestizos in Sixteenth-Century Peru: Spanish Fathers, Indigenous Mothers, and the Children In Between." *William and Mary Quarterly* 70, no. 2 (2013): 273–94.

———. *Trading Roles: Gender, Ethnicity, and the Urban Economy in Colonial Potosí.* Durham, NC: Duke University Press, 2005.

———. *Transatlantic Obligations: Creating the Bonds of Family in Conquest-Era Peru and Spain.* Oxford: Oxford University Press, 2016.

Mannarelli, María Emma. *Pecados públicos: La ilegitimidad en Lima, siglo XVII.* Lima: Flora Tristán, 1993.

Mannheim, Bruce. *The Language of the Inka since the European Invasion.* Austin: University of Texas Press, 1991.

———. "A Nation Surrounded." In Boone and Cummins, *Native Traditions,* 383–420.

Martínez, María Elena. "Archives, Bodies, and Imagination: The Case of Juana Aguilar and Queer Approaches to History, Sexuality, and Politics." *Radical History Review* no. 120 (2014): 159–82.

———. "The Black Blood of New Spain: Limpieza de Sangre, Racial Violence, and Gendered Power in Early Colonial Mexico." *William and Mary Quarterly* 61, no. 3 (2004): 479–520.

———. *Genealogical Fictions: Limpieza de Sangre, Religion, and Gender in Colonial Mexico.* Stanford, CA: Stanford University Press, 2008.

———. "Indigenous Genealogies: Lineage, History, and the Colonial Pact in Central Mexico and Peru." In Ramos and Yannakakis, *Indigenous Intellectuals,* 173–201.

Martínez-San Miguel, Yolanda, and Santa Arias, eds. *The Routledge Hispanic Studies Companion to Colonial Latin America and the Caribbean (1492–1898).* London: Routledge, 2021.

Martínez Gomis, Mario. "El control de los niños moriscos en Alicante tras el decreto de expulsión de 1690." *Revista de historia moderna: Anales de la Universidad de Alicante* 1 (1981): 251–80.

Mases, Enrique. *Estado y cuestión indígena: El destino final de los indios sometidos en el sur del territorio (1878–1930).* Buenos Aires: Prometeo, 2010.

Mazzotti, José Antonio. *Coros mestizos del Inca Garcilaso: Resonancias andinas.* Lima: Bolsa de Valores de Lima, 1996.

McClintock, Anne. *Imperial Leather: Race, Gender, and Sexuality in the Colonial Contest.* New York: Routledge, 1995.

McDonough, Kelly S. *The Learned Ones: Nahua Intellectuals in Postconquest Mexico.* Tucson: University of Arizona Press, 2014.

McKinley, Michelle A. *Fractional Freedoms: Slavery, Intimacy, and Legal Mobilization in Colonial Lima, 1600–1700.* New York: University of Cambridge Press, 2016.

———. "Till Death Do Us Part: Testamentary Manumission in Seventeenth-Century Lima, Peru." *Slavery and Abolition: A Journal of Slave and Post Slave Studies* 33, no. 3 (2012): 381–401.

Mendieta Ocampo, Ilder. *Hospitales de Lima colonial, siglos XVII-XIX.* Lima: Universidad Nacional Mayor de San Marcos, Seminario de Historia Rural Andina, 1990.

Menon, Madhavi. *Unhistorical Shakespeare: Queer Theory in Shakespearean Literature and Film.* New York: Palgrave MacMillan, 2008.

Merrim, Stephanie. "The Counter-Discourse of Bartolomé de Las Casas." In Williams and Lewis, *Early Images of the Americas,* 149–62.

Mignolo, Walter. "Cartas, crónicas y relaciones del descubrimiento y la conquista." In *Historia de la literatura hispanoamericana,* Vol. 1, *Época colonial,* edited by Luis Íñigo Madrigal, 57–116. Madrid: Cátedra, 1982.

———. *The Darker Side of the Renaissance: Literacy, Territoriality, and Colonization.* Ann Arbor: University of Michigan Press, 2003.

Milanich, Nara. "Whither Family History? A Road Map from Latin America." *American Historical Review* 112, no. 2 (2007): 439–58.

Millones Figueroa, Luis. "Colonial Andean Texts in English Translation." *Latin American Research Review* 44, no. 2 (2009): 181–92.

———. "De señores naturales a tiranos: El concepto político de los incas y sus cronistas en el siglo XVI." *Latin American Literary Review* 26, no. 52 (1998): 72–99.

Mills, Kenneth. "Bad Christians in Colonial Peru." *Colonial Latin American Review* 5, no. 2 (1996): 183–218.

———. *Idolatry and Its Enemies: Colonial Andean Religion and Extirpation, 1640–1750.* Princeton, NJ: Princeton University Press, 1997.

———. "The Limits of Religious Coercion in Mid-Colonial Peru." *Past and Present,* no. 145 (1994): 84–121.

Miranda, Deborah A. "Extermination of the *Joyas:* Gendercide in Spanish California." *GLQ: A Journal of Lesbian and Gay Studies* 16, no. 1–2 (2010): 253–84.

Molina, Cristóbal de. *Relación de las fábulas y ritos de los Incas.* c. 1575. In Urbano y Duviols, *Fábulas y mitos,* 47–134.

Morgan, Jennifer L. *Reckoning with Slavery: Gender, Kinship and Capitalism in the Early Black Atlantic.* Durham, NC: Duke University Press, 2021.

Mörner, Magnus. *Race Mixture in the History of Latin America.* Boston: Little & Brown, 1967.

Moten, Fred. *In the Break: The Aesthetics of the Black Radical Tradition.* Minneapolis: University of Minnesota Press, 2003.

Muldoon, James. "Medieval Canon Law and the Conquest of the Americas." *Jahrbuch für Geschichte Lateinamerikas* 37 (2000): 9–22.

Mumford, Jeremy Ravi. "Aristocracy on the Auction Block: Race, Lords, and the Perpetuity Controversy of Sixteenth-Century Peru." In Fisher and O' Hara, *Imperial Subjects,* 35–59.

———. "A Child Marriage in Early Colonial Cuzco." *Journal of Family History* 45, no. 4 (2020): 429–56.

———. "Francisco de Toledo, admirador y émulo de la 'tiranía' inca." *Histórica* 35, no. 2 (2011): 45–67.

———. "Litigation as Ethnography in Sixteenth-Century Peru: Polo de Ondegardo and the Mitimaes." *Hispanic American Historical Review* 88, no. 1 (2008): 5–40.

———. *Vertical Empire: The General Resettlement of Indians in the Colonial Andes.* Durham, NC: Duke University Press, 2012.

Muñoz, José Esteban. *Cruising Utopia: The Then and There of Queer Futurity.* New York: New York University Press, 2009.

Murra, John V. "'*Nos hazen mucha ventaja*': The Early European Perception of Andean Achievement." In Andrien and Adorno, *Transatlantic Encounters,* 73–89.

Nadeau, Carolyn. "Authorizing the Wife/Mother in Sixteenth-Century Advice Manuals." In *Women in the Discourse of Early Modern Spain,* edited by Joan F. Cammarata, 19–34. Gainesville: University Press of Florida, 2002.

———. "Blood Mother/Milk Mother: Breastfeeding, the Family, and the State in Antonio de Guevara's *Relox De Príncipes* (*Dial of Princes*)." *Hispanic Review* 69, no. 2 (2001): 153–74.

Nemser, Daniel. *Infrastructures of Race: Concentration and Biopolitics in Colonial Mexico.* Austin: University of Texas Press, 2017.

———. "Primitive Accumulation, Geometric Space, and the Construction of the 'Indian.'" *Journal of Latin American Cultural Studies* 24, no. 3 (2015): 335–52.

———. "Primitive Spiritual Accumulation and the Colonial Extraction Economy." *Política común* 5 (2014): n.p., https://doi.org/10.3998/pc.12322227.0005.003.

Newman, Barbara. *The Permeable Self: Five Medieval Relationships.* Philadelphia: University of Pennsylvania Press, 2021.

Nirenberg, David. *Communities of Violence: Persecution of Minorities in the Middle Ages.* Princeton, NJ: Princeton University Press, 1996.

No, Song. "La heterogeneidad suturada: Titu Cusi Yupanqui." *Revista de crítica literaria latinoamericana* 31, no. 62 (2005): 85–96.

———. "Teaching *De unico vocationis modo:* The Maternal Discourse of Bartolomé de Las Casas." In Arias and Merediz, *Teaching the Writings of Bartolomé de Las Casas,* 124–31.

Nowack, Kerstin. "Las mercedes que pedía para su salida: The Vilcabamba Inca and the Spanish State, 1593–1572." In *New World, First Nations: Native Peoples of Mesoamerica and the Andes under Colonial Rule,* edited by David Cahill and Blanca Tovías, 57–91. Brighton: Sussex Academic Press, 2006.

———. "Las provisiones de Titu Cusi Yupanqui." *Revista Andina* no. 38 (2004): 139–79.

O'Gorman, Edmundo. Introduction to the *Apologética historia sumaria: cuanto a las cualidades, disposición, descripción, cielo y suelo destas tierras* [. . .]. by Bartolomé de Las Casas. 1560–61. Mexico: Universidad Nacional Autónoma de México Instituto de Investigaciones Históricas, 1967.

Oré, Luis Jerónimo de. *Symbolo catholico indiano, en el qual se declaran los misterios dela Fè contenidos en los tres Symbolos Catholicos [. . .]*. Lima, 1598.

Orique, David T. "To Heaven or Hell: An Introduction to the Soteriology of Bartolomé de Las Casas." *Bulletin of Spanish Studies* 93, no. 9 (2016): 1495–526.

Orique, David Thomas and Rady Roldán-Figueroa, eds. *Bartolomé de las Casas, O.P.: History, Philosophy, and Theology in the Age of European Expansion*. Leiden: Brill, 2019.

O'Toole, Rachel Sarah. "The Bonds of Kinship, the Ties of Freedom in Colonial Peru." *Journal of Family History* 42, no. 1 (2017): 3–21.

———. *Bound Lives: Africans, Indians, and the Making of Race in Colonial Peru*. Pittsburgh, PA: University of Pittsburgh Press, 2012.

———. "Devotion, Domination, and the Work of Fantasy in Colonial Peru." *Radical History Review,* no. 123 (2015): 37–59.

Padden, R. C. *The Hummingbird and the Hawk: Conquest and Sovereignty in the Valley of Mexico, 1503–1541.* Columbus: Ohio State University Press, 1967.

Padrón, Ricardo. *The Indies of the Setting Sun: How Early Modern Spain Mapped the Far East as the Transpacific West.* Chicago: University of Chicago Press, 2020.

Pagden, Anthony. *The Fall of Natural Man: The American Indian and the Origins of Comparative Ethnology.* Cambridge: Cambridge University Press, 1982.

Pennington, Kenneth J., Jr. "Bartolomé de Las Casas and the Tradition of Medieval Law." *Church History* 39, no. 2 (1970): 149–61.

Penyak, Lee M. "Incestuous Natures: Consensual and Forced Relations in Mexico, 1740–1854." In *Sexuality and the Unnatural in Colonial Latin America,* edited by Zeb Tortorici, 162–87. Berkeley: University of California Press, 2016.

Pérez, Erika. "Family, Spiritual Kinship, and Social Hierarchy in Early California." *Early American Studies: An Interdisciplinary Journal* 14, no. 4 (2016): 661–87.

Pérez Bocanegra, Juan. *Ritual formulario e institucion de curas, para administrar a los naturales de este reyno, los santos sacramentos del baptismo, confirmacion, eucaristia, y viatico, penitencia, extremauncion, y matrimonio: con advertencias muy necessarias.* Lima: 1631.

Pérez Fernández, Isacio, ed. *El anónimo de Yucay frente a Bartolomé de Las Casas: estudio y edición crítica del Parecer de Yucay, anónimo (Valle de Yucay, 16 de marzo de 1571).* Cuzco: Centro de Estudios Regionales Andinos "Bartolomé de Las Casas," 1995.

Perry, Mary Elizabeth. "Between Muslim and Christian Worlds: Moriscas and Identity in Early Modern Spain." *The Muslim World* 95, no. 2 (2005): 177–97.

———. *The Handless Maiden: Moriscos and the Politics of Religion in Early Modern Spain.* Princeton, NJ: Princeton University Press, 2005.

Pierce, Joseph M. *Argentine Intimacies: Queer Kinship in an Age of Splendor, 1890–1910.* Albany: State University of New York Press, 2019.

Pillsbury, Joanne. "Writing Inca History: The Colonial Era." In Alconini and Covey, *Oxford Handbook of the Incas*, 9–30.

Povinelli, Elizabeth A. *The Empire of Love: Toward a Theory of Intimacy, Genealogy, and Carnality*. Durham, NC: Duke University Press, 2006.

Powers, Karen Vieira. "Conquering Discourses of 'Sexual Conquest': Of Women, Language, and *Mestizaje*." *Colonial Latin American Review* 11, no. 1 (2002): 7–32.

———. *Women in the Crucible of Conquest: The Gendered Genesis of Spanish American Society, 1500–1600*. Albuquerque: University of New Mexico Press, 2005.

Premo, Bianca. "Before the Law: Women's Petitions in the Eighteenth-Century Spanish Empire." *Comparative Studies in Society and History* 53, no. 2 (2011): 261–89.

———. *Children of the Father King: Youth, Authority, and Legal Minority in Colonial Lima*. Chapel Hill: University of North Carolina Press, 2005.

———. "Custom Today: Temporality, Customary Law, and Indigenous Enlightenment." *Hispanic American Historical Review* 94, no. 3 (2014): 355–79.

———. *The Enlightenment on Trial: Ordinary Litigants and Colonialism in the Spanish Empire*. New York: Oxford University Press, 2017.

———. "Familiar: Thinking beyond Lineage and across Race in Spanish Atlantic Family History." *William and Mary Quarterly* 70, no. 2 (2013): 295–316.

———. "The Maidens, the Monks, and Their Mothers: Patriarchal Authority and Holy Vows in Colonial Lima, 1650–1715." In *Women, Religion, and the Atlantic World (1600–1800)*, edited by Daniella Kostroun and Lisa Vollendorf, 275–301. Toronto: University of Toronto Press, 2009.

Prieto, Andrés I. "Confessing to Be an Indian: Penance and the Creation of a Native Self in José de Acosta's Missiology." *Colonial Latin American Review* 24, no. 4 (2015): 525–44.

Puente Luna, José Carlos de la. *Andean Cosmopolitans: Seeking Justice and Reward at the Spanish Royal Court*. Austin: University of Texas Press, 2018.

Puente Luna, José Carlos de la, and Renzo Honores, "Guardianes de la real justicia: Alcaldes de indios, costumbre y justicia local en Huarochirí colonial." *Histórica* 40, no. 2 (2016): 11–47.

Quijano, Aníbal. "Coloniality of Power, Eurocentrism, and Latin America." *Nepantla: Views from South* 1, no. 3 (2000): 533–80.

Quispe-Agnoli, Rocío. *La fe andina en la escritura: Resistencia e identidad en la obra de Guaman Poma de Ayala*. Lima: Fondo Editorial de la Universidad Nacional Mayor de San Marcos, 2006.

———. "Taking Possession of the New World: Powerful Female Agency of Early Colonial Accounts of Perú." In "Women and Early America," edited by Tamara Harvey, special issue, *Legacy* 28, no. 2 (2011): 257–89.

Rabasa, José. *Inventing America: Spanish Historiography and the Formation of Eurocentrism*. Norman: University of Oklahoma Press, 1993.

———. *Without History: Subaltern Studies, the Zapatista Insurgency, and the Specter of History*. Pittsburgh: University of Pittsburgh Press, 2010.

———. "Writing and Evangelization in Sixteenth-Century Mexico." In Williams and Lewis, *Early Images of the Americas,* 65–92.

Ramos, Gabriela. *Death and Conversion in the Andes: Lima and Cuzco, 1532–1670.* Notre Dame, IN: University of Notre Dame Press, 2010.

Ramos, Gabriela, and Yanna Yannakakis, eds. *Indigenous Intellectuals: Knowledge, Power, and Colonial Culture in Mexico and the Andes.* Durham, NC: Duke University Press, 2014.

Rappaport, Joanne. *The Disappearing Mestizo: Configuring Difference in the Colonial New Kingdom of Granada.* Durham, NC: Duke University Press, 2014.

Rappaport, Joanne, and Tom Cummins. *Beyond the Lettered City: Indigenous Literacies in the Andes.* Durham, NC: Duke University Press, 2012.

Rasmussen, Birgit Brander. *Queequeg's Coffin: Indigenous Literacies and Early American Literature.* Durham, NC: Duke University Press, 2012.

Real Academia Española. *Diccionario de autoridades.* 6 vols. Madrid. 1726–39. https://apps2.rae.es/DA.html.

Redden, Andrew. "Angelic Death and Sacrifice in Early Modern Hispanic America." In Will de Chaparro and Achim, *Death and Dying,* 142–69.

Ricard, Robert. *The Spiritual Conquest of Mexico: An Essay on the Apostolate and the Evangelizing Methods of the Mendicant Orders in New Spain, 1523–1572.* Translated by Lesley Byrd Simpson. Berkeley: University of California Press, 1966.

Rifkin, Mark. *Beyond Settler Time: Temporal Sovereignty and Indigenous Self-Determination.* Durham, NC: Duke University Press, 2017.

———. *When Did Indians Become Straight?: Kinship, the History of Sexuality, and Native Sovereignty.* Oxford: Oxford University Press, 2011.

Rípodas Ardanaz, Daisy. *El matrimonio en Indias: Realidad social y regulación jurídica.* Buenos Aires: Fundación para la Educación, la Ciencia y la Cultura, 1977.

Rivera Cusicanqui, Silvia. *Ch'ixinakax utxiwa: On Practices and Discourses of Decolonization.* Translated by Molly Geidel. Cambridge, UK: Polity, 2020.

———. "*Ch'ixinakax utxiwa:* A Reflection on the Practices and Discourses of Decolonization." *South Atlantic Quarterly* 111, no. 1 (2012): 95–109.

Rodríguez, Juana María. *Sexual Futures, Queer Gestures, and Other Latina Longings.* New York: New York University Press, 2014.

Rodríguez, María de los Ángeles and Thomas Calvo. "Sobre la práctica del aborto en el Occidente de México: documentos coloniales (siglos XVI-XVII)." *Trace: Travaux et Recherches dans les Amériques du Centre* 10 (1986): 32–38.

Rostworowski de Diez Canseco, María. "El repartimiento de doña Beatriz Coya en el valle de Yucay." *Historia y Cultura* 4 (1970): 153–267.

Rostworowski de Diez Canseco, María, and John V. Murra. "Succession, Coöption to Kingship, and Royal Incest among the Inca." *Southwestern Journal of Anthropology* 16, no. 4 (1960): 417–27.

Roxo Mexía y Ocón, Juan. *Arte de la lengua general de los indios del Peru* [...]. Lima: Jorge Lopez de Herrera, 1648.

Roy, Hélène. "El discurso neo-inca y su significado político: Vilcabamba entre sumisión, sincretismo y resistencia." *Revista de crítica literaria latinoamericana* 40, no. 80 (2014): 87–101.

Ruan, Felipe E. "Andean Activism and the Reformulation of Mestizo Agency and Identity in Early Colonial Peru." *Colonial Latin American Review* 21, no. 2 (2012): 209–37.

———. "The Probanza and Shaping a Contesting Mestizo Record in Early Colonial Peru." *Bulletin of Spanish Studies* 94, no. 5 (2017): 843–69.

Rubin, Gayle. "The Traffic in Women: Notes on the 'Political Economy' of Sex." In *Toward an Anthropology of Women,* edited by Rayna R. Reiter, 157–210. New York: Monthly View Press, 1975.

Saldaña-Portillo, María Josefina. "Indians Have Always Been Modern: *Roma,* the Settler Colonial Paradigm, and Latinx Temporality." *Aztlán: A Journal of Chicano Studies* 45, no. 2 (2020): 221–42.

Salomon, Frank. "Chronicles of the Impossible: Notes on Three Peruvian Indigenous Historians." In *From Oral to Written Expression: Native Andean Chronicles of the Early Colonial Period,* edited by Rolena Adorno, 9–39. Syracuse: Maxwell School of Citizenship and Public Affairs, Syracuse University, 1982.

———. *The Cord Keepers: Khipus and Cultural Life in a Peruvian Village.* Durham, NC: Duke University Press, 2004.

Salomon, Frank, and George L. Urioste, eds. and trans. *The Huarochirí Manuscript: A Testament of Ancient and Colonial Andean Religion.* Austin: University of Texas Press, 1991.

Salomon, Frank, and Mercedes Niño-Murcia. *The Lettered Mountain: A Peruvian Village's Way with Writing.* Durham, NC: Duke University Press, 2011.

Santaolalla, Isabel. *The Cinema of Iciar Bollaín.* Manchester: Manchester University Press, 2012.

Santo Tomás, Domingo de. "Carta al Consejo de Indias." In *Fr. Domingo de Santo Tomás, defensor y apóstol de los indios del Perú: su vida y sus escritos,* edited by José María Vargas, 15–21. Quito: Editorial Santo Domingo, 1937.

———. *Grammatica, o Arte de la lengua general de los Indios de los reynos del Perú.* Valladolid: Francisco Fernández de Cordova, 1560.

———. *Lexicon, o Vocabulario de la lengua general del Perú.* Valladolid: Francisco Fernández de Cordova, 1560.

Sarmiento de Gamboa, Pedro. *Historia de los Incas.* 1572. Edited by Ángel Rosenblat. 3rd ed. Buenos Aires: Emecé Editores, S.A., 1943.

Schneider, David. *A Critique of the Study of Kinship.* Ann Arbor: University of Michigan Press, 1984.

Schwartz, Stuart B., and Frank Salomon. "New Peoples and New Kinds of People: Adaptation, Readjustment, and Ethnogenesis in South American Indigenous Societies." In *Cambridge History of the Native Peoples of the Americas,* edited by

Frank Salomon and Stuart B. Schwartz, vol. 3, pt. 2, 443–501. Cambridge: Cambridge University Press, 1999.

Seed, Patricia. *To Love, Honor, and Obey in Colonial Mexico: Conflicts over Marriage Choice, 1574–1821.* Stanford, CA: Stanford University Press, 1988.

Segovia Gordillo, Ana. "Las gramáticas misioneras sobre la lengua quechua a través de sus paratextos." *Nueva Revista de Filología Hispánica* 68, no. 2 (2020): 451–97.

Sempat Assadourian, Carlos. "Fray Bartolomé de Las Casas obispo: La condición miserable de las naciones indianas y el derecho de la iglesia (Un escrito de 1545)." *Allpanchis* 22, no. 35/36 (1990): 29–104.

Shah, Nayan. *Stranger Intimacy: Contesting Race, Sexuality and the Law in the North American West.* Berkeley: University of California Press, 2011.

Sherbondy, Jeanette E. "Panaca Lands: Re-Invented Communities." *Journal of the Steward Anthropological Society* 24, nos. 1/2 (1996): 173–201.

Sidbury, James, and Jorge Cañizares-Esguerra. "Mapping Ethnogenesis in the Early Modern Atlantic." *William and Mary Quarterly* 68, no. 2 (2011): 181–208.

Sigal, Pete, ed. *Infamous Desire: Male Homosexuality in Colonial Latin America.* Chicago: University of Chicago Press, 2003.

———. "Queer Nahuatl: Sahagún's Faggots and Sodomites, Lesbians and Hermaphrodites." *Ethnohistory* 54, no. 1 (2007): 9–34.

Silverblatt, Irene. "Family Values in Seventeenth-Century Peru." In Boone and Cummins, *Native Traditions,* 63–89.

———. *Modern Inquisitions: Peru and the Colonial Origins of the Civilized World.* Durham, NC: Duke University Press, 2004.

———. *Moon, Sun, and Witches: Gender Ideologies and Class in Inca and Colonial Peru.* Princeton, NJ: Princeton University Press, 1987.

Simpson, Audra. *Mohawk Interruptus: Political Life Across the Borders of Settler States.* Durham, NC: Duke University Press, 2014.

Skrzypek, Jeremy W. "Editor's Introduction." *Quaestiones Disputatae* 10, no. 2 (2020): 5–27.

Smith, Andrea Meador. "Savages and Saviours in Icíar Bollaín's *También la lluvia/Even the Rain.*" *Studies in Spanish & Latin American Cinemas* 14, no. 3 (2017): 315–32.

Speed, Shannon. "Structures of Settler Capitalism in Abya Yala." *American Quarterly* 69, no. 4 (2017): 783–90.

Spillers, Hortense J. "Mama's Baby, Papa's Maybe: An American Grammar Book." *Diacritics* 17, no. 2 (1987): 64–81.

Stavig, Ward. "'Living in Offense of Our Lord': Indigenous Sexual Values and Marital Life in the Colonial Crucible." *Hispanic American Historical Review* 75, no. 4 (1995): 597–622.

Stoler, Ann Laura. *Along the Archival Grain: Epistemic Anxieties and Colonial Common Sense.* Princeton: Princeton University Press, 2009.

———. *Carnal Knowledge and Imperial Power: Race and the Intimate in Colonial Rule.* Berkeley: University of California Press, 2002.

———. "Colonial Archives and the Arts of Governance." *Archival Science* no. 2 (2002): 87–109.

———. *Haunted by Empire: Geographies of Intimacy in North American History.* Durham, NC: Duke University Press, 2006.

———. *Race and the Education of Desire: Foucault's "History of Sexuality" and the Colonial Order of Things.* Durham, NC: Duke University Press, 1995.

———. "Tense and Tender Ties: The Politics of Comparison in North American History and (Post) Colonial Studies." *Journal of American History* 88, no. 3 (2001): 829–65.

Stone, Cynthia L. "Confronting Stereotypes: The *Brevísima relación* as Homily, Not History." In Arias and Merediz, *Teaching the Writings of Bartolomé de Las Casas,* 65–72.

Summers, David. "Form and Gender." *New Literary History* 24, no. 2 (1993): 243–71.

TallBear, Kim. "Making Love and Relations beyond Settler Sex and Family." In *Making Kin not Population,* edited by Adele E. Clarke and Donna Haraway, 145–64. Chicago: Prickly Paradigm Press, 2018.

Tavárez, David. "Legally Indian: Inquisitorial Readings of Indigenous Identity in New Spain." In Fisher and O'Hara, *Imperial Subjects,* 81–100.

Tedlock, Dennis. "Torture in the Archives: Mayans Meet Europeans." *American Anthropologist* 95, no. 1 (1993): 139–52.

Timberlake, Marie. "The Painted Colonial Image: Jesuit and Andean Fabrication of History in *Matrimonio de García de Loyola con Ñusta Beatriz.*" *Journal of Medieval and Early Modern Studies* 29, no. 3 (1999): 563–98.

Titu Cusi Yupanqui, Diego de Castro. *History of How the Spaniards Arrived in Peru.* Translated by Catherine Julien. Indianapolis, IN: Hackett Publishing Company, 2006.

Todorov, Tzvetan. *The Conquest of America: The Question of the Other.* Translated by Richard Howard. New York: Harper & Row, 1984.

Toribio Medina, José, ed. *La imprenta en Lima (1584—1824).* Vol. 1. Santiago de Chile, 1904.

Torres de Mendoza, Luís, ed. *Colección de documentos inéditos relativos al descubrimiento, conquista y organización de las antiguas posesiones españolas de América y Oceanía, sacados de los Archivos del Reino, y muy especialmente del de Indias.* Vol. 16. Madrid: Imprenta del Hospicio, 1871.

Tortorici, Zeb. "Reading the (Dead) Body: Histories of Suicide in New Spain." In Will de Chaparro and Achim, *Death and Dying,* 53–77.

———. *Sins Against Nature: Sex and Archives in Colonial New Spain.* Durham, NC: Duke University Press, 2018.

Traub, Valerie. "The New Unhistoricism in Queer Studies." *PMLA* 128, no. 1 (2013): 21–39.

———. "The Present Future of Lesbian Historiography." In Haggerty and McGarry, *Companion,* 124–45.

———. *The Renaissance of Lesbianism in Early Modern England.* Cambridge: Cambridge University Press, 2002.

———. *Thinking Sex with the Early Moderns.* Philadelphia: University of Pennsylvania Press, 2016.

Tueller, James B. "The Assimilating Morisco: Four Families in Valladolid Prior to the Expulsion of 1610." *Mediterranean Studies* 7 (1998): 167–77.

Trouillot, Michel-Rolph. *Silencing the Past: Power and the Production of History.* Boston: Beacon Press, 1995.

Twinam, Ann. "The Church, the State, and the Abandoned: Expósitos in Late Eighteenth-Century Havana." In González and Premo, *Raising an Empire,* 163–86.

———. *Public Lives, Private Secrets: Gender, Honor, Sexuality, and Illegitimacy in Colonial Spanish America.* Stanford: Stanford University Press, 1999.

Urbano, Henrique, and Pierre Duviols, eds. *Fábulas y mitos de los Incas.* Madrid: Historia 16, 1989.

Urton, Gary. *Inka History in Knots: Reading Khipus as Primary Sources.* Austin: University of Texas Press, 2017.

———. "Sin, Confession, and the Arts of Book-and Cord-Keeping: An Intercontinental and Transcultural Exploration of Accounting and Governmentality." *Comparative Studies in Society and History* 51, no. 4 (2009): 801–31.

Valera, Blas. *Las costumbres antiguas del Perú y la historia de los Incas (siglo XVI).* Edited by Francisco A. Loayza. Lima: Editorial de Domingo Miranda, 1945.

van Deusen, Nancy E. *Between the Sacred and the Worldly: The Institutional and Cultural Practice of* Recogimiento *in Colonial Lima.* Stanford, CA: Stanford University Press, 2002.

———. "Diasporas, Bondage, and Intimacy in Lima, 1535 to 1555." *Colonial Latin American Review* 19, no. 2 (2010): 247–77.

———. *Embodying the Sacred: Women Mystics in Seventeenth-Century Lima.* Durham, NC: Duke University Press, 2018.

———. *Global Indios: The Indigenous Struggle for Justice in Sixteenth-Century Spain.* Durham, NC: Duke University Press, 2015.

———. "The Intimacies of Bondage: Female Indigenous Servants and Slaves and Their Spanish Masters, 1492–1555." *Journal of Women's History* 24, no. 1 (2012): 13–43.

VanValkenburgh, Parker. "Unsettling Time: Persistence and Memory in Spanish Colonial Peru." *Journal of Archeological Method and Theory* 24, no. 1 (2017): 117–48.

Vargas Ugarte, Rubén, S. J. "La instrucción primaria en el Perú virreinal." *Fénix. Revista de la Biblioteca Nacional del Perú,* no. 22 (1972): 162–67.

Verdesio, Gustavo. "Images and War: The Representation of Violence in Colonial Times and Today." In Arias and Merediz, *Teaching the Writings of Bartolomé de Las Casas,* 73–80.

———. "Traducción y contrato en la obra de Titu Cusi Yupanqui." *Bulletin of Hispanic Studies* 72 (1995): 403–12.

Villella, Peter B. *Indigenous Elites and Creole Identity in Colonial Mexico, 1500–1800.* Cambridge: Cambridge University Press, 2016.

von Germeten, Nicole. "Sexuality, Witchcraft, and Honor in Colonial Spanish America." *History Compass* 9, no. 5 (2011): 374–83.

Wagner, Henry Raup and Helen Rand Parish. *The Life and Writings of Bartolomé de las Casas.* Albuquerque: The University of New Mexico Press, 1967.

Weissberger, Barbara F. "Motherhood and Ritual Murder in Medieval Spain and England." *Journal of Medieval and Early Modern Studies* 39, no. 1 (2009): 7–30.

White, Hayden. *The Content of the Form: Narrative Discourses and Historical Representation.* Baltimore: Johns Hopkins University Press, 1987.

Will de Chaparro, Martina, and Miruna Achim. *Death and Dying in Colonial Spanish America.* Tucson: University of Arizona Press, 2011.

Williams, Jerry M. and Robert E. Lewis. *Early Images of the Americas: Transfer and Invention.* Tucson: University of Arizona Press, 2003.

Wolfe, Patrick. "Land, Labor, and Difference: Elementary Structures of Race." *American Historical Review* 106, no. 3 (2001): 866–905.

———. "Settler Colonialism and the Elimination of the Native." *Journal of Genocide Research* 8, no. 4 (2006): 387–409.

Wood, Stephanie. "Sexual Violation in the Conquest of the Americas." In *Sex and Sexuality in Early America,* edited by Merril D. Smith, 9–34. New York: New York University Press, 1998.

Wynter, Sylvia. "Unsettling the Coloniality of Being/Power/Truth/Freedom: Towards the Human, After Man, Its Overrepresentation—An Argument." *CR: The New Centennial Review* 3, no. 3 (2003): 257–337.

Yablon-Zug, Marcia. "Separation, Deportation, Termination." *Boston College Journal of Law and Social Justice* 32, no. 1 (2012): 63–117.

Yannakakis, Yanna. "Making Law Intelligible: Networks of Translation in Mid-Colonial Oaxaca." In Ramos and Yannakakis, *Indigenous Intellectuals,* 79–106.

Zevallos, Johnny. "Reflexiones en torno a la crónica de Titu Cusi Yupanqui." *Ajos y Zafiros* 6, no. 1 (2004): 201–14.

Zuidema, R. Tom. "Guaman Poma on Inca Hierarchy, Before and in Colonial Times." In *Unlocking the Doors to the Worlds of Guaman Poma and his* Nueva corónica, edited by Rolena Adorno and Ivan Boserup, 441–69. Copenhagen: Museum Tusculanum Press, 2015.

Index

abortion, 27–28, 111n64

Acosta, José de, 107n7; *De procuranda Indorum salute,* 12, 56, 60, 64, 82; *Historia natural y moral de las Indias,* 82, 131n28; on paternity, 68; and the Third Lima Council, 60

Adorno, Rolena, 105n59: on exemplarity and Guaman Poma's *Nueva corónica,* 65–66; on kinship and conquest, 19; on Las Casas's logic of natural lords, 40

Aduviri, Juan Carlos, 95, 136nn6–7. See also *También la lluvia* (Bollaín)

agency: of the enslaved, 4, 32, 112n71, 112n79; Indigenous, 90–93; masculine, 99; removal of, 31; of women, 15–33, 47–49

agrarian rhetoric, 68, 85, 93. *See also* infantilization; plants

Ahmed, Sara, 16, 88. *See also* form; use

Alaperrine-Bouyer, Monique: on elite Indigenous education, 61, 127nn68–69; on the *Inter caetera* papal bull, 121n1. *See also* education

Albornoz, Cristóbal de, and the *campañas de extirpación de idolatrías,* 93. *See also* idolatry

Alexander VI, Pope, *Inter caetera* (papal bull), 15, 54, 60, 67

Almagro, Diego, 36, 114n14

Álvarez, Bartolomé, *De las costumbres y conversión de los indios del Perú: Memorial a Felipe II,* 59–60. *See also* custom

Anónimo de Yucay frente a Bartolomé de Las Casas, 81–82, 131n28. *See also* Las Casas, Bartolomé de; Yucay

anthropology, 6–7

Arias, Santa, on Las Casas's view of Spanish intervention, 107n5

Aristotle: on custom, 57; on hylomorphism, 83

Arriaga, Pablo José de, *Extirpación de la idolatría en el Perú,* 75. *See also* idolatry

Atahualpa, 34, 42–44. *See also* bastardy; Manco Inca; Titu Cusi Yupanqui

Austin, J. L., 133n63

authorship, 10–12; and gender, 34–53; unknown, 29, 34. *See also* first-person; *Instrucción del Inca don Diego de Castro Titu Cusi Yupanqui* (Titu Cusi)

Avalle-Arce, Juan Bautista, on the *Brevísima relación,* 18

Baber, R. Jovita, on perception of behavior and community integration, 121n8

baptism: for Las Casas, 110n58; as newly allowed, 37; and politics, 50–51; and temporality, 26–27

bastardy, 41–44, 66, 116n43. *See also* legitimacy; lineage

Bauer, Ralph: on hylomorphism, 83, 131n34; on the *Instrucción,* 44–45, 114n20; on the *reducción,* 133n56

Beatriz Clara Coya: "conventing" of, 51–53, 120n91, 120n93, 120n99, 120n101; marriage arrangement of, 49–52. *See also* marriage; Quispe Titu

Bentancor, Orlando: on hylomorphism in the ideas of early modern colonialists, 83, 131n35. *See also* hylomorphism

Betanzos, Juan de, *Suma y narración de los Incas,* 41, 43

biologistic thinking, 6–7

"Black Legend," 15, 129n10

Blanco, John D., on biopolitics and colonial project, 130n18

blood: bad (maternal), 42–44, 46–47; of Christ, 134n75; healthy, 28; libel, 21–22; purity, 4, 6, 57–58, 71, 117n51; "Semitic," 58; tainted (of New Christians), 54. *See also* genealogy; *limpieza de sangre;* lineage

body: embodied examples, 61–65; and form, 10; and text, 4, 62–63, 69, 72–73, 76

Bollaín, Icíar, *También la lluvia,* 12–13, 95–99, 135n2, 136nn6–8

Writing the Early Americas

Printed in the USA
CPSIA information can be obtained
at www.ICGtesting.com
LVHW042331180823
755636LV00005B/506